2
AUSTRALIAN SOCIAL DEVELOPMENT

STUDIES IN HISTORY, ECONOMICS AND PUBLIC LAW

EDITED BY THE FACULTY OF POLITICAL SCIENCE
OF COLUMBIA UNIVERSITY

Volume LXXXI]   [Number 2

Whole Number 189

AUSTRALIAN SOCIAL DEVELOPMENT

BY

CLARENCE H. NORTHCOTT

AMS PRESS
NEW YORK

COLUMBIA UNIVERSITY
STUDIES IN THE
SOCIAL SCIENCES

189

The Series was formerly known as *Studies in History, Economics and Public Law.*

Reprinted with the permission of Columbia University Press
From the edition of 1918, New York
First AMS EDITION published 1968
Manufactured in the United States of America

Library of Congress Catalogue Card Number: 68-56676

AMS PRESS, INC.
New York, N.Y. 10003

To

THE DEMOCRACY OF AUSTRALIA

IN HOPE AND CONFIDENCE OF A

GLORIOUS DESTINY

ERRATA

Page 40, line 12, for 42 read 48
Page 42, last line, for 1792 read 1793
Page 61, line 18, for 1891 read 1801
Page 130, line 23, for 1913 read 1914

PREFACE

THE social experiments of Australia have attracted considerable attention during recent years. They have been studied by men who have brought to their research a careful training in the social sciences. These studies have been particular in nature and have been analyses generally of the methods of arbitration and conciliation in vogue during the last quarter of a century. Few attempts have been made from within to submit the same field to social analysis, and fewer still to cover the whole social development of the country.

Yet such an attempt is called for. The conditions present a unique opportunity to the sociologist. A homogeneous population, diversified enough racially to encourage variation, possessing a social inheritance of democratic institutions and ideals, living within a relatively rich territory, has worked out a unique and interesting experiment in democracy. Because its history has been short and its numbers few, the factors of its development can be analyzed, and the resulting trend of its political, economic and social institutions evaluated. With adequate scientific methods the task is feasible. In the use of such methods this work is an imperfect essay.

Other reasons call for an attempt at social analysis and evaluation at the present time. A social cycle, rich in constructive legislation, seems to have reached its conclusion. The results of that legislation are available for examination. New forces of organization and leadership have come into existence, and the future of Australian democracy depends on them. The same attitude towards social forces as is shown in Australian social legislation, namely, their control towards a consciously realized social end, challenges the social scientist to throw the light of sociological research upon the present tangled situation. Australia will only realize its destiny through a sane and well-informed leadership, a leadership conscious of the limits and potentialities of its resources, of the errors and values in its ideals, and of the lines along which a rational social development is to be attained. In hope and confidence of such a future this essay, with its concluding program of social efficiency, is put forward.

Of its imperfection no one is more clearly conscious than the author. The materials which the sociologist needs are often not available at all in Australia, or where available, need to be submitted to technical treatment. Thus, one would doubtless obtain only from diversified sources in the United Kingdom knowledge of the relative strength and the cultural standing of the various racial elements that have entered into the composition of the population of Australia. Careful research along these lines is indispensable to the beginnings of sociological study in Australia, and to an understanding of the psychology of a people characterized by courage and initiative in both peace and war. A word is due also concerning the statistical method in sociology, the one method by which sociology can be made into an exact science. The excellent social statistics collected in Australia call for examination and utilization. The relations and correlations which lie hidden within them are necessary to the scientific and accurate evaluation of the past social process and to the future control of the social environment. Until more of these rich fields have been investigated, sociological study of Australian conditions will remain imperfect, subject to various forms of bias, conscious and unconscious, or to the errors of the analytic and the impressionistic method.

No pretence is made in this work to give a complete picture of Australian social life. Nothing has been attempted except to analyze the chief factors in the process of social development, and to regard them throughout as dynamic, subject to measurement and evaluation. Consequently, much purely descriptive material has been set aside. Little, if any, account is given of the cultural life of the people, of their morality or their recreations. The stress laid in the text upon social and economic conflict must, however, not be interpreted into the inference of one of the readers of the manuscript, that Australia " is not a country where a man of ideas or spirit would expect to find much congenial company." On the contrary, there is a good deal of culture in city villa and squatting homestead alike. There is much in the thought and outlook of Australians that is spirited and idealistic, even if their philosophy of life is a reckless optimism. To have written a glowing impressionistic picture of the cultural and spiritual refinement of the people, their healthy recreations, and their far-reaching humanitarianism would have been easy. It is, however, the author's view that the sociologist must approach such a subject as the first of these three in a different way. He must obtain a measure of the relative strength and cultural standing of the various elements of the immigrant population, must estimate their reactions to the environing forces that operated upon them and finally, grade the population of today in psychological classes measured in statistical terms. In the light of such a concept, it is clear that this work is but the first sketch of what may well be the task of an organized body of students of Sociology.

It should be said, further, that this sketch of Australian social development ends with the year 1914. The oubreak of the European War has released social forces that have already marked a new epoch in the industrial and political sphere. Yet these forces were neither new nor unsuspected. Their origin and significance have been sketched in this essay, which was completed in June, 1917. Figures beyond the year 1914 have been quoted in several places to show that the general trend of the years preceding has been manifest to the latest period for which figures could be obtained. This essay is fortunate, therefore, in the moment of its appearance, inasmuch as it comes forth at a time when scientific, constructive thinking upon the past and future of Australian social development is imperatively demanded. It will be the author's fullest reward if he can contribute anything to a constructive program for that future development.

Since the materials for this dissertation were collected in Sydney, New South Wales, and their arrangement and treatment have formed part of a course in sociological research in Columbia University, New York, my obligations for assistance received are many and wide-spread. Thanks are due to the Commonwealth Statistician, Mr. G. H. Knibbs; to various friends in Sydney, particularly to Professors Anderson and Irvine, of Sydney University, and Professor Meredith Atkinson, of Melbourne University, who encouraged me to put these researches into print; to Professor Franklin H. Giddings, of Columbia University, for much insight into the meaning and significance of the forces operating in society generally; to Professor Alvan A. Tenney, for suggestions concerning both the substance and form into which the work was to be cast; to Professors Edwin R. A. Seligman and Robert E. Chaddock, who have read the statistical and more purely economic sections of the dissertation; and to Mr. Bruno Lasker, of *The Survey* (New York), whose criticisms of the manuscript from an English standpoint have been extremely valuable.

CLARENCE H. NORTHCOTT.

COLUMBIA UNIVERSITY, NEW YORK, APRIL, 1918.

TABLE OF CONTENTS

CHAPTER I
A General Survey

	PAGE
General intolerance of special privileges	17
Psychological characterization of the people	18
Conservative elements	20
Comparison of policies of Liberal and Labour parties	22
Attitudes of the Legislative Councils	27
Sociological explanations required	30

CHAPTER II
Elements of the Population

Racial factors in population	34
Elements in immigration	37
The early convicts	37
Free settlers	42
Nominated immigrants	45
Relative influence of free settlers and nominated immigrants	49
Social, economic and political consequences of their interaction	50

CHAPTER III
The Land and its Settlement

Isolation of the settlements	55
Size of the country	56
Rainfall	56
Physical configuration	58
Influence of land policy on settlement	59
System of free grants	60
System of sale at a fixed price	64
Growth and influence of the squatting interest	65
Free selection	67
System of scientific classification	71
Effects of land policy	72
Diverse interests created	75

CONTENTS

CHAPTER IV
THE STRUGGLE FOR SOCIAL REFORM

	PAGE
Social forces premonitory of conflict	76
Trade unionism	77
Political unionism	79
Rise of industrial legislation	81
A social ideal the basis for the struggle	85
Form of social pressure	86
Economic, social and political demands	87
Paradox of democracy with elements of conservatism and monopoly	91

CHAPTER V
THE CONFLICT IN ECONOMIC THEORY

Economic liberalism versus economic conservatism	94
Freedom of contract as defined by employers	95
Legislative reaction to this theory—collective bargaining, preference to unionists, and minimum wage	97
Conflicting views on question of State interference	100
Public attitude concerning competition and supply and demand	101
Attitude concerning wages and profits	104
Principles on which living wage is based	106
Social considerations implied in process of wage-fixing	110

CHAPTER VI
ECONOMIC ASPECTS OF RECENT SOCIAL DEVELOPMENT

Industrial disputes—causes	117
Industrial disputes—number and extent	119
Comparison of New South Wales and Victoria	120
Methods and results of settlement of disputes	123
Public opinion and strikes	124
Opposition of trade-union leaders	125
Penal provisions of Arbitration Acts	126
Trade unionists' explanations	127
Measures to maintain industrial peace—minimum wage, Wages Boards, Arbitration Courts	128
Effects of arbitration	130
Increased, nominal and effective wages	130
Altered distribution of wealth	131
Failure to stress increased productivity	135
Restriction of labour supply	136
Extent and influence of this restriction	137

CONTENTS

	PAGE
Movement of female labour	138
Motive and purpose of restriction of labour	139
Measures taken to prevent unemployment	141

CHAPTER VII
THE CONFLICT IN POLITICS

Political activity the conflict of groups	145
Absence of group pressure prior to 1890	145
Study of trade-union leaders	147
Contrast between leaders of opposing political parties	147
Political organization of Labour party	148
Reaction on the Liberal party	150
Social philosophy of Labour party as leavening force of idealism	151
Extension of franchise	152
Effect on attitude to land monopoly	154
Conflict of policies in regard to tropical Australia	156
White Australia policy	157
Diverse views on immigration	160
State Socialism	163
Summary	166

CHAPTER VIII
SOCIAL PHASES OF AUSTRALIAN LIFE

Social development a realization of social values	169
Care for health	170
Care for motherhood and child life	171
Consumption and syphilis	175
Food and health	177
Industry and health	179
Housing	182
Education—its place in Australian development	183
Content and purpose of Australian education	185
Dependent and delinquent children	194
Reformative treatment of criminal offender	198
Old age and invalidity pensions	200
Attitude towards women	202
Summary	206

CHAPTER IX
STRUGGLE AND FAILURE

General elements of inefficiency	209
Difficulties and efforts in primary industries	210

Irrigation	214
Development of wheat area	215
Failure in industry to grade skill	216
Apprentice question and piece-work	218
Analysis of distribution of employees in wage groups	222
Statistics of added value examined	224
Factors in diminishing value of skill:	
(a) machinery	225
(b) wage-determination in influence on cost of living	226
(c) small-scale production	229
(d) Inefficiency of *entrepreneurs*	229
(e) trade-union restrictions	230
Sociological valuation of restriction of production	232
Evidence of restrictive tendencies of Australian trade unions	234
Preference for equality in political world	242
Neglect of social sciences	243
Class consciousness and social disharmony	244
Failure of education to stimulate inventive power	246
Scarcity of playing areas for children	248
Industry and the physical needs of women	249
Restriction of birth rate	251
Summary	253

CHAPTER X
The Meaning of Social Efficiency

Meaning of efficiency	256
Efficiency applied to society	257
Nature, purpose and functioning of society	257
Factors in realization of social efficiency	260
Industrial competency	261
Social harmony	269
Organization for efficient citizenship	272

CHAPTER XI
A Program of Social Efficiency

Proposal for development of natural resources	277
Conservation of natural resources	281
Overcoming industrial strife through democratic control of industry	281
Correlation between increased wages and increased production	283
Securing skill in workmanship and giving it definite valuation	286
Division of larger states	290
Education to have a social content	293

CONTENTS

	PAGE
Democratic leadership.	294
Legislative Reference Commission.	295
Summary.	295

LIST OF TABLES

Comparison of Urban and Rural Conditions in N. S. W. 1861 and 1894	69
Value of Production in Agriculture, Pasture and Manufacture, 1910–1914	72
Industrial Disputes, Number and Magnitude in Commonwealth, 1913–1916.	119
Industrial Disputes, Number and Magnitude in New South Wales and Victoria, 1913–1916	121
Nominal and Effective Wage Index Numbers, 1911–1914.	133
Increase in Number and Average Size of Deposits in Victorian Savings Banks, 1895–1912.	133
Comparison of Occupations at Censuses of 1901 and 1911.	138
Percentage which Increase in Female Working Population Bears to Total Increase in Factory Population, Victoria, 1909–1913	140
Relative Importance of Loan Items in States of Australian Commonwealth to June 30, 1914	164
Distribution of Male Employees in Wage Groups in Manufactures November, 1912.	223
Value of Production of Manufacturing Industries, 1909–1914	235
Relative Increase in Values of Raw Materials, Plant and Machinery and Productive Activity per Employee in the Manufacturing Industry, 1909–1914	236
Distribution of Population of the States in their Capital Cities, December 31, 1914	290
Population of the Capital City of each State Expressed as a Percentage of the Total Population of the State for the Census Periods, 1871–1911.	291

LIST OF GRAPHS

Comparison of Urban and Rural Conditions in New South Wales, 1861 and 1894.	71
Percentage Increase in Number of Depositors and Amount of Average Deposit in Victoria Savings Banks, 1895–1912, Compared with Percentage Increase in Wages, Victoria, 1896–1912	134
Distribution of Male Employees in Wage Groups in Manufacturing Industries of Australia, November, 1912	222
Relative Increase in Values of Raw Material, Plant and Machinery, and Productive Activity, 1909–1914.	237

CHAPTER I

A General Survey

To the student of society, Australia appears to be characterized chiefly as a land intolerant of special privileges. He sees no aristocracy of birth, of talent or of skill. He finds in its jurisprudence none of the customs of primogeniture and entail that create rigid social classifications. There is a general equality of opportunity, increased by a liberal scheme of education, that opens a career to ability, initiative and merit. A rich political heritage has been fostered and developed. Love of liberty and a desire for self government under the fullest forms of democracy have been the dynamic forces in the political sphere. English institutions, pregnant as they are with opportunities for freedom and self-government, have been stripped of their traditional conservatism and gradually transformed into adequate organic media for the social consciousness. Elements of monopoly and privilege do not obtrude themselves. Religious hatreds, racial prejudices, social inequalities and great industrial wrongs seem never to have influenced the corporate governing life of the new nation. Industrial legislation, comprehensive in quantity and scope, daring and experimental in aim, seems to have given the working classes a large measure of social justice. The wide extension of the franchise, and the use made of political power by the working classes are equivalent to the simultaneous realization of a social and a political democracy.

In a large measure, this evaluation is true. Whatever

elements of privilege and monopoly have been, or are, present in the social structure, they have not been able to overbalance the forces that have pressed towards democracy. Social development is a conflict of forces, a struggle for power, a process of alteration in the forms and activities of the State, resulting from the effective pressure of specific groups. While later analysis will give us more clearly an estimate of the various elements of the struggle, it is sufficient in this general survey to point out that through the short period of Australian history its trend has been to destroy special privileges. In the political sphere, the early settlers struggled against the despotism and military autocracy of their governors till they obtained responsible government. Step by step, through the establishment of the ballot (1858), the liberalization of the property qualifications inserted in the early constitutions, and the granting of manhood, and later, of universal suffrage, a full and complete political democracy has been realized. The special political prerogatives attaching to the several Legislative Councils of the various states are an object of attack—and, necessarily, of defence. On the economic side of the social development, the labourer has been given a higher status. Collective bargaining has been made real, and a "sacrosanct" standard of living established. As a result, he stands nearer to the capitalist in economic rights and power than any of his fellows in other lands. In social life, the absence of great extremes of wealth and poverty, of luxury and hopeless squalor, adds another illustration of the thesis that Australian democracy as a whole is intolerant of special privileges.

A psychological characterization of the people reveals this truth from another perspective. Australia is even yet the country of the pioneer. The psychological reaction of the " frontier " is still apparent. The struggle against drought, fire and flood encouraged pluck, initiative, courage and daring, fostered freedom of thought and action and inculcated respect for individual liberty. Class distinctions, with some of the grace and charm that characterizes the Anglo-Saxon in his native home, were lost in the pioneer struggle. There was no room for the softer qualities of character. Daring, endurance, self-reliance were the only qualities that would bear the fierce strain, and in the struggle for survival they remained as the chief characteristics of the pioneer stock. The process of a peaceful expansion in commerce and industry has not led to their atrophy. The Australian has not lost his power of endurance. There remains many a bush tract unrobbed of its primeval forest, many an arid region, many a drought to test his pluck, and he is proving equal to the challenge. The versatility of his temperament, the readiness to contrive and plan, the power of initiative that answers readily the challenge of difficulty, the hopefulness born of impatience with the present and a vision of the beauty that might be made to blossom in the wilderness—all these characteristics of his are part and parcel of the enduring spirit. The vicissitudes, however, of the pioneer's lot have been correlated with another characteristic. They have tended to make the Australian careless, unthrifty, reckless of misfortune, ready to meet it, true, with a smiling face, but incurably incautious concerning the future. Such a temperament sits loose to the possibility, and is intolerant of the realization, of special privileges.

The Australian is still self-confident. Some of it is the confidence of youth, of a nation unsobered by trial and disaster. Part of it is the confidence of men who have measured themselves with a changing and hostile environment and have conquered. But much of it is the feeling stimulated and fostered in the individuals of a small democracy where man may measure himself on equal terms with his fellow man and feel his strength. He is still self-reliant. Nature has not tutored him to lean on her in easy confidence, nor have classes solidified in such a way as to make his position one of status. This self-reliance is seen in the boy with his aptitude to learn, not merely the lessons of the school room, but also the more meaningful lessons required of those who battle with the Australian bush; in the girl, with her fearlessness, her grit, and her entire absence of artificiality and diffidence; and in the adult citizen, with his independence of conduct and outlook, his capacity for leadership and his ready criticism of his own elected leaders. He has learned his own value, he realizes the potency of the political power entrusted to him, and in the light of both facts, he sets himself against the conscious creation of special privileges.

But to assert that no reactionary elements have been, or are, present in the social life of Australia would be untrue. Several are traceable in its historical development. They were the logical product of the conditions under which the country was settled, and of the political and social environment which the colonies shared with the whole British Empire. Those which exist today are rooted in the earlier environment of the Australian colonies and are to be explained by the process of their development. If, on the whole, the Australian people are intolerant of special privileges, there has, nevertheless, been developed a class that has gained power and a certain amount of prestige and has consequently become conservative. Only a false antithesis would represent it as class-conscious, as standing by its privileges. Nevertheless, in that conflict of forces and that pressure of groups which constitutes social development, this is the class standing in contrast to that which presses for the overthrow of all special privileges. The line of division today is social, industrial and, to a certain extent, cultural.

It is based on wide diversity in economic interest but not so clearly on political principles. In political activity, Australia is divided between the employer and the employed. In the former party is included almost all the professional class, and most of the small farmers. To the latter must be added a small sprinkling of men of broad social sympathies, with many of the small settlers, whose interests diverge widely from those of the big pastoralists in the former group. The division is not strictly between people who seek wealth " without reference to the feelings, reasonable wishes or even lawful privileges of their fellows " and those who seek "a share of the general prosperity out of all proportion to their share of effort in creating it." These are the extremists of the group, one set of whom concentrates on the " business of developing the country and growing rich," while the other " speculates on the possibilities of moderate affluence without excessive toil, and of wide-spread social well-being, inconceivable to countries less richly endowed, less thinly peopled and less remote." [1]

This characterization, in which extremes are contrasted, gives a clue to the conflict of interests in Australia. The line of social division is constituted by the possession of wealth. In one class, solidified politically, are to be found those who possess wealth and prestige; in the other, where even more solidarity has been realized, remain those who obtain only enough wherewith to live and rear a family in an ordinary degree of comfort. Between these two classes, there is little sympathy and much distrust. Movements started by individuals among the former for the educational or moral uplift of the latter are met with apathy and indifference on the one side, and with scarcely concealed suspicion on the other. Class bias blinds the eyes of both groups to their common interests and their mutual social

[1] *Cf.* "Australian Ideals," *The Times* (London, August 8, 1908).

responsibilities. The class of wealth and prestige has to bear the reproach of neglecting in the past to legislate otherwise than for the interests of wealth. Nor has it, in the present transitional period, such a clear concept of social progress as would enable it to regain the respect of the labouring masses. They, in their turn, organized as they are into numerous and powerful trade unions, tend to command the whole economic, industrial and political future of the country.[1] Because of their aim to abolish private employment, they offer a resolute opposition to any suggested reform that will conserve the employer as an economic factor. Their social policy is " to kill exploitation and capture capital in the interests of, and make it subserve the welfare and well-being of, humanity." [2]

If we turn to analyze the political divisions of the Australian people we find further proof of this struggle of classes. Two political parties, the Liberal and Labour parties, divided the allegiance of Australia till events connected with the European War caused a realignment. The former is the party to which the professional and commercial classes belong, with a small minority of artisans. All that is essentially good in political conservatism finds expression in its spirit and aims. Its Liberalism, in matters of government rather than of economics, is the Liberalism of Cobden and John Stuart Mill.[3] It asserts that its

[1] At the end of 1916, there were 705 registered trade unions with a membership of 546,556, of whom 506,981 were males and 39,575 females. Male members of unions form 55 per cent of the estimated total number of male employees. Of this entire membership, 412,283 or 75.4 per cent are organized in federations that cover the whole Commonwealth, and eleven of these large federations contain 40.3 per cent of the total membership of all unions. See *Labour and Industrial Report*, no. 7, pp. 339-346, or *Commonwealth Year Book*, no. 10, pp. 954-6.

[2] *The Worker*, Sydney, April 9, 1908.

[3] Compare with its program the summaries of Cobden and Mill in Hobhouse, *Liberalism*, pp. 71, 78, 81, 111.

political principles are democratic, with more or less of radicalism. Its claim to be democratic is based on its main principle, that citizenship confers equal rights, without special power or privileges. Its radicalism is not one of aim but of method. It proposes to cure social evils and remove social grievances by "root remedies" rather than by surface palliatives. Doubting the efficacy of social legislation and preferring the cultivation of a high standard of individuality, it offers to give every class of worker only "a fair show" and fair play, leaving to him the duty of using all his moral and industrial powers to obtain a living. It differs most from the Labour Party in recognizing the rights of individuals and in enforcing their responsibilities and obligations. It denies that its political principles are either conservative or individualistic, though it admits that its political method is "to go slow." [1]

The Labour party consists largely of trade unionists. It is the labouring class organized politically, with a sprinkling of men of progressive views whose fellows, in other lands, have a choice between the extreme conservative and the extreme democratic party. It has had a definite and systematic program of political reform which has found fairly wide support and has shaped Australian ideals. This program is based upon a theory of social justice involving the over-

[1] Most of the material for this and subsequent statements of the aims of the Liberal party was obtained from representative Liberals in reply to the following questionnaire:
1. Could the political principle behind Australian Liberalism be classified under any of the following heads:—individualism, laissez faire, or a sane conservatism? If none of these is satisfactory, how would you describe its political principle?
2. How far does Liberalism accept the principle of social welfare as a political ideal? What meaning does it give to it?
3. Where does Liberalism draw the limit of State control?
4. Wherein does Liberalism differ most radically from the policy of the Labour party?

throw of the present industrial system and its replacement by one in which economic equality will have been secured and poverty abolished. Negatively, it stands against monopoly and privilege and the power for exploitation of great accumulations of wealth. Its main political principle is described by its own representatives as "evolutionary socialism", which, in contrast to the revolutionary methods of syndicalism, is equivalent to the use of political methods. One of the cardinal principles of the party is humanitarianism, defined as the idea that proper regard shall be had for the health and normal necessities of the individual. Herein, humanitarianism is opposed to competition. If competition is to remain, its power must stop short at the point where society realizes its responsibility for the proper housing, clothing, feeding and educating of the people. To fix that mark and to guard it, is the chief aim and purpose of the Labour movement.

For the realization of this aim, state and municipal ownership are to be set up wherever monopolies have been established, or wherever such ownership and control would seem to produce more economical and efficient administration, or would secure what the party conceives to be the social welfare. State Socialism is the remedy adopted to replace competition, held to be "the chief method of an industrial order of robbery and exploitation," by a principle which gives priority over all other considerations to the needs and wants of man as a human being. To obtain the administrative machinery necessary, it encourages the organization of groups, industrial and political, and believes in the right of the group to discipline and coerce the individual for the furtherance of that purpose. Thus, it encourages industrial unions, compelling employers and employees alike to group themselves before they may approach the Arbitration Court. To make effective the industrial grouping of employees, the principle of "preference to unionists", or, in American phraseology, "the closed shop," has been adopted. Any new worker in an industry is compelled, within a specified time, to join the union connected with that trade, provided that specified reasonable conditions of entrance thereto are maintained. In politics, the Labour party has adopted compulsory enrolment of electors and compulsory voting, though the latter is not in actual practice, except in the state of Queensland. In short, the aim of the Labour party is to sink individual interests in the furtherance of a political and social ideal.

Other points of contrast between the parties will be clearer now that their main principles have been set forth. Fundamentally, the Liberal party sets the rights of the individual over against the socialization of all his rights and activities. It encourages competition, which it holds to be necessary to secure efficiency and afford stimulus to skill and inventiveness. It accepts State Socialism subject to certain reservations. (1) The State should interfere only to correct abuses, not, (as the Labour party is held to do), to supersede individual enterprises where no grievance or abuse exists. (2) Any enlargement of the functions of the State should take place without injustice to individuals and with fair compensation for invaded rights. This extension should be tested beforehand on business principles. Will the new proposal pay, not merely in the economic sense, but when economic advantages are weighed against social readjustments and industrial disadvantages? In its encouragement of State Socialism and a " fairer " return to workmen, the Labour party, whenever in administrative power, has adopted the day labour policy on all public works. Every workman is paid the standard wage, and is thereby held to be saved from the sweating of the contract system. The Liberal party, however, in its encouragement of competition and individual enterprise, stands by the contract system. It objects to the other system on the threefold ground that it is more expensive, less efficient, and ultimately subversive of clean government. In public works conducted by day labour, (so builders and contractors say, though the charge is not always substantiated), the estimated cost is ultimately far exceeded. This is declared to be due to the lowered efficiency of a service where the political element of appeal and criticism enters, so as to make vigorous control of large bodies of working men impossible for government officers. The system of day labour tends, in the judgment of the Australian Liberal, to create a huge civil service whose vote can influence an election, and by reason of this political power and the system of support in return for concessions, is likely to become " a quasi-political blackmailing machine."

In other matters, the same fundamental contrast between the parties is manifest. The Liberals hold to a Spencerian doctrine of liberty conceived as respect for the equal liberty of others. On this ground, they advocate freehold tenure of land as opposed to the leasehold tenure and nationalization of land advocated by the Labour party. Similarly, they object to " preference to unionists," which the Labour party has enacted as necessary for the larger freedom of association involved in the progress of the working classes, but which, the Liberals declare, robs the non-unionist of his right to work and live in his own country. The municipal franchise reveals the same cleavage. The Labour party proposes to make this franchise synonymous with the political franchise on the ground that what concerns all in a democracy should be voted upon by all. The Liberals object to this as a denial of the right of representation to the taxpayers (who are landowners), and an infringement of the principle of " no taxation without representation." Speaking generally, the emphasis of the Liberal party is upon the individual in his individuality, that of the Labour party upon him as a social unit with needs and desires to be satisfied before he can enter upon his social heritage.[1]

The contrast between the democratic elements and those which represent conservatism is deepened by a study of the political machinery. In every Australian State and in the Commonwealth, there are two legislative houses. One of these, known in the States by the term Legislative Assembly, and in the Commonwealth as the House of Representatives, is elected on the most complete form of democratic franchise. The whole territory is divided into approximately equal electorates, wherein every qualified citizen of either sex votes for a single representative. The other house, called the Legislative Council, is designed to check and criticise the onslaught of "direct leveling democracy." The Councils are of two types, nominee and elective. The members of the former are nominated by the Executive, on the advice of the party in power. There are no special qualifications for nomination, and the members have a life tenure. In actual practice, they are generally men of middle life or older, wealthy, with large professional or business interests in which they have won distinction, and

---

[1] Most of the material for the statement of the aims and policy of the Labour party was obtained from *The Worker*, Sydney, the foremost official organ of the Labour movement, and from Labour representatives through a questionnaire containing the following questions: (1) Could the political principle behind the Australian Labour movement be classified as "socialism"? If so, what does the term mean **to you?** How far is syndicalism manifest in the movement? (2) What is the relation of "humanitarianism" to labour principles? (3) Mr. B. R. Wise, speaking of the Liberal and Labour parties, says they "differ fundamentally in political principles and in their conception of the purpose and method of administration." In your opinion, how do they differ most radically in principle? (4) What is the Labour party's "conception of the purpose and method of administration"?

to which their main attention is given, and until recently they have invariably been chosen from that party that may be characterized as the conservative party. The elective Councils, which are found in Victoria, South Australia, Tasmania and Western Australia, are elected on a property, residential and social qualification which restricts their electors to from 30 to 40 per cent of those eligible to vote for members of the Assembly. The qualifications in South Australia, which was long the most democratic of the Australian States, allow as voters adult British subjects of either sex who are either owners of a freehold of the clear value of £50, owners of a leasehold of the clear annual value of £20, with at least three years to run or containing a right of purchase, occupiers of a dwelling house of the clear annual value of £25, Crown leaseholders, postmasters, schoolmasters residing on official premises, police officers in charge of stations, and ministers of religion. Two other states, Victoria and Tasmania, where the money value of the property qualifications is lower, add also graduates of British universities, matriculated students of the State University, qualified legal and medical practitioners, and naval and military officers. A mere statement of these qualifications and of the differentiations they involve reveals to the student of the science of society a departure from that equality of opportunity and privilege which political democracy involves. Granted that the members of these assemblies often surpass in ability the members of the representative chambers, still the fact that they are men of a past generation, bound to the established order by the ties of wealth, prestige and position would suggest a search of their records for evidences of opposition to democratic measures. Of this abundant evidence is available.

Nearly every measure which is claimed as democratic and

progressive has had to pass the ordeal of several rejections. The several extensions of the franchise, including women's suffrage; payment of members; land taxation; the whole range of "experimental legislation" from schemes for land settlement and compulsory purchase to wages boards and arbitration courts; the extension of governmental enterprise into the sphere of trading, have their long account of Bills rejected by the Councils. Even so well tried a measure as Workmen's Compensation is in some cases still held back. The resistance of the Councils to drastic schemes for breaking up the large pastoral holdings and to land taxation, and the brake they apply to "socialistic legislation," have driven many, if not into the ranks, at any rate to the support of the Labour Party.[1]

The Wages Board of Victoria were strongly opposed at their inauguration by the Victorian Legislative Council, where the arguments centred round the theory of freedom of contract. The Industrial Arbitration Act of 1901 in New South Wales was opposed and delayed by the Council of that State, and an Eight Hour Bill applicable to all industries was long refused in the same place.

The brief survey we have made reveals a country where a vast amount of legislation has been enacted to abolish privilege and establish a large degree of democratic equality. The Australian colonies have long been designated "laboratories of political experiment," "nurseries of practical and fearless idealism"; they have been considered as communities where a definite social principle has become the motive power behind political activity and industrial rearrangement. The establishment of social democracy has become the aim of the Australian people. Into this ideal they have read such terms as equality of opportunity, the realization of the welfare of the people as a whole, the de-

[1] Mr. Harrison Moore, "Political Systems of Australia", *Federal Handbook on Australia*, edit. G. H. Knibbs (Melbourne), p. 554.

velopment of the personality of the individual citizen and the establishment of social efficiency. They believe that the political and social meanings of democracy cannot be separated, that the latter can only be realized through the former, and that the former is incomplete without the latter. For social democracy in this sense to be brought about, society must regulate and control many of the relations of men and classes. It must create new institutions for service. It must give the individual a fair chance to live and sustain himself, to share in the ideal values of civilization.

The welfare of the people must be raised to the first place, must be the uppermost and foremost consideration. How best to secure the good of all without injury to all, should be the aim —not commercial supremacy, not cheap production, regardless of human misery following, but rather the broadest justice, the widest extension of human happiness, and the attainment of the highest intellectual and moral standard of civilized nations should be our aim.[1]

Yet accompanying this undeniable general trend, the sociologist finds several powerful conservative factors. He finds collective activity, political, economic and social, the trend and purpose of which is to steady the haste towards experimentation and check the over-sanguine confidence in political idealism. There is a social policy behind this aim, a belief in individualism, an endorsement of the social value of wealth, landed and industrial, coupled with a distrust of democratic measures untried and unproven in other countries.

Now two questions press upon the sociologist. He has to find an explanation in the process of social development in Australia for the situation above described, and then to estimate the characteristic trend of that process. He has

---

[1] Mr. W. G. Spence, *Australia's Awakening*, p. 553.

first to determine the composition of the population, its racial homogeneity or heterogeneity, and its psychic differences, since these will be reflected in its intellectual outlook, in the possibilities and forms of co-operation, in its capacity for progress and in the type of democracy developed. A homogeneous population will be more alike in character, more conscious of similar aims, and will react more surely and stably to the same impulses and ideals. Where there are no alien races, no unassimilated elements, there is likely to be a greater economic uniformity in the population. This economic and psychic uniformity will increase the possibility of co-operation. Classes that are alike in race, speech and colour, no matter how much their interests may diverge, will co-operate more readily and on more points than a heterogeneous people. The type of co-operation will be simpler. Large universal interests, such as the economic and the political, will determine the form of co-operation within classes and the lines of division among them. The capacity for progress, in turn, depends on the numbers, the similarity of type, and the harmony and co-operation of the group. There is a dynamic power in mere numbers. Competition is keener or co-operation stronger. There is greater opportunity for invention and a sharper demand for it in consequence of the number and diversity of the economic and cultural needs of the people. The harmony of the group, conditioned in its turn by the similarity of type, is not only one of the factors but also one of the measures of progress. The social composition of the population is, therefore, one of the conditioning factors explanatory of the type of democracy developed in Australia.

Social development is further a process of reaction upon the environment. Essentially the same stock settled in the Unied States, Canada, New Zealand and Australia, but their social development has been different in many important points. Natural resources, climate, rainfall, physical difficulties or advantages in regard to settlement, have been the chief conditioning factors in this regard. Upon the fullness and character of the natural resources will depend the density of the population, the number of people who can live in a given area. Their sufficiency will condition the economic and social surplus available. Where wealth can be won from Nature, the social struggle is worth while. Only a country with potential wealth of natural resources widely distributed and fairly accessible can afford to conduct democratic experiments. In such a country, the environment, especially such concrete factors as climate, rainfall and the quantity and distribution of minerals, determines the prevailing occupations, and these, in their turn, react upon the interests of the people, affecting their social, political and industrial outlook, their modes of organization and their social values. Advantages and difficulties in the way of settlement, if they lead the control of these resources to pass into the hands of a special class, give social development a specific trend, and furnish method, aim and motive to that struggle for power which is one of its dominant traits. In an analysis, therefore, of the development of a country, attention must be given to the nature of the material resources, and to the mode and extent of their use.

Further, the sociologist is concerned with an evaluation of the characteristic trend of social development. In his analysis of the factors of social development and of their interaction, he may discover that certain forces have hindered progress. In other cases, where a process of experimentation is being carried on, he may find a distinct tendency in a certain direction different from that consciously aimed at. In other matters, there may be manifest a good deal of friction, of waste and of ineffectiveness. All democracies such as that of Australia have defects. Government by the people is not necessarily nor usually a perfect form of government. Because its supreme task is that of creating and adjusting institutions which will function for the realization of ideals, it is beset with difficulties. It will not realize its fullest fruitfulness if the ideals are not conducive to the highest welfare of the state and its members, if the machinery for their realization is deficient in quantity or quality, or if the people are neither wise enough nor disinterested enough to work the machinery to its fullest capacity and for its highest purposes. It is the task of the sociologist to evaluate the ideals and estimate the defects revealed in the development of democracy. In so doing, he unfolds implicitly a program of social efficiency.

CHAPTER II

ELEMENTS OF THE POPULATION

THE population of Australia is estimated at about five million persons.[1] Both immigration and natural increase have been elements in its growth. In the earlier years of settlement the former was predominant, but in the years that have elapsed since 1861,[2] natural increase has contributed 73 per cent to the population. Racially, the Australian people are fundamentally of British descent. Of the present inhabitants, 83 per cent are native born of British parents, 13 per cent were natives of the United Kingdom, only an insignificant minority being of foreign birth.[3] To Australia there have been carried the various stocks of the Anglo-Celtic population, the Englishman, the Scot, the Welshman and the Irishman, and there they have intermarried and blended in a manner and to a degree probably unknown in any other region. In the census of 1911, those who gave their birthplaces as in the United Kingdom are tabulated. Some of these represent the new immigration from the year 1906 onwards, the others the old people left from the earlier

[1] At the end of 1915, the estimate was placed at 4,931,988. As this did not include soldiers taking part in the European war, it is clear that under normal conditions the population would have reached 5 million in the year 1914. *Vide, Official Year Book of the Commonwealth of Australia*, no. 8, p. 1085; no. 9, p. 1140.

[2] The population statistics of the Australian Commonwealth under the head of "Growth of Population" begin with this year. *Vide, op. cit.*, no. 9, p. 107.

[3] *Ibid.*, p. 100.

periods. The existence of the latter class and the proportion these older people bear to the total can be ascertained by comparing the similar figures in the census of 1901 which are larger both absolutely and relatively. The figures of 1911 indicate that of those born in the United Kingdom, who form but 591,000 persons, 60.7 per cent came from England and Wales, 15.7 per cent from Scotland, and 23.6 per cent from Ireland. An analysis of the immigration, both assisted and unassisted, is necessary to furnish complete evidence of the contribution of the various parts of the United Kingdom, but that analysis remains as one of the tasks of the Australian sociologists of the future. Such evidence as we have is indicative of an assimilation of the three main stocks of the United Kingdom into one type. To that type, Scotland and Ireland have contributed more than their respective proportions of the population of the home country. Thus of the arrivals in Australia between 1852 and 1854, it is estimated that England supplied less than one-third, Scotland one-fourth, and Ireland two-fifths.[1] A writer in *Fraser's Magazine*,[2] apparently well-informed on the life of the country, after quoting the figures for the immigration of 1855 and 1856, puts the contribution of England and Wales at 50 per cent, Ireland at 41 per cent, and Scotland at nearly 9 per cent.[3]

[1] Rusden, *History of Australia*, vol. iii, p. 13.
[2] 1858, p. 661.
[3] No adequate figures have been published to enable the student readily to separate the total population into the country of origin of their ancestors. Some little guidance concerning existing proportions can be found in the census of religions. It may be assumed that most Roman Catholics are of Irish descent, that Presbyterians are of Scotch or Scotch-Irish descent, and that the remainder of the Christian denominations, except the Lutheran, are of English or Welsh descent. The Welsh, however, form but an insignificant minority, being found almost exclusively in mining districts. In the census of 1911, out of a total population of 4,455,005,

The racial development of the Australian people, extending over a century and a quarter, has had time enough for a definite blending of hereditary elements and for the acquisition of a certain amount of stability in the resultant racial and social characteristics. In the process of assimilation each separate element has both contributed and surrendered some of its own distinctive traits. The Englishman has been dominant, and has shaped most largely the social outlook, the customs and habits of the people. Nevertheless, the Australian is not a duplicate of the Englishman. In the process of his evolution into an Australian the Englishman has lost some of his reserve, some of his insularity and lack of adaptability, some of his seriousness, some of his respect for authority and tradition, without losing any of his love of liberty or capacity for self-government. The Scot has entered into the business life of the people more particularly, and while becoming less rigid and cold, has lost none of his shrewd sense and high seriousness. The Irish form a considerable proportion of the industrial workers of the cities and may be found in smaller numbers in the farming districts. They have gained a broader horizon through contact with men of creeds and politics different from their own. Though they have not, in the main, lost their distrust towards England nor their regard for Ireland, they have put love for Australia in the place of their native patriotism.

In the immigration into Australia since its foundation,

4,274,414, or 95.9 per cent were classified as Christian, 36,785 as non-Christian (Hebrew, Confucian, Mohammedan and Buddist), while 143,806 indicated no religious preference. The Roman Catholics numbered 921,425 or 20.7 per cent of the total population, the Presbyterians 558,336 or 12.5 per cent. These figures, while inexact as measures of country of origin, nevertheless give a rough estimate of the contributions of the Irish and Scotch to the social composition. See *Official Year Book of the Commonwealth*, no. 10, p. 136.

there have been four distinct elements—convicts, free settlers, gold diggers and assisted immigrants. These have interacted one upon the other and upon the environment, so that the rate and nature of the settlement of the country, the method of its economic development, and the trend of its political and social organization are their resultants. As long as the colony seemed destined to be nothing but a penal settlement, free settlers could not be induced to come in large numbers. While convict labor was available, early settlers were able, in many cases, to take up large areas of land proportioned to the number of convicts they employed. With the cessation of transportation there coincided roughly a period during which the Crown lands of the colony were sold at a low price, and the proceeds used in bringing out settlers. With the advent of the gold diggers came a demand for agricultural expansion, to provide food for the new population. The assisted immigrants who followed the gold-digging period, in conjunction with those of the diggers who remained after the gold fever had subsided, were the main factors, sociologically considered, in the social composition of the present day.

The contribution of the convict to the social development of Australia has never been thoroughly studied. The materials for such a study are not present in large quantity or in accurate statistical form. Nevertheless, sufficient evidence is available to enable us to make several important sociological inferences. Let us first examine the evidence.

The settlement of the colony of New South Wales in 1788 was made by a party composed of convicts and their officers. Of the convicts, who amounted to 756, 36 had been transported for life, 20 for 14 years, while the remainder, forming seven-eighths of the total, had been sentenced to seven years, the shortest term allowed by the harsh criminal code of those days. Presently, however, political prisoners from Ireland and Scotland were sent out, and were so incorrigible that they had to be segregated in secondary penal settlements. During the Napoleonic wars, most of the convicts were of this type. From 1815 onwards, they were men and women whose crimes were of a milder type. Transportation to New South Wales ceased in 1840, and to Tasmania in 1852, after about 120,000 men and women had been transported. An estimate made in 1837, just prior to abolition, showed that nearly 50,000 of them were then living in the country.[1] Many of these, having completed their terms, were settled on the land, or were engaged in trades. Others, whose sentences had not expired, were assigned to free settlers to perform compulsory labour for them, while the remainder were employed upon government works under strict supervision. It should be added that Western Australia, at its own request, was supplied with convict labour from 1843 to 1868, during which period 10,000 convicts were received.

As the sentences of the short-term convicts expired, they became freedmen, or, in the language of the settlement, "emancipists." They were thus free to marry, and as the proportion of free women was small, it is certain that convict women were largely the mothers of the first generation of Australian born. It will be of significance, therefore, to examine such figures as are available for computing their influence, numerically considered.

In the first years of settlement, from 1788 to 1795, 5,765 men and women were transported to New South Wales, and of these 3,377 either died or returned to England at the expiration of their sentences. But 1633 men and 755 women remained in the colony in 1795 who had either served their time, been pardoned or emancipated, or were still prisoners. In the next

---

[1] Scott, "History of Australia," *Federal Handbook*, 1914.

fifteen years, that is, till the beginning of 1710, 6,525 convicts were despatched to Sydney. . . . Taking the percentage of those who remained in the preceding seven years, there would in 1810 be 3,232 men and 1905 women who had arrived as convicts. As in the whole population of 10,452, there were 2,654 children, not more than 2,346 men and women in the settlement had not been transported.[1]

Thus, at the end of 22 years of settlement, the children formed 25 per cent of the population. Persons who were, or who had been, convicts formed one-half of the total, while convict women were six times as numerous as free women.

In 1820 it was estimated that free settlers, who had emigrated voluntarily, totalled only 1,588 men and women, with 878 children, while the emancipists, or freed convicts, amounted to 7,556 persons with 5,859 children.[2] In 1821, a muster of the population took place in which no distinction was made between those who arrived as free settlers, and those who had become freed, when the total reached 29,783. Of these 15,969 were free and freed, while 13,814 were convicts. The former comprised 5,323 men, 3,422 women, and 7,224 children, while the latter were divided into 11,608 men and 1,206 women.[3] In 1828 the population had grown to 34,418, of whom 13,400, including children, were free, 7,350 had been freed, while the convicts were 15,668 in number.[4] The influx of free settlers, which began to assume steady proportions after 1820, altered the relative proportion of the convict population. By 1833 the population was estimated at 60,794, in 1836

[1] M. Phillips, *A Colonial Autocracy*, pp. 6-7.

[2] Wentworth, *Statistical Account of the British Settlements in Australasia*, vol. i, p. 415.

[3] *Ibid.*, p. 481.

[4] R. C. Mills, *The Colonisation of Australia*, p. 173.

at 77,096.[1] At the census of 1841 taken in the year after the cessation of transportation, the total population was 128,726, of whom 26,977 remained convicts, 19,395 had been freed, the rest being free.[2] The census of March 2, 1846 is available for us in a useful form. It shows a total of 187,413, of whom only 6.6 per cent of the male population, and 1.4 per cent of the female population remained bond-servants. Of the male population over 27 per cent had been born in the colony, nearly 55 per cent had arrived as free settlers, while the liberated formed but 11 per cent. Of the female population, 41 per cent had been born in the colony, and 42 per cent in the United Kingdom.[3]

The sociological significance of this experiment in colonization is great. It is customary in Australia to dismiss the whole subject with a deprecatory reference to "a birth-stain." It is possible to discount the enormity of the crimes committed by the convicts, to point out that political prisoners from Ireland at the close of the eighteenth century, or men convicted of breaches of such acts as the Game Laws or the Combination Laws, or Chartist agitators, were among the convicts. All this must be admitted, and may form a justification for the view that such men "were in reality rough-hewn foundation stones of the best kind."[4] But it must be admitted, further, that thieves, forgers, coiners and highway robbers, criminals of a low moral and mental type, formed the majority, and that, whatever may have been their rank in the moral scale before conviction, the convict system was sufficient to degrade most men and women. Sociologically, we can afford to disregard the nature of

[1] *Journal of the Statistical Society of London*, vol. xi, p. 38.
[2] Barton, *History of N. S. Wales*, vol. i, p. 484.
[3] *Journal of the Statistical Society of London*, vol. xi, p. 38.
[4] Frank Fox, *Letters from an Old Dog*, p. 84.

their crimes and the fact that many of them died unreformed. The facts go to prove that they have handed down no heritage of moral obliquity, industrial incapacity or helpless and irremediable poverty. The selective process involved in the method of their treatment tended to enable only those to become freed, and thus marry, who were trustworthy as servants, and energetic as freedmen. Similarly the concerted opinion of the early settlement, where the fewness in numbers of the free settlers compelled them to maintain their exclusiveness, was selective in regard to marriage, yet we find that marriages of traders and settlers with children of freedmen or even of prisoners was frequent and socially approved.[1] In 1828 we have William Charles Wentworth, the most striking figure in early colonial life, speaking proudly of 6,067 men and women who had become freed, were house-holders and proprietors of landed and other property to the value of above one million and a half pounds sterling, and had upwards of 9,000 children, whom they were educating in industrious habits.[2]

The explanation of this situation is simple. Moral turpitude, however serious may be its consequences in society, is after all an acquired characteristic and is not transmissible by heredity. A new land, where social customs were not strong enough to fix an irredeemable brand upon the children, gave them, and even their parents, that fresh opportunity which is so frequently curative of moral disorders. The dangers and difficulties of Australia offered them those opportunities for adventure which they had been denied, and they responded to them, so that they grew to the physical and moral height of the average man. Even though their influence cannot have been great, either for evil or for

[1] Phillips, *op. cit.*, p. 11.
[2] Wentworth, *op. cit.*, vol. ii, p. 157.

good, the positive view seems to be correct, that, because of their courage and vigour, the early convicts who succeeded in leaving children were individually, to use words already quoted, " rough-hewn foundation stones of the best kind."

The influence of the convicts on Australia's social development was not merely individual, it was social, political and economic. Because so much of the early population was bond, its early governors were men of the navy and the army. Some of them, like Philip and Macquarie, had useful notions concerning the method of administration and settlement of a virgin land, but the more practical difficulties of securing discipline, both among the convicts and the soldiers and officers sent to control them, absorbed most of their attention. The disposal of the Crown lands was profoundly affected by the presence of convict labourers, whom the governor was only too willing to assign to settlers, in order to relieve the government of their charge, their maintenance being made, further, the basis of grants of land. The unprofitable nature of their labour, especially in agriculture, tended, in conjunction with other circumstances to fasten upon the young colony a decided trend towards pastoral life, and a consequent slow development of agriculture. Even when freed, the emancipists, without the capital necessary for taking up pasture and with a certain reluctance towards agricultural labour, tended to centre around Sydney, which from the year 1820 began to assume a preponderating position relatively to the rural population. At the same time, the free labourer, who had emigrated at his own expense or with assistance, found himself in competition with the emancipated convict, who was preferred in the squatting pastoral districts, and through the conditions affecting the acquisition of land, tended also to be driven into the cities.

Free settlers came only slowly into the young country. The first of them arrived in 1792, five years after the foundation of Sydney. In 1805 there were something like 600 of them, but in 1810 they had not increased beyond 700, and in 1815 a more careful estimate showed not more than 900 men and 200 women who belonged to that class.[1] In 1819 their numbers did not exceed 1,400, excluding children.[2] In 1820, Wentworth estimated free settlers at 1,558 and their children at 878, while at the same time he claimed that the emancipists, or liberated convicts, totaled 7,556 and their children 5,859.[3] From 1821 onwards the tide of immigration set in more steadily, and in the decade averaged 880 settlers per year, reaching over 1000 each year after 1828.

The explanation of this slow rate of development of settlement is to be found in the circumstances of the early settlement. In the first place, the colony was designed almost solely as a penal settlement. Its first governor, Captain Arthur Phillip, after his brief and restricted glimpse of its possibilities, advocated its development by free settlers aided by convict labour. "If fifty farmers were sent out with their families, they would do more in one year in rendering this colony independent of the mother country as to provisions than a thousand convicts."[4] But the British government had come to a decision on the matter which was not to be shaken for many years. A proposal had been made that American loyalists should be given the opportunity of emigrating to the new land. But not even the greatest statesmen of the England of that time had a colonial policy which would provide for the self-government which such colonists would demand. Crowded gaols and prison hulks

---

[1] Phillips, *op. cit.*, p. 7.
[2] *Ibid.*, p. 109.
[3] Wentworth, *op. cit.*, vol. i, p. 415.
[4] Barton, *op. cit.*, vol. i, pp. 315-317, 324-5.

were a more pressing problem. It was not England herself that was overcrowded, as in the next century; it was her prisons that were full to overflowing. Hence, even when Phillip urged that no more convicts should be sent to the new settlement till there were enough farms in use to supply food, the British Home Secretary announced the resolution of the government "' to send out all the convicts sentenced for transportation in order that His Majesty's gaols in this kingdom may be at once quite cleared." [1]

Even when the wisdom of Phillip's suggestion that free settlers should be introduced was recognized, the spirit and tendency of early colonial administration and the absence of any effective measures to promote immigration acted as a decisive check till about 1830. A convict settlement permitted of modes of discipline with which naval and military men like the early governors were familiar. The addition of free settlers not only complicated their problem, making it equivalent to the rule of a community half free and half convict, but by the dispersion of the settlers made police precautions an immense financial and administrative burden. Hence the effective opposition of the early governors. Governor Macquarie (1809-1821) endorsed the principle that the colony existed to give a chance for reformation to every convict who had served his sentence. " My principle is that when once a man is free, his former state should no longer be remembered, or allowed to act against him: let him then feel himself eligible for any situation which he has, by a long term of upright conduct, proved himself worthy of filling." [2] This patronage of the emancipists, who continued to surpass the free settlers in numbers for many years, hindered the advent of free settlers.

[1] Quoted in Barton, *op. cit.*, p. 365.
[2] Quoted in Jose, " *History of Australasia,*" p. 43.

ELEMENTS OF THE POPULATION

But two other valid reasons existed for the slowness of settlement, the ignorance of the British public and the expense and difficulty of the journey to Australia. The former reason was in part removed in 1821 by the report of Mr. Bigge, a Commissioner sent out by the British Parliament to report on the administration of Governor Macquarie. His long, careful accounts of the position and possibilities of the young colony started a steady stream of emigration of young, adventurous men, each with a little capital. This stream steadily increased in volume, as we have seen, during that decade. Almost at the same time, the publication of William Charles Wentworth's book [1] furnished the British public with a glowing and detailed account of the colony and of the opportunities it afforded even to the man devoid of capital.

But the outstanding obstacle to emigration to Australia was the length and expense of the journey, which occupied from four to six months and cost up to £40 per head. During these years emigrants, all of whom paid their own fare, were going out from England to America at the rate of 20,000 a year. The journey was short, the fare relatively small, and the land so near that return was possible, if not easy. If so distant a settlement as Australia was to participate in this tide of emigration, it must find some means of giving assistance to those who wished to seek its shores. Such a policy was determined upon from the year 1830, and means were found through the use of the proceeds of the sale of Crown lands.[2] The colonial and home governments both gave assistance to intending settlers. The former paid half the passage money for unmarried females, who were destined as wives for the numerically preponderant males of

[1] *Statistical Account of the British Settlements in Australasia.*
[2] *Vide infra*, p. 64, for treatment of this matter.

the community, and loaned £20 to any married mechanic to emigrate with his family, an assistance extended afterwards to agricultural labourers. As these advances were practically never repaid, emigration of females was made free in 1835, and emigration of males in 1837. In the colonies, from 1835 onwards till the crash at the end of 1841, bounties were paid to private settlers who introduced mechanics and farm settlers. In 1840 the bounty was increased, and extended to agricultural labourers, shepherds, carpenters, bricklayers, masons, female domestics and farm labourers. A systematic advertising of the opportunities offered in Australia led to emigrant ships being despatched from many parts of the United Kingdom. One of these interesting pamphlets [1] tells us that

during the eight and a half years previous to 30th June 1836. it appears that 10,284 emigrants had arrived in the colony of New South Wales. . . . Early in spring a vessel sailed from Dundee, with a number of respectable farm-servants and mechanics: afterwards there were three vessels from the Highlands. Ships have also sailed from the Clyde and from England and Ireland.

The increased bounties offered in 1840 gave an immense impetus to immigration. Altogether, between 1832 and 1842, New South Wales received from land sales no less than £1,090,583, expended £950,000 of it on immigration, and obtained 50,000 settlers.[2] Land speculations had been responsible for this immense revenue. A financial crisis which lasted from 1841 to 1843 put an end to assisted immigration for some time.

During all this time men and women were coming in who

[1] "Notes on Australia for the information of intending Emigrants," by John Bowie, Writer of the Signet (Edinburgh, 1837), p. 23.

[2] Mills, *Colonisation of Australia*, p. 322.

had paid for their own passage. In 1829, 564 came; next year, 309; in 1831, 457; in 1832, 1,214. In 1833 the total had reached 1,432, in that year exceeding the assisted immigrants, who totaled 1,253.[1] Figures fail us for the period of the great rush of assisted immigration, but the settlements at Swan River, afterwards Western Australia, and at Adelaide, in South Australia, brought in many free settlers. On the whole, the incoming of free settlers prior to 1851 was a mere trickle, the precursor of a flood that was again to die down.

The flood burst with the discovery of gold (1851) in New South Wales and Victoria. The rich alluvial gold fields of the latter colony, which had just started on its career of independence and self-government, attracted shiploads of men from England and California. Its population in 1850 was 76,162, but the immigrants had carried the figure in 1855 to 364,324, and by 1861 to 541,800.[2] The population of the whole of Australia in 1850 was 405,356; the influx of gold-digging into the two auriferous states and the consequent stimulation of settlement in all the states had raised the figure in 1855 to 793,260. By 1861, when the ebb and flow of the tide of gold-seekers had attained a state of equilibrium, the population stood at 1,145,585.[3]

This great influx altered the nature and the trend of Australian development. It brought in a new population, with greater economic needs and larger economic possibilities. Its social and political effects were even greater. It reduced the convict section and their children to a minority, which was to diminish in proportion and significance. It broke up the tendency to an aristocratic stratification of the new society, towards which the mode of land settlement

[1] Jose, *op. cit.*, p. 210.
[2] *Victorian Year Book*, 1915-1916, p. 9.
[3] See *Commonwealth Year Book*, no. 10, p. 101.

and the use of convict labour were contributing. Not only were many of the gold-diggers frankly republican in their views and sentiments, as riots on the Victorian gold-diggings showed, but there was a stronger and more significant leaven of Chartism. This leaven was infused between the granting of self-government in 1851 and the operation of the new constitutions in 1856. Though this new population had little influence in the shaping of the constitutions, it had much to do with their working and their early liberalization. In consequence of the number, nature and character of those who came in the gold rush, they are rightly estimated as one of the most significant elements in the settlement of Australia. The gold-digging immigration "precipitated Australia into manhood."

During the period of the gold rush the tide of assisted immigration was flowing strongly. Each state was anxious to participate in the flow of wealth and prosperity which had obviously followed the influx of population. Assistance was given to those who wished to bring family or other relatives to Australia, or to those of certain occupations in the United Kingdom who wished to emigrate. In the years 1852-1854, when 224,000 unassisted immigrants arrived, those who were assisted totaled 46,373, and of these more than 60 per cent were women.[1] After the gold rush there was little abatement of the stream. In 1855 New South Wales received 14,567 nominated immigrants as contrasted with 3,116 who paid for their own passages. Next year the numbers were 7,210 and 8,791, respectively.[2] But as financial depression and difficulties in obtaining land set in, the states gave less encouragement, and immigration was unaided from about 1887 to 1906. In the first five years of

[1] Rusden, *History of Australia*, p. 13.
[2] *Fraser's Magazine*, 1858, p. 661.

this century the tide was reversed, 16,793 more departures than arrivals being registered. But from 1906 onwards agricultural labourers, domestic servants and artisans were introduced in large numbers, a quarter of a million immigrants being received in the period ending with the year 1913.

Our analysis has shown us two main sources for the Australian population, both alike in race, speech and political tradition, differing merely in economic circumstances and in their manner of entrance into Australia. One was possessed of at least sufficient capital to pay the cost of the lengthy voyage to Australia, the other had every qualification for worthy citizenship in a new and unexplored land except sufficient passage money. In the latter fact there is no suggestion of pauperism. Never, except by a philanthropic blunder which aroused so much indignation that its repetition was impossible, were English paupers shipped to Australia. The assisted emigrants were as free from pauperism as the average English labourer of the years following the reform of the Poor Laws. The gold-diggers were certainly above the average of their class. A comparison has been made of the relative literacy of the United Kingdom and of the State of Victoria during the years 1853-1855, the years of the gold rush, the comparison being based on signatures to marriage registers. " The record seems to indicate that the early arrivals in Victoria from the United Kingdom were better educated on the average than their compatriots who remained in that country." [1] An English estimate of them in the year 1868, made by one apparently well acquainted with the social composition and political development of Victoria, is interesting. " The mass of the people are certainly more intellectual, more ardent, better educated and more independent, than

[1] *Victorian Year Book*, 1915-1916, pp. 513, 514.

the parallel classes of any European population. . . . The very fact of a large portion of them having voluntarily emigrated from the old country and accepted all the hazards of a new career in an unknown land, argues in them a certain moral and intellectual superiority." [1]

Despite this general likeness, the free settler and the assisted immigrant have contributed two distinct strains to the Australian population. These are traceable through the opportunities of settlement on the land which fell to the one, and of employment in cities which fell to the other, as well as through the psychological reaction to these varying opportunities. Among the former class, it is not incorrect to include the officers of the army corps who were sent to keep order among the convicts, and the officials who came to administer the laws, many of whom remained. As we shall point out in our treatment of the reaction of the settlement of the land upon social development, the leading officers of the New South Wales Army Corps were able to reward themselves with large blocks of land, selected from the most fertile areas that the young colony offered for appropriation. When their military position was lost, on the disbanding of the Army Corps, they settled down as landed proprietors. Being the only capitalists, and having acquired further wealth by the infamous traffic in rum, they were in a position to buy the grants of dissatisfied or bankrupt free settlers. With the advent of other young men of capital, many of them members of the untitled nobility of England, and the possibility after 1813 of obtaining large areas of land on the western plains of New South Wales, an attempt was made to introduce the aristocratic traditions and customs of the mother country. The spirit, bearing and outlook of the English squire, the desire for wide-flung acres, and for social position and distinction based on landed

[1] *Fraser's Magazine*, 1868, p. 480.

property, the combination of the parochial spirit with a strong sense of local independence, entered with them into Australian life. Evidence of the arguments on which the desirability of such an aristocratic society is affirmed, is found in an article in *Fraser's Magazine*.[1] The writer asserts that the physical geography of the country has made a distinction between the farmer and the grazier, who exist side by side in permanent rivalry. Starting from the assertion that "universal suffrage, equal electoral districts, vote by ballot, and triennial parliaments are instruments of fatal mischief in a society which contains the remnants of a convict population, largely recruited by invading hosts of goldfinders," the need of a legitimate aristocracy with hereditary titles is established to the writer's satisfaction. Then "the three classes of Australian society would fall into their natural relations, and would exhibit a social hierarchy such as no other British colony can present." Nevertheless, apart from the land monopoly which was associated therewith, and the unsuccessful attempt in 1851 to create an hereditary political aristocracy,[2] this spirit, tempered as it has been with the more radically democratic movements, has added a useful individualistic leaven.

The English official was the instrument whereby there was recreated under altered skies the best features of English life. The aims and ideals of England, the love of law and order, the desire for self-government, the idea of justice, of freedom, of liberty — all that is the birthright of Englishmen was incorporated into the social structure of the new nation. Australians had not, like the American colonists, to undertake the formation of a mode of government which contained the essentials of British liberty with-

---

[1] 1858, p. 666.
[2] See Cramp, *State and Federal Constitutions of Australia*, p. 55.

out guidance from those who understood the inner spirit of the unwritten English constitution. Further, these British officials established a tradition of probity in public service which makes the official life of Australia free from any taint of conscious injustice, political partisanship or personal self-seeking.

Of the free settlers who were neither officials nor army officers, it must be said that they were the men who opened up mountain pastures, who followed the explorer out into the interior along the banks of the inland rivers or who penetrated the dense forests of the coastal rivers and planted their farms. Theirs was, in every case, a life of adventure and daring. For if Nature deprived the early Australian settler of the American colonists' struggle with a savage foe and equally savage wild beasts, she faced him with a hostile environment more forbidding than any other country presents. The fight with the naked elements was the pioneers' battle. Only men of inherent courage and initiative, men in strength and breadth of outlook above the average, would have faced the long voyage and the uncertainty of life in a new land. Nature was fickle in this new country. Flood and fire and drought might come to rob the settlers of the rewards of their efforts. Hence they tended not only to become individualists, fighting each his own battle, but to assume some of the gambler's optimism, some of the hopefulness and confidence of those who take great risks, who are often thrown down, but arise again with smiling faces.

In this psychological reaction the large number of assisted immigrants who did not become tillers of the soil were not sharers. Their position and outlook were different. Their entry into the country was facilitated by the use of government funds. They came to accept employment, though some of the farm labourers thus brought in were able to get selections of their own after 1861. But the majority were unfortunate in the moment of their entry and in the inadequacy of the opportunities for settlement on the land. Until 1861, at least, the largest influxes of nominated immigrants occurred at periods of acute financial crisis. Land speculation had produced large revenues which had been expended in introducing immigrants. When the crash occurred, shiploads of intending immigrants were on their way. Thus in 1842, the year following the failure of the first land boom, 27,000 assisted immigrants arrived. Men and women, introduced in this way and under such circumstances, were likely to rely upon state aid. Cheap lodgings had to be found for them on arrival, they had to be assisted with work and with transportation facilities to that part of the country where work was to be found. Further, the aggregation into cities became fixed in the social process of Australian life by the arrival of the nominated immigrant. The influence of land monopoly had been at work from the earliest day of the settlement, forcing emancipated convicts and free settlers, as well as nominated immigrants, into the cities. But from the forties onwards through the gold-digging rush, this tendency took definite shape and direction. When the gold-diggers of Victoria had worked out the alluvial deposits, they fell back upon their trades in many cases, and crowded into the few cities. Among the nominated immigrants were many artisans, since the nomination was neither wisely regulated nor restricted. Hence with the demand for employment and a supply of labor available on the one hand, and on the other a supply of wool, which was the country's chief industry at that date, manufactures sprang up. With them the grouping of a large proportion of the population of Australia in cities, with all that is implied of altered psychic traits and an altered political development. City and country are not only distinct in Australia, as in other lands, but there is less interchange between them than elsewhere. The city is not recruited mainly from an overflowing countryside. On the contrary, the industries for which the few good ports and capital cities of the Commonwealth are the natural centers are carried on by people who have never been stimulated by the hardship, the restricted opportunities, the individualism of country life and work. Historically the city has been built up, and many of its industries are still carried on, by the immigration of the town dwellers of the United Kingdom. The cities have social wants and desires that find expression in a definite social policy, and they have become the stronghold of the Labour party. As a result, Australian development has taken a line in which it challenges contrast with that of countries like the United States and Canada. An Australia of open spaces, climatically adapted for wide-flung settlement, would have developed, like the United States, into a land of individualism, with little of the communal feeling, and with no strong sense of the reliance of the individual upon society. The Australia of to-day, where country and city are so historically separate, is a land in which the strong, practical, independent and daring spirit of the pioneer beats side by side with the socialized consciousness of the city-dwellers that finds in a radical democracy the natural outlet for its faiths and ideals.

CHAPTER III

THE LAND AND ITS SETTLEMENT

GIVEN the people whose manner of arrival and whose character we have described, we have to analyze the physical and social environment into which they were thrown, before we have completed our outline of the conditioning factors of Australian social development. The nature of the country, its climate, its rainfall, its natural resources, and the advantages and difficulties, natural and artificial, which its settlers met, must be taken into account as affecting the rate, nature and degree of settlement, and this, in its turn, as conditioning its economic and political development. Into the full analysis of these factors this dissertation cannot enter. Let it suffice to say that neither can the Australia of the past and the present be intelligently understood, nor the Australia of the future intelligently guided till sociological investigation along these lines has been begun.

The effect of the isolation of Australia as a selective factor in the composition of its population has been already discussed. This isolation has had economic effects as well, mainly through the general ignorance which tends to prevail concerning a place so far removed from the chief centers of trade and industry. In the days when it was in need of railways and of other accessories towards opening it up, private capital was not greatly interested in so small a settlement and so distant a land. Hence, the State, which alone could attract the investment of capital and guarantee its repayment, came to be the chief entrepreneur, and the

Australian states became, in this sense, socialistic. This isolation, with its economic effects, is passing away. Large investments of capital from outside the country have been made, in addition to that accumulated in the debts of the various States.

The very size of the country, involving as it does, varieties of climate, soil and surface, with varying rainfall and the possibility of diverse and numerous products, becomes a weighty factor in its social development. It is a spacious land of mighty distances. In size, it is almost equal to continental United States, and only one fourth smaller than Europe. Its coastline is over 12,000 miles. The greatest distance east and west is over 3,000 miles. Five-thirteenths of its area lie within the Tropics, the rest being within the Temperate zone. The most northern point of the mainland is 10° S, the southern point is 39° S, while Tasmania runs down to 43° S. By reason of its insular geographic position and the general uniformity of its physical features, Australia is less subject to extremes of weather, and is on the whole more temperate than regions of similar area and in similar latitude. The extreme range of shade temperatures in summer and winter is probably only 81°, while that of North America is 153°. The range between the mean summer and mean winter temperatures in the six capital cities is under 20 degrees, except in Adelaide, South Australia, where this range is slightly exceeded. There is, however, a fairly large part of the country where the average summer temperature is over 90 degrees, constituting the problem in tropical colonisation which confronts the country. The degree of relative humidity is found to be greatest when, and where, the temperature is low. That is, humidity is greatest in the winter months and in Hobart, the most southern of the capitals.

The rainfall varies greatly. Tropical regions on the

north-east coast of Queensland receive at times over 200 inches per year, while an area around Lake Eyre in South Australia has but 5 inches per year. It is estimated that at least one million square miles, over one-third of the whole continent, has a rainfall of less than 10 inches a year. A minimum of 15 or 16 inches per year is essential for close settlement, though dry farming is possible in certain countries where the rainfall is only 13 inches. The great evaporation in Australia, however, raises the minimum for dry farming to about 15 inches. This low rainfall tends to make settlement difficult in more than half of the continent. Nevertheless, the area which remains and has a rainfall sufficient for settlement and production, is almost equal to that of the whole of Europe, exclusive of Russia. The distribution of rainfall is significant for the economic development of the country. Summer rains fall mainly within the tropical North, and along the East, covering the whole of the state of Queensland, and a part of New South Wales, and contributing during the hot months from 60 to 90 per cent of the total rainfall for that area. Winter rains are experienced over the same regions in varying amounts, but are more characteristic of the whole western and southern coast, from Western Australia to Victoria. From 60 to 70 per cent of the rainfall of this region occurs in winter. But this distribution is not regular. There is no fatal uniformity about it, as in the monsoons of India, and a threatened drought is often broken up by the arrival of rain long over-due. On the other hand, the fact that such a large proportion of the rain of certain areas falls in the winter months, when evaporation is less rapid and when the soil gets the full benefit in the spring time, gives wheat growing and the rearing of sheep greater assistance than the same rainfall distributed evenly throughout the year. The result is that large areas, though unadapted for close settlement, are yet suitable for pasture and in part for wheat, and will become increasingly so under scientific methods of conservation.

The physical configuration of the country is simple and uniform. It has no central backbone, no mountains clothed with perennial snows to feed its rivers. Along the eastern coast, at distances varying upwards from 50 miles, lies one long divide, which runs from Northern Queensland, through New South Wales into Victoria. Between this and the Pacific coast on the east and the south is a rich coastal plain with an abundant rainfall and numerous rivers. The mountain chain itself is rather a plateau, and in places comprises areas of rich soil, as well as mineral areas of all sorts. Westwards of the Great Divide stretch fairly level plains, the eastern limits of which are well watered by the rivers which rise in the mountains. Some of the rivers, however, run over the porous outcrop of a vast artesian basin, in area equal to 569,000 square miles, so that a large proportion of their waters sinks undergound. The rolling country in New South Wales within the 20 inch limit of rainfall is the home of the wheat industry, while farther west, horses and cattle range in Queensland and sheep in New South Wales. Central Australia, the more arid section of the continent, is a vast plateau from 1,000 to 1,500 feet high. This runs up towards the Northern Territory, and ends in a tropical plain. To the North West, it passes into the tropical portion of Western Australia, some parts of which are fairly well watered. In the South West, there is an auriferous region around Kalgoorlie where a population of over 60,000 lives in several large towns in a region where the rainfall is only 8 inches per year. Nearer the coast is a region forming but a small proportion of the vast area of Western Australia, where the mountain chains are low, and the rainfall is sufficient, on the eastern edge, for pasture and, nearer the coast for wheat and dairying.

This brief sketch is sufficient to show a land with great potentialities, but with enormous hindrances to its economic development. Scanty rainfall operates to prevent agriculture in sections where the soil is rich in nitrogen. Tropical heat has hindered the settlement and development of large, fertile and well watered areas. The productive areas are not naturally restricted relatively to a population of five million persons. But wise choice is needed concerning their relative values in pasture and in agriculture, scientific knowledge concerning their capacities and the mode of their highest utilization, and organized social effort towards securing that utilization. As indicated above, the rate, nature and degree of settlement, and the economic and political development of the country will depend on these measures. Scientific knowledge is, however, only possible after exploration and the opening up of the country, and organized social effort appears only after the creation of a community informed concerning its opportunities and responsibilities. The distribution of the available land, the size and nature of the holdings and the mode of their tenure may be considered by the sociologist, in his investigation, as factors affecting the first conditions of a wise choice concerning their relative value and use.

It is clear that much has depended on the distribution of land from the beginning of the settlement. The foundation of such a colony as New South Wales, where the virgin lands of a whole continent lay open for distribution by the Crown, afforded a unique opportunity for social prevision. The distribution of the land might have been so controlled and directed as to foster the settlement of a numerous yeomanry, conserve the natural resources of mine and forest, and endow the future educational institutions of the land. To effect the former object, it would have been necessary to control the first settlement, to regulate the later distribution of land, and prevent the holding back of large territories from their more effective use in agriculture. This, and other modes of conserving natural resources, however, required a more thorough and scientific survey than was feasible in the early days of settlement. The use of the land to endow future educational establishments never entered into the vision or the practice of a colony destined first to be a penal establishment, and controlled later by a landowning aristocracy to whom education was a matter for private arrangement.

The land policy of the new colony was short-sighted in aim, formless in content, and shifty and faulty in execution. From the foundation of the first colony to the end of the 19th century, no regular or uniform system, based on scientific knowledge of the potentialities of the country and regard for its future intensive settlement, and adaptable to its growing needs, had been suggested. Land was given away wastefully, or sold in quantities which enabled a relatively small group of persons to obtain control of large areas used mainly for pastoral purposes, although, in many cases, suited for cultivation. As a result, the distribution of the population, the economic development of the country, its political institutions and its psychological characteristics were profoundly affected. The effect of the land policy will be seen more clearly after a description of its various forms.

In the beginning, the tilling of agricultural land was necessary to obtain food for a colony so distant from the world centers of production. This need led Governor Phillip to seek the introduction of free settlers, to whom as well as to freed convicts he gave grants of small farms, always less than 100 acres in size. Settlers were guaranteed two years provisions and furnished with convict labour free of expense, one year's clothing and two years' food being supplied with each convict. Settlement thus came to be not so much a matter of the intensive cultivation of small farms as a means for the easing of the exchequer from the burden of convict expenses, as well as an opportunity for men of capital. Hence, the military officers, the only men of capital in the early settlement, came to acquire large areas, a process rendered the easier by the fact that their superior officers were acting governors during three of the earlier years. These men systematically allotted among their officers large areas of land and the convicts with which to work them. As a result of such grants and of the ease with which the lands of small settlers could be bought up, one of these officers, John Macarthur, who bears an honoured name in Australian history because of his contribution to the development of the pastoral industry, obtained possession, as early as 1891, of 4,000 out of 18,000 acres available for pasture land. Possession of land by no means indicated an intention to cultivate it. In 1805 we have Governor King complaining of "the common practice pursued by the colonists of obtaining larger grants than they could afford to cultivate."[1] In 1810, when the population was estimated at 11,590[2] the area alienated was 95,937 acres, held by 808 proprietors.[3] With the opening up of the plains beyond the Blue Mountains in 1813, the system of free grants and assisted convict labor came to fruition. Sheep rearing had been introduced after 1805 by John Macarthur, whom George III, keenly interested in agriculture, had presented with a few merino sheep and a grant of 5,000 acres in perpetuity. The

[1] Quoted in M. Phillips, *A Colonial Autocracy*, p. 15.
[2] See *Commonwealth Year Book*, no. 8, p. 33.
[3] M. Phillips, *op. cit.*, p. 14.

pastoral industry called for larger areas, the governor still had the power of granting free land, convict labour was abundant, but the capital necessary was scarcer than free settlers. Hence land was given more and more lavishly and fell into relatively fewer hands. Governor Macquarie (1809-1821) granted 239,576 acres, five persons receiving 3,000 acres each, four receiving 2,000 acres each. Thus two results, long to remain characteristic of Australia, were brought about. More than one-half of the land passed into the hands of the free settlers, who comprised less than one-fifth of the population, while not one-eighth of the population was occupied in agricultural pursuits.

In 1820 a report was made to the British Parliament on the administration of Governor Macquarie. The Commissioner, Mr. Bigge, has given us much valuable material concerning the state of the colony. On the question of the land, he expressed the opinion held by the wealthier settlers with whom he sided very largely in their quarrel with the governor.

The whole tendency of that [Bigge's] report was to favor the aggregation of large areas under private ownership: to make it easy for the capitalist to procure land, and thus, with the convict labour, develop the wool export of the country. Bigge looked for the prosperity of the colony to capitalist farmers with large estates, cultivated by forced labour, or to proprietary companies holding sway over immense tracts, where great herds of sheep should be guarded by lonely convict shepherds. He looked with cold and unfeeling eyes upon the colony's attempt to start manufactures. Minor trading ventures were to be allowed a chance of existence, and men with small capital were to be given land, though with a sparing hand. But to the wealthy land and labour were to be dispensed liberally, with two chief objects in view, one, to encourage immigrants who

[1] M. Phillips, *op. cit.*, pp. 110, 111.

might relieve the government of the charge of convicts, and the other to provide England with an important raw material.[1]

One gets a glimpse of the contradictions of the land policy of the period by quoting together with this report the view of Lord Goulburn, Under Secretary of State for the Colonies, who wrote in the same year as Bigge's report (1820) :—" Large grants of land to individuals have been the bane of all our colonies and it has been the main object of Lord Bathurst's administration to prevent the extension of this evil by every means in his power." [2] Within a few years, however, land companies, formed in London, were given large areas of Australian soil. In 1824, the Australian Agricultural Company, which had a capital of a million pounds, was granted a million acres of land, on condition that it expend the equivalent of its capital on the improvement of land. Similar grants were made in Van Dieman's Land and Western Australia. The first two companies made large use of convict labour, thus reducing the cost of the penal settlement.

In 1830, the system of crown grants ended. The colony's first experiment in the disposal of public lands was finished. With a population that could not have exceeded 50,000 there had been alienated in New South Wales alone an area of 3,344,030 acres.[3] Had this been divided among the occupiers, taking them in family units, it would have made possible the settlement of a series of small holdings. Australia would have had a fine nucleus of early settlers cultivating the soil with their own hands and the labour of their families. Unjust as the system of free grants was to posterity, the use of the system in promoting immigration

[1] M. Phillips, *op. cit.*, pp. 322, 323.
[2] Quoted in M. Phillips, *op. cit.*, p. 111.
[3] Mills, *Colonisation of Australia*, p. 158.

and fostering agricultural settlement on small holdings has had advantages in a new country which go far to outweigh its social inequity. But the crown grants of Australia were less for agriculture than for pasture, were in increasingly large areas, and were not so much a bounty on immigration, as a reward for the possession of capital sufficient to employ and care for convict servants. The insufficiency of convict labour which gave better returns in the pastoral industry, the large areas granted, as well as the suitability of the country for pasture, especially for sheep, gave agriculture a great set-back. For many a long year " wool was king " of the industries of the young land. A colonial aristocracy based on land tended to arise. Had the system of free grants continued, the first comers would have succeeded in occupying all the best lands of the country in large holdings long before there was any considerable population.

The system of sale at a fixed price, which succeeded the crown grant system in 1830 achieved no greater success. It brought settlers into the country in great numbers, since the funds obtained were used to promote immigration. Western Australia and South Australia were settled under the stimulus of the ideas of Wakefield. The experiment in the latter colony shows how the notion of the class distinctions and class interests of England permeated Australian land policy at that period. Wakefield, who counted among his friends Lord Durham, Earl Grey, Grote, the historian of Greece, Jeremy Bentham and John Stuart Mill, brought forward a scheme for the foundation of a colony based on the aristocratic control of high-priced land. He declared that the ease with which poor men could obtain land had made unprofitable the employment of large capital in the colonies, and had restricted the close settlement of the country under English conditions. If the public lands of an unsettled part of Australia were sold at a "sufficient price," labourers would be unable to buy land and become farmers. On the other hand, English gentlemen might go out to invest their capital in such land, and with a retinue of servants, among whom were no convicts, live in leisured ease amid the Arcadian simplicity of colonial life. The experiment failed badly, but it had the effect of raising the price of land throughout Australia from five shillings, the minimum fixed in New South Wales in 1830, to twelve shillings and later twenty shillings per acre. The latter figure, without regard to situation and fertility, has been the standard price at which most of the rural land of Australia has been alienated since that date.

From this period and this system arose another phenomenon of great sociological significance, namely, the squatting interest. Squatters were the owners of large herds and flocks who moved them, without license or right of occupation, into the crown lands. Unable to buy the large areas needed for their sheep, they preferred to trespass like nomads over the grassy plains. Their action showed many of the qualities of courage, energy and self-reliance that the pioneer life brings forth. The recognition of this and of the value of their industry led to their being granted licenses at a nominal fee. Squatting having been thus legally recognized, the squatters proceeded to occupy large areas, thereby monopolizing settlement on some of the most fertile lands of the colony, at the same time paying a ridiculously low rental, which bore no proportion to the size or value of the holdings. Thus, Governor Gipps, in the course of his fight with these land monopolists, reported to the Under Secretary of State for the Colonies that four squatters occupied 12,110 square miles among them on the fertile Liverpool Plains, an area greater than that of Belgium, while nine other men paid only £10 a year more for a total of 486 square miles in the same district. Eight others occupied 1,747,840 acres among them, and five more a million acres. On the other hand, five persons paying the same license fee could not procure together more than 2,000 to 3,000 acres. One squatter, who held 381,000 acres, or 625 square miles, an area as large as that of several counties, paid only £80 a year for the privilege.[1]

In 1844 Governor Gipps sought to restrain the squatters, to limit their runs, to transform the licenses into leases and thereby to secure a more adequate rental. Accordingly, he issued regulations requiring squatters to purchase 320 acres of their runs at one pound an acre. This would have given room for a homestead, and, coupled with the right to graze over the surrounding country until it was required for sale, was a just proposal. But the squatters, having an advantage over the Governor in that he had issued this order without consulting the Legislative Council, carried on a bitter fight for the right to lease blocks of five miles square for periods of fourteen years, with the right to purchase 640 acres at the upset price, to renew the lease for five years, and to preclude the sale of their run during the period of their lease. This fight they won when Earl Grey, a disciple of Wakefield, passed through the Imperial Parliament in 1846 a Crown Lands Sales Act, which, when applied to Australia by Orders-in-Council, contained regulations granting the squatters' demands. The effects of this action were serious.

Huge acres of land were secured by men at an absurdly low rental, with the right to purchase practically as they might please. As was only to be expected, the latter provision was well taken advantage of. Choice blocks with river frontages and positions the possession of which would prevent other per-

[1] Rusden, *History of Australia*, vol. ii, p. 331.

sons in the future from using the surrounding land, were speedily alienated. And thus was placed in the hands of a comparatively few men a power fraught with incalculable danger to the generations then unborn. Among the evils brought to the birth at this time, and which have since grown to the full development of maturity, was an absentee landlordism: the locking-up of land in the hands of a few which might have carried a population a hundredfold larger than its existing occupiers, and which would have doubled its productive power: an unnecessary antagonism between agriculturists and pastoralists. . . . [1]

When the flood tides of the gold immigration burst upon the country, it found a land of large pastoral estates, where wool was the chief product, and where agriculture was correspondingly retarded. Into these pastoral estates went the money of the successful miners. There was no other great or more profitable industry. But agricultural land for the new population thereby grew relatively scarcer. The knowledge that rich agricultural areas were occupied by squatters led to a demand for free selection throughout the public lands of the colonies. It was thought that a population of farmers could be substituted for one of a few squatters if the public lands were made available on three conditions:

(1) The area selected must not be less than 40 acres nor more than 320 acres.

(2) A price of £1 per acre must be paid, one-fourth of it immediately, the rest in instalments.

(3) The selector personally must live on his selection and improve it to the value of another £1 per acre.

Hence from 1861 onwards this system was applied in most of the states. It made no distinction between soils, or con-

[1] Epps, *Land Systems of Australasia*, p. 23.

sidered either their location or their potentialities. No scientific demarcation of agricultural areas took place, and no stipulations were made as to the cultivation of lands that were primarily agricultural. The right of any person to enter upon a leasehold and select the most fertile and best watered areas led to a bitter class war between settler and squatter, to a reckless and illegal system of selection by the latter, and to practices on the part of the former involving fraud and blackmail. In Victoria there was produced "a mad scramble for the soil, conflict between pastoralists and settlers, public and private immorality, the taking up of land for speculation rather than cultivation, and the aggregation of large estates."[1] In Queensland the same results followed.

Injurious tendencies of the law were heightened by its abuse. Fraudulent selections enabled speculators to grasp larger blocks than the spirit of the law allowed. Combinations by members of a family gathered into one hand tens of thousands of acres in coveted districts. Those who had taken part in the lotteries of New South Wales and Victoria carried their experience to new pastures in order to overreach the authorities of Queensland. Some settlers incurred heavy liabilities by purchasing at auction lands which, if selected by others, would have rendered it impossible for the settlers to follow their previous pastoral pursuits.[2]

South Australia, which insisted on survey before selection, and had provisions concerning cultivation and re-sale of its more restricted public lands, and Western Australia, where railway companies or syndicates had received grants of land to be subsequently thrown open for settlement, escaped from the iniquity and paralysis of the period.

[1] Epps, *op. cit.*, pp. 70, 71.
[2] Rusden, *op. cit.*, vol. iii, pp. 606, 607.

Evidence of what this land policy has meant for Australia is abundant. Some of the most significant points are contained in a speech delivered in September, 1894, by the Hon. Sir Joseph Carruthers, at that time Minister for Lands for New South Wales.

In 1861 we had 159,834 residents in our towns and 189,116 in the country, but after thirty years under our present land system we have 730,100 residents in towns, as against only 388,321 in the country districts. . . . We have alienated no less than 49,600,000 acres of land since 1861 to settle only an additional 199,000 souls in country districts, . . . whilst prior to 1861, 189,000 residents were settled upon 7,350,000 acres of alienated land. . . . The holdings in the country in 1861 were represented by 15,650 occupants (proprietors). . . . To-day (September, 1894), with our enormous alienation, the holdings are represented by 41,400 occupants, or, in other words, over fifty million acres of land have been alienated since 1861, or are in course of alienation now, for an increase of 25,750 rural occupants—that is, at the rate of 2,000 acres for each occupant. In 1861 the average size of a holding was 280 acres, but in 1893 the average size of a holding was 762 acres.[1]

These results, may be summarized in the following table:

COMPARISON OF URBAN AND RURAL CONDITIONS IN NEW SOUTH WALES 1861 AND 1894

	1861	1894	Percentage Increase
Urban population	159,834	730,100	356.8
Rural population	189,116	388,322	105.3
Occupants of Land	15,650	41,400	164.5
Average size of holdings in acres	280	762	172.1
Alienations of land in acres	7,350,000	49,600,000	574.8

[1] New South Wales, *Hansard*, vol. lxx, p. 434.

These figures, as illustrated by the accompanying chart, show several paradoxes in social development. Along with an immense increase in alienated land is to be found an immense actual and relative increase in urban population, with a growth in rural population that bears no relation to the increase of alienated land, and is not equal to the proportionate increase of occupiers. The latter fact suggests the presence of an absentee-landlordism that finds no place in the statistics of rural residence. There is a further disparity between the increase in occupiers and the greater increase in the average size of holding, explicable by the immense alienation and the use made of the land. Plainly, this alienation is not one of land to be settled in small agricultural holdings. On the contrary, it is one where vast estates are in the hands of companies and single holders, where agriculture is restricted, and where the tide of immigration that might have flowed in fertilizing vigor over the land has been stayed in capital cities on the margin of the continent.

The figures for land under cultivation illustrate the retarding effect upon agriculture of the whole course of land legislation. New South Wales, a state later proved to be eminently suited for agricultural development, but one where the pastoral industry had made its home, remained absolutely and relatively behind the states of Victoria and South Australia until another method of dealing with land became operative in 1894. Victoria began to attack land monopoly in 1877 with a land tax, and in the nineties forged ahead of the other states in area under cultivation. South Australia discovered the wheat-bearing capacity of its lands in the days of the gold rush, and by reason also of her wiser land legislation, was cultivating by 1880 an area absolutely and relatively larger than that of any other state.

COMPARISON OF URBAN AND RURAL CONDITIONS IN NEW SOUTH WALES, 1861 AND 1894

DISTRIBUTION OF URBAN AND RURAL POPULATIONS

URBAN	RURAL
45.8%	54.2%
65.3%	34.7%

PERCENTAGE INCREASE OF RURAL POPULATION, OCCUPIERS, HOLDINGS AND ALIENATIONS OF LAND DURING 1861-1894, ON THE BASIS OF THE YEAR 1861

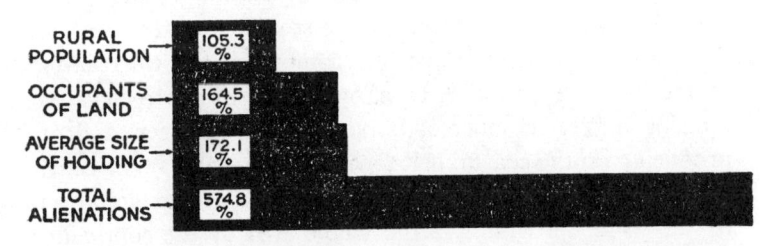

RURAL POPULATION	105.3%
OCCUPANTS OF LAND	164.5%
AVERAGE SIZE OF HOLDING	172.1%
TOTAL ALIENATIONS	574.8%

From about the middle of the last decade of the nineteenth century measures have been taken to obtain smaller holdings for agricultural settlement and to put lands to their best use. The latter aim involved scientific classification, not only of the Crown lands not yet alienated, but also of certain entire sections of the country. The former aim was sought by two methods, the imposition of land taxation so as to make the owner prefer to subdivide and and resell his land, and the repurchase of large pastoral estates by the government. These estates are divided into smaller blocks and offered to settlers on reasonable terms of repayment. In 1907 the areas thus acquired totaled 1,270,595 acres. In 1916 they had reached 3,156,087 acres, of which over 2,700,000 acres had been allotted in farms to about 11,700 settlers.[1] Along these lines of scientific classification of the highest potentialities of land and social effort towards the utilization of all land for the purpose for which it is naturally fitted, lies the future increase of settlement in Australia.

Yet Australia remains an empty continent, where nature has put greater difficulties in the way of settlement than any other country has. The pastoral industry, which till 1911 was supreme, and is now second in value,[2] is limited through climatic conditions in respect of rainfall and temperature, to about 28 per cent of the country. An area embracing another 19½ per cent would be useful, if provision could be made for the transport of stock to wetter areas in dry seasons.[3] Tropical Australia, comprising five-thirteenths of the total area, capable of carrying, on its more elevated interior, a great number of horses, cattle and sheep, and of producing on the coastal belt tobacco, cotton and sugar cane, has so far baffled the capacity and ingenuity in exploitation of the white settlers. Of the whole area of the continent, only eight per cent is settled,[4] and but little of that is in

---

[1] *Commonwealth Year Book*, no. 6, p. 295; no. 10, p. 258.

[2] The following figures concerning the estimated value of production from agricultural, pastoral and manufacturing industries 1910-1914 will show the period of transition. *Commonwealth Year Book*, no. 9, p. 1132.

Year	Agricultural Industry	Pastoral Industry	Manufacturing Industry
	£1000	£1000	£1000
1910	39,752	56,993	45,598
1911	38,774	50,725	50,767
1912	45,754	51,615	57,022
1913	46,162	57,866	61,586
1914	36,052	60,265	62,922

[3] Griffith Taylor, *Australia, Physiographic and Economic*, p. 252.

[4] *Commonwealth Year Book*, no. 9, p. 278.

agriculture. Small holdings of 100 acres or less, which are mainly agricultural or dairying, form nearly 45 per cent of the total number, but their aggregate area is but a very small part of the whole commonwealth and only 2.24 per cent of that of the total holdings. On the other hand, 90 large holdings, each over 50,000 acres, aggregate nearly three times the area of the small holdings. Holdings between 10,000 and 50,000 acres total 1,150 in number and cover an area of over twenty million acres. Counted with the 90 holdings each over 50,000 acres, these 1,240 holdings form almost one-quarter of the whole occupied area of the continent. The largest aggregations of property are in New South Wales, where 698 holdings, each over 10,000 acres, cover more than nineteen million acres, or 32 per cent of the total area of holdings over one acre in area, and nearly 10 per cent of the whole state. In Queensland, where no statistics concerning the number of holdings are available, three-quarters of the state is occupied under leases and licenses, mainly in unsettled districts.[1] These figures would have less significance for the sociologist if they represented the best use of the land, or if they stood for stern Nature's rigid limitations upon settlement. As stated earlier, the scientific survey of the soil and its capacities on which alone accurate statement or wise social action can be based, is lacking. In regard to agriculture, however, it has been estimated by the Commonwealth Meteorologist, after weighing all the conditioning factors, that 500,000 square miles are suitable for wheat growing.[2] Out of this possible area, only 14,511 square miles were cultivated in 1913-1914, yielding over 103 million bushels,[3] instead of 900 to 1,000

[1] *Commonwealth Year Book*, no. 8, pp. 264-270.
[2] *Federal Hand Book*, 1914, p. 149.
[3] *Commonwealth Year Book*, no. 8, pp. 310, 313.

million bushels, the potential output, as estimated by the Commonwealth Meteorologist.[1]

Our survey of the physical environment into which the Australian settler came, has revealed the forces which have operated upon him to produce the Australian of to-day. Scarcity of rainfall and fear of recurrent droughts diminish the productivity of the great central heart of the land, and tropical heat hinders the settlement and exploitation of another great section. Nature has made the coastal plains of the continent the most fertile parts, and has determined the chief ports of the land as its commercial centers. The absence of large navigable rivers will prevent large inland centers of commerce and administration. The chief ports of the land will, therefore, always be the centers toward which by means of railways, the chief modes of transportation, the products of the interior must concentrate. The need of this transportation in early days, when the wealth of the land consisted in wool reared in the inland plains, when capital could not be obtained by the sparse population itself, but only by its government, led to the building of state-owned railways. Within the habitable area, a gigantic wasteful and impolitic distribution of the public lands has profoundly altered the rate, nature and degree of settlement. Settlement has been pastoral longer and to a greater degree than it need have been. The economic development of the country has been both checked and diverted. The pastoral industry, carried on over large areas, is not so productive as the same industry carried on upon smaller irrigated areas, and far from as productive as a combination of wheat farming and sheep raising upon areas of about 1,000 acres. The difficulties in the way of easy settlement of the land have tended all along to keep the

[1] *Federal Hand Book*, p. 150.

immigrants in the cities and thus to make the city distinct from the country. The relatively small countryside prevents it from being a breeding-ground for the city.

Thus have been created in the short historical development of Australia those diverse interests which are the basis of the class antagonism that marks off its political groups. No single differentiating principle can readily be discovered. The physical environment, with its promise of golden harvests followed by years of drought and hardship, marks off the toiling adventurer of mine and field from the commercial, professional and labouring classes of the city. The distribution of wealth which went first to the pastoralist, then to the mine-owner and manufacturer, is possibly the chief distinguishing factor. The make-up of the population, the altered proportions in which the Celt stands to the Anglo-Saxon, the superior prestige acquired and sustained by English officers, officials and owners of large estates, are distinct elements in bringing one or more sets of persons into conflict with the activities and interests of other groups. The relations between city and country, the social attitude of the former in contrast with the individualistic attitude of the latter, and, finally the organization of each, politically and economically, with the reactions of government itself upon the problems created, justify a further study of social development in terms of conflicting interests and group struggles. For this study, the period of Australian history from 1890 onwards offers abundant material.

CHAPTER IV

THE STRUGGLE FOR SOCIAL REFORM

WITH the year 1890 the most recent epoch of Australian social development begins. From that year dates the operation of those political, economic and social forces which have made Australia a country of such deep interest to the student of social reform. Those forces had their genesis in the national temperament and in the conditions described in the two previous chapters. Their eruption, volcanic as it was in intensity, was preceded by much that was premonitory of a new order. The speculation in land which was characteristic of the period had led to a great inflation of land and rental values, which later precipitated a financial crisis. Periods of drought in New South Wales and South Australia in the middle of the decade prior to 1890, with a general fall in prices, made employment more difficult to obtain and wages began to fall. About the same time the state governments, which had been spending large sums of money in opening up the country, ceased their expenditures, and thereby increased unemployment. Large numbers of men gathered in Sydney, New South Wales, where relief work of an unproductive nature was found for them at the rate of five shillings a day. Already industrial trouble and social reform on principles that were considered novel and heterodox, the two distinctive traits of later social development, were becoming manifest. An interesting revelation of the conflicting principles which were to clash so bitterly afterwards is found in a letter from Sydney, written in

October, 1886, to the *Fortnightly Review*.[1] The writer, after telling of the numbers and conduct of the unemployed, and their refusal to accept wages of 15 shillings per week and rations, says:

Were the rate of wages regulated by supply and demand, there would not be a sober and capable man out of work in any of the Australian colonies. . . . The right to live, or rather to receive good wages, is being recognized by the Australian governments, who are making, and are perhaps compelled to make, humiliating concessions to the unemployed. It requires no prophet to foretell from this combination of circumstances great difficulties in the relations of labour and capital. The working class of Australia frankly admit that they will not allow wages to follow the laws of supply and demand.

The student of economics recognizes in this antithesis of the laws of supply and demand in relation to wages and in the demand for a living wage the rise of the new factor of association by means of trade unions. The agrarian question, with the tendency, on the one hand, towards large estates, and the demand, on the other for closer settlement, was being replaced by the industrial question as the workers of the cities became organized.

Trade-unionism in Australia began in the decade of the gold rush.[2] The early unions sought for the eight-hour day, and were able to make its adoption fairly general. As wage questions, however, came into prominence during the reaction after the gold rush, the unions manifested a tendency to deal with them on a basis different to the law of supply and demand. Owing to expanding trade after the gold discoveries, and industrial activity due to a great command over outside capital, no serious decline in wages

[1] Vol. xli, N. S., p. 314.
[2] See "The Historical Development of Trade Unionism in Australia" in *Trade Unionism in Australia*, edited by M. Atkinson, p. 49 *et seq.*

occurred till the year 1886. In the meantime trade-unionism had become firmly established. In 1885 the unions had an estimated membership of 50,000, and by 1890 had received legal recognition and protection in all states but Western Australia.[1] When, therefore, serious unemployment set in during the year 1886 the unions had both the motive and the power to fight for liberty of association and for the recognition of the right of collective bargaining. But another element was entering into the struggle that was to differentiate the unionism of the last quarter of a century from that which preceded it. An awakened social conscience became manifest. A social ideal, embodied in a new order of society, where fuller rights and larger opportunities for the masses of mankind seemed possible, became a guiding principle in the struggle for higher wages and better conditions. The wave of sympathy with the London dockers in 1880, when £30,000 was contributed from Australia to their strike funds, the great interest in Single Tax and land reforms fostered by the visit of Henry George, and the foundation of the communistic " New Australia " in Paraguay, furnish evidence of the presence of this new spirit that was bound to clash with the economic individualism prevalent in the industrial and political life of the time.

The first struggle came in 1886 because the pastoralists, at a time when the wool market was not yet experiencing a fall in prices, proposed to reduce shearing rates and charge increased prices for rations. The shearers, many of whom were small, independent settlers, objected and organized themselves. Sporadic and scattered strikes during the succeeding years enabled them to educate non-union shearers to the value of unionism. In 1890 came the great maritime strike. Members of the Marine Officers' Association, whose

[1] This State, which was then in its legislative infancy, gave similar recognition in 1902.

pay was in some cases less than that of the union seaman, asked for an advance of wages. Before doing so, they had affiliated with the Melbourne Trades Hall Council. The employers signified their willingness to treat with their men, but demanded, as a condition, their secession from the Council. The employers were ready to fight for " freedom of contract," and would have nothing to do with organized labour. They refused to arbitrate or enter into conferences, as such action implied a readiness to make concessions. Even if "hollow sentimental notions" urged them, in a time of crisis to yield, their better judgment counseled them to stand firm.[1] They signified their sympathy with the old, conservative unionism, while objecting to the new, "illegitimate" unionism, with its social program. On the other hand, shearers and miners joined with the marine officers and transport workers to secure the recognition of unionism. In 1891 the shearers struck when the employers adopted the same tactics as in 1886. A request from the shearers for a conference to arbitrate and settle the points at issue was rejected as an interference with free contract because the shearers insisted on collective bargaining. The disorder accompanying these two strikes necessitated government interference, while the final swerving of public opinion against the employees led to their decisive defeat.

The reaction was twofold. On the part of the unionists, political activity was introduced to reinforce the more conservative activities of trade unionism. "The failure of these widespread strikes, the intervention of the government in the struggles, the general social discontent consequent on the collapse of the boom, and acute financial and industrial depression, were the immediate causes that brought organized labour into politics."[2] Smarting under the defeat of

[1] See Reeves, *State Experiments in Australia*, vol. ii, p. 91.
[2] *Ibid.*, p. 61.

the maritime strike, the Australian Labour Federation met in Brisbane in August, 1890, to formulate a plan for political action. The general objects of the Federation, as outlined, were to extend labour organizations, to seek means of settlement of differences or by " an aggregation of power to enforce legitimate and necessary claims," to promote productive and distributive co-operation;

to consolidate the eight hour system by legislation or otherwise, to secure direct representation of labour in Parliament, to assist members in securing a fair wage and reasonable conditions of labour, and to take steps for the ultimate establishment of a minimum wage for all men and women in Australia, which, with a statute day, would prevent Australians from being degraded by competition to the level of Chinese and European labourers.[1]

After deliberation, the Federation set out its political objective or ultimate aim, which embraced as its first plank " the nationalisation of all sources of wealth and all means of production, distribution and exchanging of wealth." Other planks were state pensions, free educational institutions, state controlled " sanitary " institutions, and a just distribution of wealth. The immediate political program comprised universal adult suffrage, abolition of plural voting and of all nominee or property qualification chambers, equal electoral districts, complete and adequate registration of electors and annual parliaments.[2] These aims were to be obtained by organizing the trade unionists and general labourers of the country into a solid Labour party who would elect candidates to Parliament pledged to support the Labour platform. In 1891, at the general elections in New South Wales the Labour party won 36 seats out of a house of 120,

[1] Rules of the Australian Labour Federation, Brisbane, 1890.
[2] See St. Ledger, *Australian Socialism*, pp. 38, 39, 42.

and by 1899 had won a total of 70 seats in the legislative chambers of the continent. When the first Commonwealth Parliament met in 1901, it contained 24 Labour members in both houses out of a total membership of 111. By 1906 it had reached a total of 41 members, and in 1910 secured a majority in both houses. A Labour ministry held office for a few months in 1904, and again in 1908-1909. By this time it had emerged from an insignificant third party to considerable strength. In 1910 it attained office for three years, and again from 1914 till the end of 1916, when a conscription referendum rent the party in twain. In the meantime the same process had been repeated in the legislatures of the various states. Coming in as a third party, demanding, as the price of its support to one of the other parties, such reforms as cheap land, land taxation, adult suffrage, abolition of plural voting, equal electoral districts, early closing laws, minimum wage legislation, arbitration acts, and state pensions, it was able to achieve much. Gradually, as the altered political emphasis obliterated the party divisions of the pre-federation period and led to the consolidation of the opponents, it became the party in opposition, and by 1913 there had been a Labour administration in every State. Thus out of the defeated strikes of 1890 came a political party whose rise and achievements are the most significant items in the social and political development of Australia since that period.

The second reaction of public opinion upon the strike was equally significant. A demand arose for measures to prevent the repetition of such wasteful and damaging conflicts. Industrial legislation in response to the demand assumed a twofold form. In Victoria the problem was attacked indirectly. An effort was made to remove those economic abuses which give questions of wages their primacy as causes of industrial disputes. Legislation was endorsed to mitigate or abolish sweating. Wages Boards were created, composed of a chairman and equal numbers of employers and employees, who were thus "a jury of trade experts," competent to fix rates of pay, forms of work, hours of labour and conditions of employment. In the beginning, this legislation was restricted to four trades where sweating was more prominent. Notwithstanding their humanitarian aim, " these proposals were received with violent hostility in one quarter, namely by those who resisted what is known as any interference with the liberty of the subject, and also by those who made a fetish of the law of supply and demand."[1] The advocates of *laissez faire* boldly asserted that "any interference with the relations of private employers and their employees, however well-intentioned that interference might be, would do more mischief than good." Others argued that the Boards would do away with personal liberty, and would " determine whether a poor widow was to be allowed to work for an honest living for herself and her fatherless children." "Nothing," it was boldly asserted, " that Parliament could do would stop sweating, which existed in every large city in the world."[2] On this occasion most of the opposition came from the Legislative Council, which contained some of the largest employers of the State. When in 1900 a proposal was made to extend the system to other trades, a protest was raised by the Chamber of Manufactures, on the ground that the absence of sweating in those trades did not furnish the original motive, and that further interference with economic liberty was undesirable. Nevertheless the system is now firmly

[1] Sir Alexander Peacock, author of the measure, in a ms. statement, quoted by Prof. M. B. Hammond in *Annals of the American Academy of Political and Social Science*, July, 1913, p. 28.

[2] Quoted by Prof. M. B. Hammond, in *Quarterly Journal of Economics*, Nov., 1914, p. 116, from the *Victorian Parliament Debates*, vol. lxxix, pp. 4405, 4412.

established, though supported by employers rather on the ground of its unique success in preventing strikes than through any belief in the principles on which the system is based.

The second method of avoiding industrial disputes, that of arbitration, arose in New Zealand, whither the maritime strike of 1890 had spread. The priority in time in this matter belongs to New Zealand, but in complexity of method, in industrial strategy, and in the formulation of social principles the primacy has passed to Australia. The New Zealand system, in its beginning, laid more stress on conciliation than on arbitration. The Australian workers, and some of the employers, were in favor of the method of conciliation. The Victorian Wages Boards were in principle but a method of conciliation. In New South Wales, however, neither employers nor employees favored it. The former were responsible for the failure of several voluntary measures of conciliation and arbitration enacted prior to 1901. An act passed in 1892 created councils of conciliation and arbitration, but the employers treated them with contempt, refusing to submit industrial disputes to their jurisdiction. Since the boards had no power to compel the attendance of witnesses or the production of necessary documents, the efforts of workmen to have their cases heard were baffled by the refusal of the other side to appear. An amendment of the act in 1899 proved ineffective. The same attitude was adopted by employers towards a similar act for which the late Mr. C. C. Kingston was responsible in South Australia in 1894.

The workers saw in the methods of conciliation an opportunity for the successful assertion of collective bargaining, but they were anxious for a law which would make it impossible for conciliation or arbitration to be refused. Alleged breaches of voluntary agreements on the part of employers, spread over years of conflict,[1] converted the workers' preference for conciliation into one for compulsion. They wanted a court with power not only to intervene to settle disputes, but also to enforce awards. The court, when appointed, would aim primarily to settle disputes, but since disputes arose largely out of questions of wages and conditions of employment, it would, in the last resort, have to settle and enforce a minimum wage and minimum standard conditions of employment. Hence, when in 1901 the late Mr. B. R. Wise, K. C., introduced the first Arbitration Act into New South Wales, he brought forward a measure of compulsory arbitration instead of conciliation. In 1904 the Commonwealth Parliament passed an act of a similar nature, conferring jurisdiction, in the case of disputes extending beyond the limits of one or more States, on a specially constituted Federal Court of Arbitration.

The foregoing sketch of the events of 1891 and of their consequences shows the beginning of a period of social conflict. The consolidation of large towns, the growth of the manufacturing industry and the aggressiveness of trade-unionism produced the conditions under which industrial struggles became possible. The generally free franchise of the country afforded trade-unionism, when organized politically, an opportunity to bid for democratic control of government. But neither the form of economic development nor the extent and nature of political organization is adequate to account for the social struggle of the last quarter of a century. It is customary to advance the rise of the Labour party as the sole reason for this phenomenon. Its detractors blame the number, frequency and bitterness of industrial disputes to its organized power in trade-unionism and its influence in legislative chambers. Its adherents and

---

[1] See Spence, *Australia's Awakening*, p. 108.

some of its opponents attribute its growth and consequent influence to this organization and solidarity. This analysis is not deep enough. The organization and solidarity of the Labour party have been effective means towards the realization of the program. The program, however, is more significant and more fundamental. Industrial disputes, whether peaceful demands or more violent strikes for increased wages and better conditions, are not necessary results of either organized trade-unionism or of its legislative activity. Again, they are but means to an end, and that end is to be found expressed in the platform and aims of the Labour movement. But even when we have analyzed these phenomena back to organic expression of the aim sought therein, we have yet to explain the support which the platform of the Labour movement has secured. That support is to be found in a deep-rooted sentiment latent in the country, a sentiment born of the reaction from conditions of social development in the preceding century, and fostered by an "ideal of social progress" which would "control and rationalize the prevailing doctrine of wealth accumulation at any price."[1]

The sociological history of the last quarter of a century is therefore the logical development of that of the previous century. It is the history of the struggle of a social ideal to manifest itself. That ideal became an impulse to the political organization of a new party and a resolvent of previously existing parties. It formed the watchword of the new party, and gradually, partially and perhaps sullenly secured the grudging acquiescence of other parties. To one group or class it was a stimulus to collective action towards its realization, to another or other groups or classes

[1] See an admirable interpretation of this matter in a series of six articles, entitled "Australian Ideals" in *The Times* (London, July-Aug. 1908).

it was a provocative to combined action to prevent its realization, to modify its form or mitigate what was feared would be its evil effects. As, however, behind the resistance of the opponents of this ideal there was another ideal, the conflict resolved itself into one between two groups, two classes, with antagonistic ideals. Rapid economic expansion, material advance as measured in terms of exports and imports, on the one hand, was set up over against social progress obtained by restraining individualism and asserting the rights of the enfranchised individual to all that is implied in the recognition of a common humanity. In other words, the social struggle in Australia has been, and still is between two groups, one of which concentrates on the "business of developing the country and growing rich," while the other speculates upon the "possibilities of moderate affluence without excessive toil, and wide-spread social well-being, inconceivable to countries less richly endowed, less thinly peopled, and less remote." [1]

One direct consequence of the manner in which this social struggle was precipitated is that the pressure in the direction of social reform comes from the groups most concerned. It is the workers of city and country, of factory and shearing-shed who have given momentum to the forces inherent in the social situation prior to 1890. Hence the strategy of the social conflict has been influenced by their views, their methods, their outlook. It is idle to look to the conservative, employing class for any considerable constructive efforts in the direction of social reform. Criticism, not always hostile, but seldom sympathetic, and never potent to alter the form of industrial strategy, is all they have given. A few men of progressive views and broad popular sympathies, such as the Hon. W. Pember Reeves in

[1] "Australian Ideals," *The Times* (London, Aug. 8, 1908).

New Zealand, the late Mr. B. R. Wise and Mr. Geo. S. Beeby, M.L.A., in New South Wales, Sir Alexander Peacock, M.L.A., in Victoria, and the late Mr. C. C. Kingston in South Australia have been the creative minds who have shaped the legislative enactments of most importance as means to social reform. But in all methods of attaining their ends other than that of constructive law, the workers of Australia have followed their own devices. The national temperament, heedless of experience, unchecked by expert leaders, experimental in method, reckless of consequences, is to be found reflected in the struggle. The initiative in the onset has come from the workers. Strikes, *i. e.*, concerted refusals on the part of the workers to accept employment, have been far more frequent than lockouts, or refusals on the part of employers to permit the workers to continue at work. In fact, lockouts are rare, the men almost invariably acting first, and, in addition, are costly, since they involve a heavy fine under the Arbitration Act. Strikes, further, are often undertaken against the advice of the leaders of trade-unionism. Their barbarity, futility and unwisdom are abundantly recognized by them, yet the rank and file never stop to weigh consequences. Whether the loss in wages to the workers, and in general well-being to the community is ever compensated for by the results of strikes is not a criterion in general use among Australian trade-unionists. In the matter of compulsory arbitration, in the question of preference to unionists, in the distinction between skilled and unskilled labor, in the choice between piece work and fixed wages, in the whole economic problem of production and distribution, the action taken in Australia has been along the line of the collective interests of the working class.

Their aims are economic, social and political. First stands a demand for economic justice, for a distribution of wealth that will enhance social well-being. They do not object to wealth as such, nor to the wealthy man who has become wealthy in developing the resources of the country. What they do object to is wealth obtained by means of monopolistic enterprises in industry or on the land. In place of the insistence on profits as the aim of industry, they have stressed a greater equality of industrial opportunity and a more equitable distribution of the social wealth. They are not anxious that their primary products shall increase rapidly, nor that their manufacturing industry shall grow till it becomes adequate to meet the needs of the people. They do not desire to be distinguished, as America does, for the sum-total of their wealth or for the power which they, as a nation, may possess thereby. They would rather that their country's industrial development should be slow than that there should be created, in consequence of a speedier exploitation, vast aggregations of wealth in the hands of a few. A distribution of wealth as scientifically controlled as is its production is a part of the social philosophy of the Labour movement.[1] To that end, a demand is made that the worker shall receive such a reward for his labour as will enable him to live as a human being in a civilized community. The Australian people generally argue that if labour be a duty, subsistence becomes a right, the enforcement of which society must guarantee because of the powerlessness of the labourer, under modern economic conditions, to enforce his rights. Accepting the family as an economic and social unit, and every male as actually or potentially the head of a family, the workers ask for a living wage that will enable them to maintain their own physical strength and social status, and rear a family in accordance with a certain definite standard of comfort and decency. Society is expected

[1] See a striking article, entitled "Labour's Philosophy," *The Worker*, August 18, 1910.

to enforce this wage by making it a first charge upon the proceeds of industry, to be calculated without regard to profits.

The economic demands have been enforced through a political program and by the political method. The right of the franchise, based on a concept of personality, was the first step in the political program. With its realization came a wide-spread confidence in the power of legislation, and that multiplication of laws in furtherance of a social ideal which has made the statute books of Australia "laboratories of political experiment." The basis for this supreme confidence in the power of legislation is twofold. In the first place, democratic legislation is the assertion of the responsibility felt by the individual for his own and his fellow's efficiency. Hence, in its enforcement he does not destroy, but rather increases, his own independence. He realizes his own personality in caring for his fellows. Secondly, legislation is coming to be the invention of new political formulæ for the satisfaction of social wants. It has often been more than the expression of public opinion; it is tending to become an instrument for the actualization of collective needs and purposes. As such it becomes increasingly sensitive, not to public opinion merely, but to the needs that it has to meet, or to the advancing purposes with which it must keep pace. Of the larger constructive measures in the Australian political program of the last twenty-five years, it is only partly true to say that they expressed public opinion. Rather were they bold endeavors to find methods for the realization of political principles or to solve pressing social problems. As such, they tended at times to go beyond what party opinion endorsed, while falling short of a solution of the problem at issue. For instance, the Industrial Disputes Act of New South Wales, 1908, which had a stormy career, is declared to have introduced a larger measure of industrial socialism than the leaders of the party which passed it realized at the time.[1] While this concept prevails, the true test of Australian legislation will lie in its efficiency, in its power to realize the collective purposes, and in its ability to give full scope to social personality.

Included in the social program have been such rights of a common humanity as are possible only by the payment of an increased wage. Of these, leisure is a first condition. It is realized by competent observers that the successful assertion of the right to a certain amount of leisure is one of the foremost achievements of Australian national life. The Australian feels that its value, as shown in the case of those who can buy it with their wealth, is so great that it ought to be added to the needs of life and made a part of those conditions which are one's natural birthright. Without it, personal freedom is curtailed, personal dignity lowered, and the full play of mind and soul checked. The socialistic conception of production for public use, rather than for private profit, is in part the basis for this demand. " With machinery put to its proper use, that of contributing to the happiness of mankind," so runs the unionist argument," increased leisure will give opportunities for the cultivation of all those higher faculties latent in man but now repressed by the pressure of a social system which makes the satisfaction of mere material wants an all-absorbing struggle." [2]

To the demand for leisure as a condition for the development of a higher national life has been added one for a free education for every child. " Education is one of the measures which will strike at the root of the injustice from

---

[1] See Russell, "Industrial Arbitration in relation to Socialism," *Economic Journal*, September, 1915.

[2] Rules of the Australian Workers' Union, quoted in Spence, *Australia's Awakening*, p. 74.

which the masses now suffer." " Labour stands for giving to Australians the opportunity to become an enlightened people. Every child must be educated at the expense of the community. Education must be made free right through, from the primary school to the University." [1] By means of free education, national efficiency is to be secured and every member become equipped for industrial, political and social life. Democracy is to be enlightened and efficient, its best brains selected and trained for its service, and by so doing, the congealing of the social strata and the crystallization of class feeling be prevented, as far as possible.

Finally, a demand for better conditions of health and recreation has been included in the social program. That the Australian people shall be healthy citizens rearing healthy families has been a national aspiration. Hence, as expressed in the program of the Labour party, and in general ultimately endorsed by all, have been proposals for the care of maternity, the protection of child life, the medical inspection and care of school children, the purity of food, the extension of the scope and methods of public health even to the nationalization of hospitals, and finally, for housing regulations that will prevent the erection of the slums of old-world cities, under sunnier skies and happier conditions.

We have reached now the explanation of the paradox with which our sociological analysis began. The intolerance of special privileges is the reaction from a period when special privileges tended to become entrenched in the economic and political development of the country. The great mass of democratic legislation represents the effort of a people, politically emancipated, to correct the abuses of the past and realize the fulness of individual and social development for which the term "democracy" in a young, free, rich country is an adequate expression. The State Socialism

[1] Spence, *op. cit.*, p. 588.

of Australia is the direct consequence of its isolation, the nature of its immigration, the conditions of its settlement, the long distances of the continent, the sparseness of its population, the concentration in cities, and, finally, the nature of the social ideals. State ownership of land, an assisted immigration, the priority of pastoral development, the long carriage of wool and wheat to a few distant ports, the scarcity of capital within the country, these were the conditions that have given impulse and form to Australian state socialism. Government enterprise has meant the use of the state's capital and resources for the purpose of securing to the whole of society the rich return to be derived from nature in a new and undeveloped country. Without such expenditure, the development of the machinery of civilization in the country would have been less speedy, and the rich profits arising from its exploitation would have been distributed differently. The bitter lessons of an era of land monopoly and class privilege, combined with the more pleasant lessons of the period of state aid, bear fruit in the social attitude of to-day.

In parallel fashion, we have found the explanation of the presence in Australian life of a class that gained power and privilege, became conservative and formed the nucleus around which the commercial and professional classes have formulated their interests and organized their political activities. Through the control which this class achieved over the land, there was created by 1845 a wealthy territorial aristocracy. The perversion of the various acts seeking to establish a yeomanry upon the soil only increased the power of this territorial aristocracy and established a feud between squatters and free selectors. The adoption of property franchises in elections, and the consequent control for many years of both representative houses in each State and of the Legislative Councils, even to-day, by the conservative class, explains the slowness with which the admitted evils of land monopoly have been dealt with, as well as the bitterness of the political struggle. Fundamentally, the conservatives of Australia are individualists. They have inherited the social temper of those bold men who faced the Australian bush, and, each for his own, careless of the interests of others, carved out his fortune upon the land. As suggested, they are a valuable element in Australian life, but it is the clash of their aims, interests and purposes with those who follow a program of social reform, which constitutes the social struggle of Australia to-day.

It remains for us, then, to analyze this struggle in its major phases, economic, political and social. Therein we shall see vividly the principles which differentiate these two classes. We shall see the measures taken to reform the admitted abuses of the past, and those which aim to realize a new social ideal. Land monopoly and restricted settlement are attacked. Into the old bottles of political conservatism is poured the new wine of democracy. Individualism is submitted to the acid resolvents of new economic theories. The problems pressing for solution concerning industrial disputes, living wages and decent conditions of labour are attacked. Finally, we shall see, a care for human happiness is so extended as to cover the life of man almost from the cradle to the grave. These, we shall find, are the great strides Australia has made towards the realization of a social democracy.

CHAPTER V

The Conflict in Economic Theory

In Australia, two antithetical social theories are found, and each has many adherents. An economic liberalism coexists in complete contrast with an economic conservatism. To one group of persons economic activity is governed by what they believe to be immutable laws, interference with which tends to endanger private interests and social welfare. The other group has "swallowed economic formulae", and is seeking to find economic laws which will not conflict with social rights. To the classic individualism, entrenched in Australia through land monopoly, the latter group opposes an ideal of social and economic justice, to be realized by a collective control of monopolies and the extension of the industrial and economic functions of the state and municipality. The doctrine of supply and demand, with its corollary of competition, is superseded by that of a living wage as the first charge on industry. Freedom of contract has given place to a legally established collective bargaining, enforced through courts of conciliation and arbitration. In the principles which guide the decisions of these courts are to be found the clearest instances of the conflict in economic theory.[1]

[1] Among the most valuable materials for sociological study in Australian life are the reports issued by the various Arbitration Courts, especially those of the Commonwealth Arbitration Court, which, because of its status and the character and ability of its President, Mr. Justice Higgins, is the industrial arbiter of the continent.

The doctrine of freedom of contract dominated the thought and action of the pastoralists and employers of Australia till within recent years. This view of relations between masters and workers determined their attitudes during the strikes of 1890. In 1891 the President of the Employers' Union declared that "all that employers insisted on was that they should be allowed to conduct their business as they pleased, and to employ whom they pleased, whether the men were in unions or not."[1] In addition they held the view that they alone should have the right to determine the rate of wages and the conditions of employment, while denying to workmen the right to combine.[2] Any attempt on the part of the employees acting collectively to appraise their services was regarded as an act of "outside interference" that must be fought at all costs as detrimental to individual and social welfare. That freedom of contract meant, on the part of the employer, "the power to withhold bread" was freely recognized. Thus, the Institute of Marine Engineers had accepted a reduction of wages for a term, with the proviso that three months' notice of any desired alteration should be given. In November 1896, as the bad conditions which led them to accept reduced wages were passing, they gave notice of the termination of their agreement. "The shipowners' reply was a menacing letter, sent—not to the Institute, but to each individual employee—asking him whether he was, or was not, satisfied with the existing conditions, for, if not, he was 'jeopardising his position.'"[3] In this case there was no recognition by the employers of the fact

[1] Quoted from *The Argus* (Melbourne, Feb. 27, 1891), in Spence, *Australia's Awakening*, p. 113.

[2] See Spence, *op. cit.*, p. 113 for instances of such interpretations.

[3] *Commonwealth Arbitration Reports*, vol. vi, p. 100. Henceforth to be cited thus: 6 C. A. R., p. 100.

that the worker was not really free. " This same argument, ' Why do you take the job?' is used as to all complaints about low wages and bad conditions " without consideration of " how human beings are driven to enter the services of others by the grim spectre of unemployment at their heels, and by the still more terrible spectre of hopeless pauperism never far behind." [1]

Against this view of the relations of employer and employee the social sense of the community has come to rebel. Nevertheless the notion still exists that the employer, who by thrift begins life as a capitalist, and by managerial ability renders a social service, is thereby best fitted to arrange the terms of employment. Much that has been done to restore true freedom of contract is still denounced as unwarrantable interference. But the old freedom of contract is no longer acknowledged as such. " The power of the employer to withhold bread is a much more effective weapon than the power of the employee to refuse to labour. Freedom of contract under such circumstances is surely misnamed: it should rather be called despotism in contract." [2] The general helplessness of individual employees against employers proves that the contracting parties are not on the same level; the contract is not free. In the case of the members of the Federated Gas Employees' Industrial Union, evidence before the Arbitration Court showed that owing to the absence of a union prior to 1912 the men always got a smaller increase in wages than they asked for. Further, when a Wages Board was formed, covering some of the members of this industry among others, " the numerous wood and coal merchants who dominated the Board " granted their employees a wage

[1] 2 C. A. R., p. 72.
[2] 5 C. A. R., p. 27.

equal only to 77 per cent of that obtained by similar workers in the employ of the various gas companies, who were not represented on the Board.[1] "Under the misnomer of 'free contract', it [the contract system] throws the worker back on the old unfair dilemma of insufficient rates, or else unemployment and a hungry home."[2]

To remedy this situation, three measures have been taken. Collective bargaining is legalized and encouraged. In the Commonwealth Court of Arbitration, and in that of New South Wales, this action is followed by what is held to be its logical complement, preference to unionists. Finally, a minimum wage is enforced as a bulwark of economic freedom, a check on the despotic contractual power of the employer. Collective bargaining is established by law. Among the chief objects of the Act which established the Commonwealth Arbitration Court[3] are:

(a) to facilitate and encourage the organization of representative bodies of employers and of employees, and the submission of industrial disputes to the Court by organization . . . (b) to provide for the making and enforcement of industrial agreements between employers and employees in relation to industrial disputes.

The Act encourages collective bargaining by refusing the right of approach to the Court to any other than organized bodies of employers and employees, termed "industrial unions", and by registering and enforcing industrial agreements made between such corporate bodies. It provides also for the registration of such industrial unions, and a body of regulations exists covering the conditions of their registration and the exercise of their powers.

[1] 7 C. R. R., p. 65.
[2] 3 C. A. R., p. 36.
[3] The Commonwealth Conciliation and Arbitration Act 1904-1911.

The same Act provides that preference to unionists shall be granted whenever in the opinion of the court it is necessary for the prevention or settlement of industrial disputes, for the maintenance of industrial peace, or for the welfare of society. Similarly the establishment and enforcement of a living wage is the main measure towards securing " what is fair and right in relation to any industrial matter, having regard to the interests of the persons immediately concerned, and of society as a whole." [1]

The struggle has now shifted from the right of collective bargaining and the value of the minimum wage to some of their corollaries. Few persons would be found to dispute the benefits of unionism, though many object to its methods. Few, too, deny the principle of a living wage, through controversy exists as to the rate of the wage, the method by which it is determined, and its effect upon industry. Over the questions of preference, of the extent and nature of state interference, and the principle on which the living wage shall be decided, with its juxtaposition of social aims and economic consequences, the differences of opinion are profound and far-reaching.

Preference to unionists is regarded, on the one hand, as a corollary to compulsory arbitration, without which industrial peace and the securing of equitable industrial conditions would be impossible. Three reasons are advanced for its necessity. (1) The opportunity for preference in employment tends to act as an incentive to working men to enroll themselves in unions, thus perfecting the legal machinery and extending its scope. "It may seem very shocking in some quarters, but it is my clear duty, in obedience to the law, to treat unionism as a desirable aid in securing industrial peace." [2] (2) The economic and social

[1] See Commonwealth Conciliation and Arbitration Act 1904-1911, sec. iv.
[2] Mr. Justice Higgins, in 5 *C. A. R.*, p. 25.

advantages derived from arbitration have been won at much cost by the trade-unionists, who have the right to be recompensed by such a favor. " There is much force, one must confess, in the position . . . that the union men have to fight for non-unionists, as well as for themselves, in the efforts to obtain better terms from the employers; that the unionists have to pay subscriptions and levies, sacrifice time and energy and (not infrequently) their employment." [1] (3) There is a third reason that has great weight in practice. It is felt that without preference, there would be no security for the conditions of remuneration and employment so far won. The non-unionist is a tool in the hands of the capitalist, used by him as a lever to reduce wages in a time of industrial depression, and by his presence, a constant menace to the unionist and his cherished industrial ideals. " The truth is, preference is sought for unionists in order to prevent preference of non-unionists or anti-unionists, to prevent the gradual bleeding of unionists by the feeding of non-unionism. It is a weapon of defence." [2]

On the other hand, those who object to the principle advance three reasons. They declare that, since employment is to be made conditional upon joining a union, the unions would control the primary right which every man has to earn his living in the way he may choose. They hold that, since not only the right to work, but also one's political thought and action would be conditioned by membership in unions which are becoming increasingly political, the principle of preference is subversive of liberty. It would deprive a man of the right to act, think, and speak for himself. Lastly, there is raised the objection that the discrimination between the two classes of union and non-union workers is opposed to

[1] 5 *C. A. R.*, p. 25.
[2] 7 *C. A. R.*, p. 233.

the institutions and traditions of England, and, when used by a Labour government to reward its followers, is but a form of the vicious " spoils " system. Thus, logical necessity stands opposed to expediency. To one group, preference is a vital necessity to the securing and enforcement of collective bargaining; to the other it is an inexpedient and partisan act.

On the question of State interference, the objectors are governed less by expediency, though their basic principles do not now receive the general support in current economic opinion that they formerly did. They endorse the doctrine of supply and demand in relation to wages, with its corollary of competition. They hold that a natural law, such as they believe that of supply and demand to be, controls the fixing of wages. This law of political economy is believed to have the certainty of operation and the inexorable character of the law of gravitation. To attempt therefore by state action to regulate, restrain or control its operation is foolish and futile. To leave wages to the natural play of economic forces would be better than to create a fictitious standard of remuneration. Thus, on January 25, 1916, the Employers' Federation and similar bodies approached the Premier of New South Wales with regard to increased wages in war time. The requests and the argument ran thus:

We urge, therefore, that in the interests not only of employers of labour but as a protection to our industries, and in view of the serious financial and industrial crisis which is fast developing as a result of the great and disastrous war which is sapping the very foundations of our national industrial fabric, it is incumbent upon the Government of the country to take such steps as will restore and maintain industrial peace. We believe that a declaration by the Government that no applications for increased wages excepting in cases where workers are being paid less than the minimum of 8s 9d per day fixed by his Honor Mr. Justice Heydon, or shorter hours, would be considered by wages boards during the period of the war, would have a beneficial effect in the industrial arena, and would put an end to a condition of things which is fraught with the gravest consequences to the whole community. The present tendency of wages board awards is to create a fictitious standard of remuneration which cannot possibly be maintained after the war, and the necessity for an ultimate readjustment of wages will be likely to create further industrial strife. . . . It is only courting disaster, therefore, to leave in the hands of wages boards' chairmen at this critical period the full power to adjust wages and hours of labour to temporary economic conditions.[1]

Without discussing the whole situation, one may point out, first, that the view of the employers in this matter seems to have been based on the erroneous idea that in Great Britain " Mr. Lloyd George has announced that no further increases in industrial wages will be permitted except those governed by existing industrial agreements."[2] Nevertheless, allowing for this error, the employers seem to regard the regulation of wages as an incentive towards industrial strife, and competition as the ultimate method of readjustment after the war. It is no unfair inference, therefore, to regard competition as a method of wage adjustment which they prefer to one of state regulation.

In the social ideal which guides most of the legislative activity promoted or supported by the Labour party, and endorsed by large sections in Australia to-day, supply and demand and competition are alike superseded. The theory of supply and demand is found by Mr. Justice Higgins, after an experience of over 10 years in the Commonwealth

[1] Statement of the Employers' Federation, published in *Sydney Morning Herald*, Jan. 28, 1916.
[2] Statement *ut supra*.

Arbitration Court, " to be responsible for much industrial friction, and to be at the root of many industrial disputes."[1] Industrial peace cannot be secured while human life is " treated in the game of competition as if it were the ball to be kicked. This, the most valuable asset of the State, must be protected, whatever else suffers."[2] Competition, though not abrogated, has its definite limits. Unless these are fixed at a point at which a worker can obtain a wage sufficient to satisfy " the normal needs of the average employee regarded as a human being living in a civilized community,"[3] there will result nothing but bitter industrial disputes.

I cannot conceive of any such industrial dispute as this being settled effectively which fails to secure to the worker enough wherewith to renew his strength and to maintain his home from day to day. He will dispute, he must dispute, until he gets this minimum: even as a man immersed can never rest until he gets his head above water.[4]

Industrial peace will never be possible till the right of every human being to a sufficiency of the primary wants of life is met. This result can only be achieved by regulating the anti-social operation of the economic law of supply and demand, and by lifting the burden of a wasteful and damaging competition off the shoulders of the worker.

My function is to secure peace if possible; and, in order to secure peace, to provide that the employee shall have a reasonable return for his labour—above all, sufficient means to meet the primary wants of human life—including opportunities for rest and recreation. A growing sense of the value of human life seems to be at the back of all these methods of regulating

[1] 5 C. A. R., p. 27.
[2] 4 C. A. R., p. 18.
[3] 2 C. A. R., p. 3.
[4] 3 C. A. R., p. 20.

labour; a growing conviction that human life is too valuable to be the shuttlecock in the game of money-making and competition; a growing resolve that the injurious strain of the contest, but only so far as it is injurious, shall, so far as possible, be shifted from the human instruments.[1]

There cannot be competion among workers for a wage lower than one fixed by Arbitration Courts or Wages Boards as sufficient to afford them a frugal livelihood. Just as the State interferes to secure sanitation and pure food, in the interests of those not able nor wise enough to secure such for themselves, and thereby, in the interests of the whole community, so it interferes with competitive wage fixing.

When however, a living wage has been fixed, a large measure of true freedom of contract has been secured and competitive bargaining may begin. The industrial legislation of Australia, considered apart from the organized action of trade unionists, makes no attempt to fix a maximum wage, to dictate the conditions of employment, or to interfere with the free choice of the employer in selecting his workmen. Abrogation of the employers' freedom of contract is not equivalent to the subjection of employers to the dictation of unions.[2] The employer is free to dispense with the services of any worker who does not come up to his standard and to obtain the best men available by offering them higher wages. He may carry on his own business in his own way, and make what profits he can, provided he does not create industrial trouble or endanger industrial peace by insufficient wages or other injustice.

In the strain of competition, the pressure on the employer is often very great, and he ought to be free to choose his em-

[1] 4 *C. A. R.*, p. 101.
[2] See 5 *C. A. R.*, p. 168 and 7 *C. A. R.*, p. 232.

ployees on their merits and according to his own exigencies, free to make use of new machines, of improved methods, of financial advantages, of advantages of locality, of superior knowledge, free, in short, to put the utmost pressure on anything and everything, except human life.[1]

"In every case that has come before me," said Mr. Justice Powers, Deputy President of the Commonwealth Arbitration Court, "employers are voluntarily paying to some employees for special work, or qualifications, or responsibility, or for long or trustworthy service, more than the rate fixed by the Court from time to time. Nothing should be done to check that."[2] A powerful incentive to efficiency, to higher technical skill and to increased productivity would be checked and destroyed if superior skill could not demand increased wages.

When we consider the attitude taken towards profits we see the same conflict of views. Profits are not regarded as opposed to social justice. They are only taken into account so far as they affect the standard wage. The principle on which the latter is based is not one of profit-sharing. The right to fair wages is not equivalent to the right to be awarded a fair proportion of the profits. A fair and reasonable remuneration is a first charge on the products of industry, standing on the same level as the cost of the raw material of manufacture. It has to be paid whatever may be the profits. If the latter are high, if skilful management, enterprise, largeness of output or mere good fortune has enabled an employer to obtain large profits, it is not a part of the purpose of industrial legislation that he should be made to pay higher wages. The workers run no risks, incur no liabilities, and the profits of the employer are his return

[1] 4 C. A. R., p. 18.
[2] Federated Mining Employees' Case, No. 13 of 1916, p. 24.

for those risks and liabilities. But profits must not be made at the cost of the primary needs of the worker, nor at the cost of society. "No one ventures to contend that profits are legitimate which are made by means of stinting the labourer and his family in necessaries or which are made to the detriment of human life, the ultimate riches."[1] Yet, if wages are to be reduced where a mine has not been paying a dividend or where the whole venture is speculative, the dividend " would be distributed at the cost of the workmen's breakfast tables, by reducing the food necessary for the worker and for his wife and children,"[2] or the companies would be speculating on a part of the employees' proper wages.[3] If a new industry is arising or is struggling for existence, its inability to make profits ought not to affect the addition which is made to the basic wage as a recompense for skill.[4] Should an industry contain employers who are, through want of managerial ability, enterprise and equipment, unable to make profits, that is no ground for either reduced or differentiated wages in that industry. A distinction exists between the profits that are possible in an industry and those which individual employers make.[5] Under these conditions, the needy employer must pay the same rate of wages as his more successful rival. Parasitic industries, which cannot maintain themselves without sweating or cutting down wages below a living minimum, had better be abandoned.[6] There can be no industrial peace, no social or economic justice, unless the living wage is kept sacrosanct, beyond the reach of alteration by either neces-

[1] 8 *C. A. R.*, p. 63.
[2] 3 *C. A. R.*, p. 35.
[3] 7 *C. A. R.*, p. 139.
[4] 5 *C. A. R.*, p. 73.
[5] 2 *C. A. R.*, p. 65.
[6] 3 *C. A. R.*, p. 32.

sitious or greedy employers or more necessitous workers. Thus does the notion of social justice conflict with the idea of profit-making as the end of private enterprise.

An analysis of the principles on which the living wage is based reveals the same conflict of social principles with economic theories. When, in 1906, the first case was tried before the newly-created Commonwealth Arbitration Court, the President, the late Mr. Justice O'Connor, laid down the principle that the wages paid should be " fair and reasonable." When the employing company engaged in the dispute suggested that the market value of the services rendered was the true test of fair rates, the President replied:

That cannot be so. The whole body of modern legislation against sweating is founded on the experience that competition, which fixes market value, may under certain conditions produce a market rate of wages which literally is not enough to keep body and soul together. Market value cannot therefore be the only test, but market value must always be the most important element in any test which is to be applied.

Accepting the market value, and adding something for risk or responsibility such as special vocations call for,

there must also be added something for the increased cost of living in Australia, not only by reason of the higher cost of some of life's necessaries, but also by reason of the increased comfort of living and the higher standard of social conditions which the general sense of the community in Australia allows to those who live by labour.[1]

Thus early was it judicially recognized that the minimum wages, on whatever principle it was fixed, should be more than a merely competitive wage, and should accord with a fair standard of living.

[1] 1 C. A. R., p. 27.

Then in 1906, by the Excise Act, the Federal Parliament made an interesting experiment, known as the " New Protection." The old Protection had made good wages possible, the new Protection was to make them actual. The Excise Act imposed on locally manufactured goods, protected by a moderate tariff, a further excise duty which was to be remitted if the employer paid fair and reasonable wages. Because of the difficulty attaching to the interpretation of the term " fair and reasonable," the whole matter was to be referred to a well-informed and impartial tribunal, possessing full powers of investigation, consideration and variation. Though the whole act was declared, on appeal to the High Court, an unconstitutional exercise of the power of taxation, it furnished the opportunity for a most important and far-reaching decision concerning the living wage. In 1907 Mr. H. V. McKay, a large manufacturer of harvesters and agricultural machinery, whose enterprise, energy and business organization had given him first rank in his industry, made application for a declaration from the President of the Arbitration Court, Mr. Justice Higgins, that the conditions as to the remuneration of labour in his factory were fair and reasonable. The President, faced with the necessity and confronted by the duty of giving these terms adequate meaning, based his interpretation on the needs of the unskilled worker. His whole argument runs thus:

The provision for fair and reasonable remuneration is obviously designed for the benefit of the employees in the industry: and it must be meant to secure to them something which they cannot get by the ordinary system of individual bargaining with employers. If Parliament meant that the conditions should be such as they can get by individual bargaining, if it meant that those conditions are to be fair and reasonable, which employees will accept and employers will give, in contracts of service—there would have been no need for this provision. The remuneration could safely have been left to the usual, but unequal, contest, the "higgling of the market" for labour, with the pressure for bread on one side, and the pressure for profits on the other. The standard of "fair and reasonable" must therefore, be something else; and I cannot think of any other standard appropriate than the normal needs of an average employee, regarded as a human being in a civilized community.[1]

Examining the employers' methods of assessing wages, the President found that one employer

did not consider the quality of the men at all, but the class of work. . . . The one-sided nature of an employer's valuation of an employee is indicated clearly by the frank statements of Mr. Geo. McKay: "I pay the men what I consider them to be honestly worth. In fixing the wages I have endeavoured to get labour at the cheapest price that I honestly could." Mr. Rigby says that his idea of a fair wage is what the employer, on looking at the men, chooses to give him for his work.[2]

The President, however, refused to consider an agreement "reasonable" if it did not carry a wage "sufficient to insure the workman food, shelter, clothing, frugal comfort, provision for evil days, *etc.*, as well as reward for the special skill of an artisan if he is one."[3] The basic wage was, therefore, to be dictated by the needs of the unskilled labour in regard to food, clothing and shelter. To that was to be added, in case of artisans, such reward for skill as was commonly used and accepted by the employers and employees. As the Court came to deal with casual employees, paid by the hour, it found itself compelled to pay attention, in determining the basic wage,

[1] 2 *C. A. R.*, p. 3.
[2] *Ibid.*, p. 14.
[3] *Ibid.*, p. 4.

to the short periods of employment, to the expenditure of money and of time in getting to the work, to the "broken time" of the employees, to the fact that they are paid by the hours of actual work, and to the general rise of wages in the community, whether effected by wages boards, or awards, or not.[1]

Thus, in the case of unskilled labourers, who lose a large amount of time in consequence of the nature and conditions of their employment, the wage is fixed at a rate per hour which will enable them, while working the average number of hours per week, to obtain a living wage.[2] These rates per hour are high, and in times of good business tend to increase the necessarily demoralizing effects of casual labour, though, based as they are on average hours of employment, they are fair to the individual and the industry.[3]

The living wage has thus been divorced from any standard inherent in custom, except in regard to the gradations of skill which are recognized alike by employer and employee. No considerable account either is taken of the measure of productivity, the amount of value added to the raw material of manufacture by the labour employed upon it. It has thus become a standard wage, one marking a definite necessary standard of comfort. It is not a matter of philanthropy, not a mere humanitarian wage, but one based on the requirements of a worker "as a man in a civilized community which has resolved that, so far as laws can do it, competition shall no longer be allowed to crush him into sweated conditions."[4] It is a matter of justice, that is, it is felt to be as inherent a feature of the social system as

[1] 6 C. A. R., p. 67.
[2] Cf. 7 C. A. R., pp. 217-220, 8 C. A. R., pp. 65-74.
[3] Vide Federated Storemen and Packers Case. No. 41 of 1915, p. 22.
[4] Mr. Justice Heydon, President of the N. S. W. Arbitration Court, N. S. W. Industrial Gazette, March, 1914.

man's rights to life and property. Industry has tended to intrench on the rights of personality and to rob humanity of certain elements of dignity and personal freedom. These can only be restored by the payment of a sufficient wage.

An analysis of the social considerations implied in the process of wage-fixing in Australia shows how firmly this idea has seized the public mind. The basic wage is founded on the theory of responsibility for an actual or potential family, hence a wage that makes marriage a luxury is neither fair nor reasonable.[1] Family life is intimately related to "efficiency, sobriety and morality," and family life is dependent on economic conditions.[2] The living wage must therefore be enough to enable the worker to marry and bring up a family. No distinction is made between the wages of the single and the married man, since the former is potentially the head of a family, and one of the normal needs of an average employee is the need for domestic life.[3] When, however, we come to the question of a minimum wage for women, and are met by the demand of "equal pay for equal work," the principle of the living wage requires that women shall be paid on the assumption that they have to find their own food, shelter and clothing, not the food, shelter and clothing of a family. The minimum rate in the industry, moreover, must be such as meets the needs of that sex which is usually found therein. Thus, in the millinery trade the women usually found they would be protected by a minimum wage, while any man would be left to bargain with employers for a reward adequate for the extra skill which alone would attract him to that industry. In the case of fruit-picking, for example, where in numbers the men only slightly predominate and where

[1] 2 C. A. R., p. 64.
[2] 5 C. A. R., p. 164.
[3] 6 C. A. R., p. 71.

women do equal work, men and women are to be paid at the same rate, thus leaving the employer free to select whichever person or sex he prefers.[1] Thus even the demand for equal pay for equal work, apparently equitable on economic grounds, is overruled by social considerations.

Considerations of health enter also into the question of the conditions of labour and the rate of wages. Thus, from the beginning of the Federal Arbitration Court, opposition was offered by the President to any use of extra wages to counteract the effect of unduly long hours on duty.[2] Neither economically nor socially was it wise to give employees a direct interest in overtime work.[3] Nor should a complainant be allowed to bring in,

as a reason for higher wages, certain conditions which were alleged to be unnecessarily hard, . . . hours which were said to be grossly excessive, sleeping, and living accommodations which were said to be unhealthy and degrading. . . . I decline to make an award on the basis of conditions which are unnecessarily unwholesome or degrading.[4]

Health is to be put before money; labour is not to be bought at the cost of health or safety. "I cannot encourage the notion that by paying extra money an employer is justified in putting the employee under unnecessary risk of his life."[5] A hodman required to carry a load of bricks beyond a height of 20 feet cannot claim extra wages because the task is laborious. To grant his request would be to hinder the introduction of effective mechanical appliances

[1] 6 *C. A. R.*, p. 73.
[2] 1 *C. A. R.*, p. 24.
[3] 2 *C. A. R.*, p. 75.
[4] *Ibid.*, p. 60.
[5] 5 *C. A. R.*, p. 164.

as well as endanger his health.[1] In the case of sailors, the forecastle must be cleaned out daily, even if that action increases the wages bill by adding the services of another man.[2] Health is superior to wealth.

Leisure, too, enters into the normal needs of the employee. It is a condition essential to health and industrial peace. To enforce it under certain circumstances might involve great infringement of the employers' liberty of action, but the infringement is held to be justified.

Even if shipowners, accustomed to the old order of things, shake their heads at innovations in the direction of restraining their freedom of action, I conceive it to be my duty, in order to gain this great end of greater home life and greater contentment, to make an effort, even experimental, to meet the wants of the employees. . . . In addition to the eight hours' rule, each officer shall be free from duty at his home port—from an hour after safe mooring till two hours before departure. This would largely tend to compensate for the officer having to work (practically) seven days in the week—most Sundays and public holidays.[3]

Nor is it enough that certain periods of leisure should be granted each month or so. Body and mind alike demand that hours per day must be regulated, in the interests of public safety and individual welfare. Sleepy and tired men are unfit to control vehicles of public transportation. Overtime has to be paid for at increased rates; but even so, it is shunned by workmen, not because they can afford to despise the addition to their wages, but on the ground that a man is physically spent after eight hours' toil, and that further labour is dangerous to health, conducive to accident and

[1] 7 C. A. R., p. 231.
[2] 5 C. A. R., p. 168.
[3] 4 C. A. R., p. 99.

economically unprofitable. Leisure periods during the work of the day are sought for, and are, to a certain extent, obtained. Some shops and factories give ten minutes at eleven o'clock, others, like the printing trades of New South Wales, obtain a break at any time of the day most convenient to the factory. One hour is generally allowed for lunch, on the grounds of health. Thus, the demands of the postal electricians before the Arbitration Court for one hour for lunch instead of one-half hour were granted as being conducive to the health and contentment, and thereby to the efficiency, of the men.[1] It is noteworthy that, in the same award, the hours worked by the men were reduced to 44 per week by this device of giving greater leisure, but the reduction was contingent on the promise of the union that energy and productivity should not thereby be diminished. On the other hand, when the boot manufacturers sought to compress the working week of 48 hours into five days, instead of five and a half, as hitherto, in order to leave the whole of Saturday free, the proposal was refused on the ground of possible injury to the health of the women and youths who are so largely employed in that industry.[2]

Labour conditions, as they are enforced by awards, are regulated by considerations of public interest. Every case put before an arbitration tribunal affects the lives and well-being of multitudes. The public interest, therefore, stands before the interests of either employers or employees. The public interest, on its economic side, is primarily in efficiency. The public interest is therefore served when higher wages mean better machinery, better organization in the factory, and greater enterprise on the part of the employer. If piece-work would benefit employer, employees and the

[1] 7 C. A. R., p. 16.
[2] See *The Worker*, March 7, 1912.

public alike, this is a serious argument against those who oppose it. But if the piece-work bargain is not free, if piece-work tends to excessive speed, the " skimping " of work and inefficiency, to that extent the public interest would be served by its prohibition.[1] The best illustration, however, of this new governing principle is to be found in the consideration given to the question of " improvers." These were persons, sometimes youths, very often adults, who had not gone through a regular or complete course of apprenticeship, who were not capable of earning the standard wage, and in most cases never would be. " The existence of this class," said Mr. Justice Higgins of them in 1907,[2]

is a standing menace to industrial order and industrial peace, as well as a hindrance to industrial proficiency. . . . It is this body of half-trained men, hanging on to the skirts of a trade, that is used for the purpose of pulling down the wages of men fully trained. On this irregular force of industrial inefficients an employer can always rely for temporary assistance in industrial crises.

Not only are these men " a perpetual menace to the peace of the community,"[3] but they are the signs and symbols of industrial inefficiency. They show an industrial order too indolent, too short-sighted to train its youths for industrial efficiency and good workmanship, and ready to allow the " pestilent manufacture of imperfect tradesmen." To continue the system would be to endanger the minimum wage, disturb industrial peace, and encourage inefficiency. On these grounds the employment of improvers is now forbidden. Discussing the matter in its legal and social relations, Mr. Justice Heydon, President of the New South

[1] *Cf.* 4 *C. A. R.*, p. 26 and 6 *C. A. R.*, p. 75 on this point.
[2] 2 *C. A. R.*, p. 14.
[3] See 4 *C. A. R.*, pp. 15-23 for an exhaustive discussion of the matter.

Wales Arbitration Court, admitted that he could discover no principle of liberty or fair-play that would debar a man of his common-law right to earn his living as an improver or what not, at any wage he chose, but there might be considerations of public interest in favor of such restriction.[1] It is these social considerations that override economic utility and legal individualism.

The whole arbitration machinery of Australia, operating for the realization of an ideal of social justice, is based on three related grounds that find much support in Australian sentiment and opinion. (1) The process of production is not individual, but social. Man does not produce as a solitary unit, but as a member of a fast and increasingly complex association. The co-ordinated and systematized efforts of his fellows, crystallized in the institutions of society, or plastic in the activities of the industrial world, are essential to his activity. The factory system and machine production are accentuating this relationship. Society cannot, therefore, disregard the conditions under which its units work. (2) The state is interested in human happiness. The economic process has a moral side. It arises from human wants. Society is interested in the mode and measure in which the satisfaction of those wants is achieved. If conditions of employment in the production of goods, or the distribution of the same, restrict the freedom of the individual and limit his possibilities of happiness, it is the right and the duty of society to intervene. Just as sanitary laws limit the freedom of the individual to injure the health of the individual, so industrial laws seek to prevent injury to his social and industrial efficiency. They aim at transcending legal rights by social justice. (3) The interest of the State in human happiness logically leads to a collective re-

[1] See Appeal from Farriers' Wages Board, quoted in *The Worker*, Jan. 6, 1910.

sponsibility for the same. The State cannot stop at a certain point and, having established a fair field with no favor, leave the contestants to fight out the matter. Should a dispute arise between the directors of production and their employees, society cannot afford to let the dispute continue to its usual unsatisfactory finish. Production must go on, not in the interests of the directors, but in the interests of society which suffers in restricted supplies. Hence the prevention and settlement of industrial disputes is logically involved in a correct social attitude towards the economic world. "This Court, as I take it, represents the public between the two conflicting factions, and the public are suffering grievously by the contest."[1] Even if the economic conflict is inherent in the normal relations of employer and employee, society's interest lies in reducing the seriousness, the frequency and the costliness of the conflict. No doctrinaire views, but just plain common sense, fortified by bitter experience, lie behind this position. Production is becoming increasingly invested with a social interest, and therefore, regardless of older theories, a new social ideal calls forth new facts, arrangements and dispositions which become the basis of new theories.

[1] 3 C. A. R., p. 19.

CHAPTER VI

Economic Aspects of Recent Social Development

In Australia, as in other parts of the world, the relations between capital and labour are greatly strained. The process, which began in 1890 with the shearers' and maritime strikes, has continued without cessation. The industrial world has been organized into two hostile camps. Between these there is a never-ending series of strikes, lockouts, and other disputes which lessen production and cause a direct loss in consumptive power by a great loss in wages. In general, these strikes are evidence of class feeling. They are not in every case a struggle for the realization of the principles enumerated in the last chapter. The determination of those principles has been taken out of the arena of strife into the calmer atmosphere of a judicial court. A series of strikes is equivalent to industrial war, and manifests the usual phenomena of confused and conflicting issues, of depreciation of motives and of bitter feeling that are associated with war. Further, there has been developed what may correctly be termed "industrial strategy," the chief characteristic of which is to strike at the moment when the greatest harm can be done the unoffending and sympathetic public. In so far as the public is sympathetic or the employers unorganized and irresolute in their opposition, the strike succeeds. When the employers are organized a strike never completely succeeds; when the public conscience becomes satisfied with the social advance made, or becomes dissatisfied with and unsympathetic towards the aims of unionists, strikes will have less success.

The causes of industrial dislocations cover a wide area

of industrial action and opinion. They may, however, be grouped for purposes of explanation under four heads:

(1) The fear that the standard of living, so hardly won, will be affected detrimentally by certain alterations in industrial conditions affecting wages and hours of labour. Thus, men will strike for an increase of wages when the increased cost of living has made their present wage equivalent to a decreased standard of comfort. Quite 40 per cent of the dislocations are due to this cause.

(2) Resentment caused by the conduct of employers, managers or foremen in making what are considered unjust dismissals or in victimising prominent trade-unionists. On this question of the employment of particular classes or persons a large number of strikes take place, especially in the mining districts.

(3) The determination to assert certain broad union principles which are not merely matters of trade-unionism but also cover questions of working conditions and discipline. Thus men strike for the right to combine and to be represented by unions, as *e. g.* the Brisbane Tramway strike (1912). Demarcation troubles concerning the right to a certain area of industry, and the question of handling " black " or " boycotted " goods are frequent causes of dispute.

(4) There is a last cause which parallels the second cause. Just as employers are guilty of abusing their power and position, so unions and groups of workers wilfully abuse their power. Lazy, " selective " and sympathetic strikes, with certain arrogant demonstrations of strength come under this head. There are also certain minor sets of circumstances which cause dislocations and are only allowed because of the power of unionism, and its failure to exercise control of its own members. Thus, while a group of miners are holding what will be a short meeting, the

"wheelers" will refuse to wait, will return their horses to the stables, leave the colliery and throw the mine idle for the whole day. Workmen stay away from work to attend the police court to hear prosecutions against fellow employees, to witness some amusement, or for other reasons which trade-union leaders cannot and do not endorse. Again, these causes of industrial dislocations recur most frequently in the mining industry.[1]

The figures published concerning the number and extent of industrial disputes in the whole commonwealth are astounding. They show in the year 1916 a total of 508 disputes, involving 1,536 establishments, directly affecting 128,546 work people and indirectly affecting 42,137 more, with a total loss of over a million and a half work days and an estimated loss in wages of £967,604. The figures for recent years are supplied in the following table:[2]

INDUSTRIAL DISPUTES—NUMBER AND MAGNITUDE FOR THE COMMONWEALTH OF AUSTRALIA, 1913-1916

Year	No. of Disputes	No. of Establishments involved in disputes	Number of Work-people Involved Directly	Indirectly	Total	Number of Working days Lost	Total Estimated Loss in Wages, £
1913	208	921	33,493	16,790	50,283	623,528	287,739
1914	337	1,203	43,073	27,976	71,049	1,090,395	551,228
1915	358	942	57,005	24,287	81,292	583,225	299,635
1916	508	1,536	128,546	42,137	170,683	1,678,930	967,604

It should be said in explanation of this table that some duplication and consequent increase in the size of all the figures is unavoidable in the compilation of such statistics. Thus the same persons might be involved in two or more disputes in the course of a year, and the number of work

[1] *Commonwealth Labour and Industrial Branch Report*, no. 6, p. 101.
[2] *Ibid.*, no. 7, p. 489.

people affected thereby increased. Similarly, in estimating the number of working days lost, no account can be taken of actual unemployment or of broken time, which in the case of all unskilled labour averages about 20 per cent. In the estimated loss in wages, the same factor enters to swell the total, while a second objection may be raised that seasonal work, such as sugar-cane cutting and shearing, is only delayed, not lost, by a strike.[1] Nevertheless, in most industries a large sum of wages is sacrificed, the employers also suffer an immediate and direct loss, due to the restriction of production, and calculated as equal to one-half of the wages lost,[2] while the indirect loss to the country's trade as a whole must always be great.

An interesting and significant sidelight upon the cause of such frequent and costly strikes is presented in a comparison of similar figures for New South Wales and Victoria, the two leading industrial states. The former state was estimated during the years 1913 and 1914 to have 453,600 persons in receipt of wages and salary, the latter to have 346,800. They differ mainly in the facts that New South Wales has most of the coal-mining areas of the Commonwealth, has a larger number of persons employed in industries other than manufacturing and mining, has a stronger and better organized unionism, which has achieved political success, holding office from 1910 onwards, and, lastly, has a mixed system of Arbitration Court and Wages Boards which provide for the settlement of industrial disputes, instead of the Victorian system of wages boards alone, with no provision for such settlement. The record for the two states during the years 1913-1916 is shown in the following table: [3]

[1] See *Report ut supra*, p. 102.
[2] *Commonwealth Year Book*, vol. viii, p. 1040.
[3] See *Commonwealth Labour and Industrial Branch Report*, no. 6, pp. 103-106, no. 7, p. 491.

INDUSTRIAL DISPUTES—NUMBER AND MAGNITUDE IN NEW SOUTH WALES AND VICTORIA 1913–1916

	New South Wales				Victoria			
	1913	1914	1915	1916	1913	1914	1915	1916
No. of disputes	134	235	272	336	29	44	38	55
No. of establishments involved	466	908	694	719	63	164	154	449
No. of workpeople involved—								
Directly	25,647	33,955	47,006	91,762	4,151	5,699	5,434	13,576
Indirectly	14,364	22,326	22,608	31,638	2,026	1,352	809	2,092
Total	40,011	56,281	69,614	123,400	6,177	7,051	6,243	15,668
No. of working days lost	468,957	836,948	464,343	1,145,222	85,212	84,106	64,878	228,269
Total estimated loss in wages £	216,368	419,656	240,322	674,064	35,744	39,619	28,476	114,683
Working days lost in mining group	....	650,649	321,773	762,581	....	34,641	28,511	72,564
Estimated loss in wages in mining group £	....	324,668	176,977	481,307	....	16,884	12,073	38,552

An analysis of this table and a comparison with that for the whole Commonwealth shows that the years 1914 and 1916 were abnormal years, in which the mining industry in New South Wales was engaged in a bitter and prolonged dispute. So much the figures reveal on their surface. As a matter of fact, the miners on the northern coal fields of that state, after prolonged efforts before arbitration courts, after endeavors to obtain their demands by conference with employers, and, finally, after legislative efforts had failed, refused in 1914 to work the afternoon shift. This dispute alone was responsible for a loss of over half a million working days and an estimated loss of more than £250,000 in wages. In 1916 they struck over the eight-hour question, and held up the industries of the country during the month of November.

It is clear, then, that one single industry, if large enough, and if its members are either so averse to guidance on the part of their leaders or believe themselves to be so unjustly treated that no law can restrain them, can seriously imperil industrial peace. Now the position of the miners differs from that of other workers. They live in close communities where few, if any, other industries are found. They, therefore, lack the educational and restraining influence in trade and industrial affairs which a strong body of iron or steel workers in their midst would exert. They have a strong community spirit born of the fact that a dismissed coal miner can find no other work in the district, and must break up his home and move elsewhere. Consequently they scrutinize carefully the decisions of managers, foremen and overseers, and more than any other group strike for the second cause outlined above.[1] Further, such is the irregularity of work in coal mines that out of a possible working year of 276 days, slightly less than 200 days are worked,

[1] See p. 118.

and the wage product of this reduced period has to maintain the miner for a whole year of 365 days. Out of the 76 days which are lost, not more than 20, it is calculated, are lost through industrial disputes.

If this abnormal cause of inflated figures be put aside, the statistics show a progressive decrease in the average duration of disputes and in the average loss of wages caused. The average duration of a dispute in 1913 was approximately 12½ working days, in 1914 8⅓ days, in 1915 7¼ days. The estimated loss in wages for these years per worker involved was £5 14s, £4 2s, and £3 14s, respectively. It is noteworthy that an increased proportion of disputes last one day or less. Many of these are for trivial reasons which do no credit to the persons involved, but others of them are for matters which a little conciliation or explanation rectifies.

Of the 337 disputes which took place in 1914, 118 were settled in favor of the workers, 98 in favor of the employers, 110 were settled by compromise, and the remaining 11 were indefinite in their results. Of the 358 disputes in 1915, 190 resulted in the workers enforcing their demands, 78 resulted in the employers' favor, 68 were again compromised, and 22 were indefinite. Out of 508 disputes in 1916, the corresponding figures were 223, 178, 84 and 23, respectively. Since a compromise is interpreted to mean the enforcement of part of the demands of the workers, or successful resistance to a substantial part of the demands of employers, and as indefinite includes sympathetic strikes and those arising from misconception of the terms of awards, it seems that strikes tend to result in favor of the workers in the majority of cases. This in part is due to the justice of their cause, in part to the power, industrial and political, of unionism, and in part to public opinion, which is, in general, too apathetic either to assist or resist, generally remaining passive.

The methods of settlement of these disputes reveal an overwhelming preponderance of direct negotiation between employers and employees or their representatives. Thus, in 1914, 247 disputes out of a total of 337 were settled by this method, in 1915, 254 out of 358, and in 1916, 319 out of 508. Arbitrators, not under the Commonwealth or State Industrial Act, settled 11 disputes in 1914, 29 in 1915 and 34 in 1916. The industrial machinery of the respective states was invoked in 24 cases in 1914, only 8 in 1915 and 19 in 1916, while the Commonwealth Arbitration and Conciliation Act was called into force in only 5 disputes in 1914, 2 in 1915, and 6 in 1916.[1]

These figures concerning the number, nature, causes and results of industrial disputes show that strikes are blind and clumsy acts of revolt against conditions or agreements that are regarded as irritating and obnoxious. Further, they are a paradox in a land where the arbitration machinery is so perfected, and where so much support is given in legislation and in social opinion to the just demands of an industrial democracy. No matter how lax public opinion may have become in regard to the continued repetition of strikes, no one would attempt to justify them. The leaders of unionism recognize the barbarity of the strike. They regard it as an obsolete weapon, which has been superseded by more civilized methods. In 1910 a motion was carried unanimously in the Trades Union Congress, Sydney, affirming " that this Congress is in favour of obtaining its ideals, and redressing its grievances, by constitutional methods, and is of the opinion that strikes should only be resorted to when every possible hope of conciliation has failed." Mr. David Watson, representing the Newcastle miners, in seconding the above motion, said that success did not run along

[1] See *Commonwealth Labour Reports*, nos. 5, 6, 7.
[2] *The Worker* (Sydney, April 14, 1910).

the line of strikes, but of political action, while the mover declared that strikes were contrary to the principles for which their forefathers fought. Two years later, when heavy penalties for striking had been imposed in New South Wales, a motion was put forward in the same Congress, demanding the repeal of all industrial legislation that took away the right of combination and the right to strike, but it was defeated.[1] The general strike is advocated only by the Industrial Workers of the World, a small but aggressive minority. The sympathetic strike "is, or ought to be, an anachronism."[2] These representative statements show that, prior to 1914, most strikes have been sporadic outbreaks, not carefully-planned industrial conflicts. They have arisen from the impulsive action of unionists who have neither asked for nor received the sanction of their executive officers, and rely on class loyalty and solidarity to gain sufficient support to ensure victory. Against this tendency also, the responsible leaders of unionism are definitely arrayed. It is felt that "individual members must not be permitted to violate the terms of any agreement arrived at by a union with the employers. No one union should be allowed to plunge a whole country into industrial chaos."[3] The reasoned verdict of the leaders of unionism is that the strike "is a weapon which becomes more evil in its effects as society becomes more complex, and as the union movement, the collective system, becomes stronger and more widespread."[4]

The prevalence of strikes in Australia is contrary to both

[1] *The Worker*, June 13, 1912.
[2] Hughes, *Case for Labour*, p. 51.
[3] *Ibid.*, p. 50.
[4] See speech of Mr. W. G. Spence, M. P., President of the A. W. U. delivered in the Federal House of Representatives, July 29, 1910, reported in *The Worker* (Sydney, August 3, 1910).

the ideals and the policy of the leaders of trades-unionism. Again, strikes exist in the face of far-reaching machinery for the removal of the causes of disputes. This machinery has had a twofold effect. In the first place, it has stimulated industrial organizations by allowing only unions, not individuals, to obtain redress of economic and industrial grievances. The chief increase in organization took place in unskilled trades, where the opposition to the higher standard of living demanded before the arbitration court was proportionate to the advance in the standard. Hence there occurred among unskilled workers many minor strikes for various changes in industrial conditions. On the other hand, the power vested in the courts for summoning compulsory conferences when a dispute is imminent or contingent, for enforcing awards, and for penalizing striking, has diminished the number of serious strikes and has lessened the intensity and duration of those which do occur.

The paradox, therefore, presents itself that strikes are more numerous but less violent. The paradox is intensified by the fact that the states which have made the greatest provision for the settlement of industrial disputes are those which have the most strikes. These states have also penal provisions against strikes. The arbitration courts may punish a union which strikes by cancelling its registration, by cancelling the award under which it is working, or by cancelling or suspending preference to the members of the union. A monetary fine up to a maximum of £1000 may be imposed on the industrial union, and each individual is subject to a penalty with a maximum of £50. Individuals are fined regularly and systematically for taking part in strikes, and the maximum penalties have been imposed alike on organizations and on individuals. Strikes are, therefore, at the best, an ingrained bad habit; at the worst, instances of lawlessness strangely out of place in an advanced democracy.

The explanation of this paradox is to be found in a sentiment common to all members of the industrial classes which leads them to disregard the advice of their leaders and the requirements of law. This view is summarized, though not endorsed, by Mr. Justice Heydon of the N. S. W. Arbitration Court, when he says that " striking is not, in itself, an act of moral turpitude, but a right to which, in cases of oppression, men instinctively fly. Strikers are not, therefore, criminals in the opprobrious sense of the term, and may even in certain cases engage one's strong sympathy." [1] The right to work is held by them to include the right not to work, to refuse to work wherever conditions seem unjust. To strike under such circumstances is not considered by Australian workmen as a crime, but an assertion of one's inalienable natural rights, for the surrender of which no other advantages can repay them.

This valuation of the strike as the ultimate means of redress does not justify its frequent use. It explains why men throw down their tools without using any of the machinery for testing the justice of their demands. In their estimation, the strike is as legitimate as arbitration: to refuse to work is a right as natural and inalienable as the right to have grievances redressed. Men might hold this view, and resort to strikes as nations resort to war, only as the last resource. But another factor enters in to condition the frequency of disputes. Moderate trade-unionists calculate that up to 40 per cent of the members of most unions are men holding extreme views on the present social system. They are desirous of overthrowing it as speedily as possible, and will tolerate nothing that will support or conserve capitalism. Hence the most trivial matters are seized upon as excuses for the dislocation of industry, and in unions where the extremists are numerous, strikes are most fre-

[1] See *N. S. W. Industrial Gazette*, vol. vi, p. 338.

quent. Such views as these lead the Australian workers to prefer the strike to its alternative, the ballot-box. A free and equal political democracy can register its will in legislation and enforce its decrees. Its laws and the conditions which prevail are its own creation. It presents frequent opportunities for redress of unjust legislation and the amendment of ineffective machinery. A strike is, therefore, not only a ridiculous and obsolete weapon for industrial betterment, it is a crime against social enlightenment, and against the justest and most effective form of social organization that has yet been devised. Considered on its economic side, it is wasteful and inefficient. It inflicts more damage than can be compensated for by any advance in wages or in conditions of employment. Its effects are cumulative. The economic injury done and the social bitterness created will be sore burdens on a country seeking to realize social efficiency.

The machinery referred to as auxiliary to the maintenance of industrial peace and the establishment of social justice is of a threefold order. In the first place, legislation fixes a minimum wage below which no person may be engaged. This minimum, which ranges from half a crown in Victoria to five shillings in Queensland, prevents the employment of girls and boys, or, in women's trades like millinery and dress-making, of women on terms which are equivalent to a premium for employment or which give no economic return for labour. This legislation is important and valuable in the case of the industries referred to, since those employed are now more carefully trained during the period of their apprenticeship and are more certain of continued employment at the close of that period. The second type of administrative machinery is that of wages boards, which are found either singly, as in Tasmania, or in combination with industrial courts in every state but Western

Australia. The boards of Tasmania and Queensland (up till 1912) followed the original Victorian model, which is restricted to wages, hours of labour and the question of apprentices. In these states the wages boards are not in any real sense subordinate, as wage-fixing instruments, to the industrial courts to which appeals from their jurisdiction lie. The New South Wales system which has been adopted in South Australia and in Queensland (since 1912) makes the boards subordinate to the court, and at the same time extends their jurisdiction to any subject that may become the cause of a dispute. By reason of their composition and legal mode of procedure, these latter boards make little use of the Victorian method of conciliation, but proceed by that of judicial determination.

The third type of administrative machinery consists of Arbitration Courts. These do not exist primarily to regulate wages, but to prevent and settle industrial disputes. Because of their appellate jurisdiction over wages boards, their power in the Commonwealth and in Western Australia to perform all the functions of a wages board, their action in registering industrial agreements, and the preponderance of wages questions in industrial disputes, they have, however, a large voice in the determination of wages. In this respect, though beginning at the other end of the problem, they come to undertake similar functions to the wages boards. They cannot, however, begin the work of settling conditions of employment till there has been a dispute, whereas a wages board is so constituted that on its formation it usually begins its work. The Victorian Act contains no provisions for the settlement of, and no penalty for, industrial disputes, except the suspension of the award, neither does it demand or encourage the formation of unions. The system of wages boards, on the Victorian model, seems eminently suited to poorly paid trades, where, in conference, employees can convince their employers of the justice of higher wages, and the latter can show their workers the difficulties of their business. The system of industrial arbitration, with its encouragement of industrial unions, gives opportunity to vigorous trade unions to establish themselves, enforce large and sweeping demands for social justice, organize themselves politically, and thus intensify the social conflict.

The effect of the operations of this economic machinery has been to secure a better return for labour. Sweating has been suppressed except in the case of "home workers," mainly deserted wives and widows, who are driven by economic necessity to take "white work" at very low rates, and who succeed in contravening the legislative measures requiring the registration of outworkers. The wages of men, based on the principle discussed above,[1] have been fixed so as to give a reasonable standard of life to the unskilled worker. In 1907 Mr. Justice Higgins, of the Commonwealth Arbitration Court, in the epoch-making award of the "Harvester Case,"[2] declined to certify a wage of six shillings per day as "fair and reasonable," and placed the minimum living wage at the rate of seven shillings per day, or two guineas per week. In 1913, Mr. Justice Heydon, president of the New South Wales Arbitration Court, in an exhaustive judgment that took into account the increased cost of living, increased the minimum living wage to eight shillings per day, or £2-8-0 per week of six days, at which rate it stood at the beginning of the present war. The average nominal weekly wage throughout the Commonwealth on December 31, 1915, was £2-15-6 for adult males and £1-7-4 for adult females.[3] Where the minimum

[1] See Chapter V.
[2] 2 C. A. R., pp. 1-19.
[3] See *Commonwealth Year Book*, vol. ix, pp. 1058-1059.

wage has advanced in this proportion, it is to be expected that there has been each year a considerable advance in the wages paid in the various industries, as well as great activity on the part of wage tribunals in altering and varying awards. During 1915 awards and agreements affecting the rate of wages were made to the number of 401, affecting 197,410 persons, and the average increase in wages per head per week for the employees affected by the altered awards was five shillings and three pence. During 1914 the corresponding figures showed that 384 changes, affecting 125,-218 persons, led to an average increase per head per week of four shillings and eleven pence.[1] Investigations and comparisons made by the Commonwealth Statistician show that nominal wages increased from 1901 to 1912 by no less than 24 per cent,[2] and the increase has continued to date. The total amount of wages paid in the Commonwealth during the period 1908-1913 increased 69 per cent, while the increase in the average paid per employee, despite the great proportionate increase in female labour, was 28.5 per cent The increase in wages paid was due to industrial development; the increase in average wages was mainly the effect of action by industrial tribunals. Simultaneously there has been, during a portion of the last decade, a slight advance in the proportion of wages paid to profits earned. On the surface, then, it would seem that there has been a change in the distribution of wealth, and that the wage-earners are receiving a larger share of the produce of their labour.

A more definite illustration of the actual movement of wages in regard to income is found in figures collected by the Commonwealth statistician, relating mainly to Victoria. These figures cover the period 1896-1912, and are based

[1] *Commonwealth Year Book*, vol. ix, p. 1053.

[2] Quoted in *Federal Handbook British Science Association* (Australia), p. 477.

upon returns of income supplied to the income tax commissioners. They show a small decrease of 4.2 per cent in the average net income per taxpayer during the first five years (1896-1901), a large increase of 49.6 per cent from 1901-1906, and a substantial increase of 11.6 per cent during the remainder of the period. The total increase during the whole period reached 60 per cent. Taking corresponding periods for wages, they increased in the first quinquennium by 5.4 per cent, during the second 1.2 per cent, but during the next six years by no less than 28.5 per cent, resulting in an increase on the whole period of 40 per cent.[1] In these figures we note that during the years of decreased income, wages kept up: during the period of largely increased income they made little advance, while in the third period, when incomes were still steadily rising, the wage-earners began to share in the growing wealth of the community to a considerable degree.

If, however, variations in the cost of living, with their effect upon the purchasing power of wages as well as unemployment, be taken into account, it will be seen that since 1911 there has been a steady decrease in effective wages. While the rate of wages has increased, the cost of living has increased in greater proportion, with the result that effective wages have decreased nearly five per cent since 1911 and stand 1 per cent lower than in 1901. The following table,[2] computed in index numbers, shows the position. It should be noted that the advance in the cost of living, which is due in part to the increased wages being passed on to the consuming public, has led to a demand for social regulation of the factors which have contributed to the increased cost of living. The regulation of prices, the control

[1] Quoted from *Sydney Morning Herald*, March 1, 1915.

[2] See *Commonwealth Labour Report*, no. 7, p. 436 also *Commonwealth Year Book*, no. 9, pp. 1095-1104 for cost of living index numbers.

NOMINAL AND EFFECTIVE WAGE INDEX NUMBERS, 1911-14

Year	Nominal Wages Index Numbers	Rate of Wages allowing for lost time	Cost of living Index Numbers	Effective Wages (Fullwork)
1911	1000	1000	1000	1000
1912	1051	1042	1101	955
1913	1076	1071	1104	975
1914	1085	1014	1140	952
1915	1102	1078	1278	862

of monopolies, the substitution of state enterprise as a rival to combines, and the establishment of courts to regulate rents, are among the proposals for carrying this idea into effect.

The figures relating to savings banks show a great advance in the wealth of those who use them. Figures prepared by the Victorian statistician [1] should be put alongside those quoted in an earlier paragraph concerning the increase in wages. In tabular form they give the following results:

INCREASE IN NUMBER AND AVERAGE SIZE OF DEPOSITS IN VICTORIAN SAVINGS BANKS, 1895-1912

Year	Depositors per 1000 of Population	Average Deposit £	Increase % in No. of Depositors	Increase % in Average Deposit
1895	286	21.61	....	....
1901	327	24.58	14.3	13.7
1906	380	25.20	16.2	2.5
1912	474	30.64	24.7	21.5

[1] See *Victorian Year Book*, 1913-1914, p. 607.

PERCENTAGE INCREASE IN NUMBER OF DEPOSITORS AND AMOUNT OF
AVERAGE DEPOSIT IN VICTORIAN SAVINGS BANKS, 1895-1912,
COMPARED WITH PERCENTAGE INCREASE IN WAGES,
VICTORIA, 1896-1912

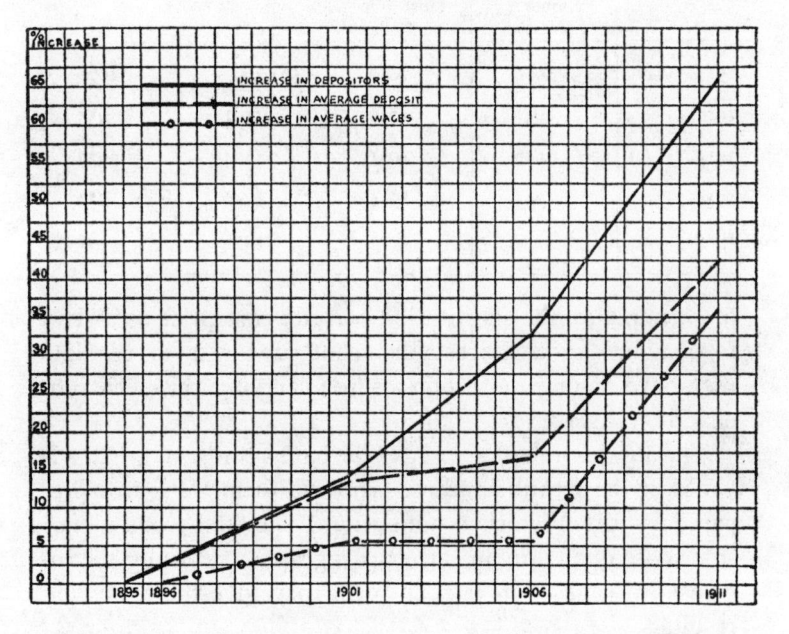

The statistical returns in the other states and in the Commonwealth reveal the same growing habit of thrift and an increasing diffusion of wealth. Forty-nine per cent of the population of the Commonwealth are depositors in the state savings banks, and have an average balance of over £40.[1] When the amounts held by banks other than the savings banks, and those paid yearly in life, industrial and fire insurance premiums are added to those savings and the larger profits of industry, it will be seen that Australia is a land where a very large proportion of the population is at least quite above the "poverty line."

[1] See *Commonwealth Year Book*, vol. x, pp. 786-8.

The effect upon material advancement of the machinery for fixing wages cannot yet be definitely measured. It is obvious, however, that it has produced greatly increased nominal wages, while amid all this increased outlay the employer's profits have not been seriously affected. This large increase has been effected without putting any appreciable strain upon the resources of the country. The nation has not been led into poverty, nor, as yet, has it attained the economic millenium. It has discovered the truth of Professor Marshall's dictum,

that any change in the distribution of wealth which gives more to the wage receivers and less to the capitalists is likely, other things being equal, to hasten the increase of material production and that it will not perceptibly retard the storing-up of material wealth.[1]

One would expect that the shortening of hours would produce greater energy and vigilance on the part of the workers, and that juster and fairer conditions would be a stimulus, in the absence of any harsher dynamic, towards a reasonable output. It is distinctly doubtful if these results have been achieved. The efficiency and productivity of the worker is checked by conventional restrictions which find no place in industrial law, but which are the unwritten code of the industrial process. On the whole, it is true to say that Australia has not realized that increased productivity is rightly demanded by a community which has sought to obtain a just distribution of the wealth produced.[2] The establishment of social justice resulting in a poorer state is social suicide. A nation seeks to give to each man the full product of his labour only that he may be inspired by this act of justice to give greater service to the community.

[1] Marshall, *Economics of Industry*, p. 135.
[2] See Chapter IX for fuller criticism.

This ultimate purpose does not yet seem to have become part and parcel of the social consciousness of Australia, a fact that will become clearer if we examine the question of the quantity of the labour supply.

There is in Australia among the industrial classes a desire to restrict the quantity of labour offering. There is a definite opposition to the economic fetish of a reserve of labour. The trade unions seek by legislative measures and industrial regulations to reduce unemployment to its lowest terms. By restricting overtime, by limiting the normal working day, and by discouraging immigration, they aim at compelling every industry to absorb all the labour offering. The result has been that during recent years there has not been available labour sufficient for the development of the natural resources consistently with the growth of population. Abundant evidence of the trend of public sentiment above described may be found. Measures restricting overtime were passed primarily in the interests of the public health. They have come to operate in the direction of the employment of a relatively larger quantity of labour, and hence of the depletion of the almost non-existent "reserve of labour." The week of 48 hours having been standardized in most occupations, there has arisen a strong demand for a week of 44 hours, worked in five days of eight hours each and a half-day of four hours on Saturday. The discouragement of immigration, except under certain useful but hitherto impracticable conditions, was until about 1912 the public policy of Australia. The Commonwealth Contract Immigrants Act of 1905 controls the introduction into the Commonwealth of immigrants under contract to perform manual labour. Approval will not be given for the immigrant to enter unless the contract conforms to the industrial and economic standard prevalent in Australia, and if he is not a British subject, it must be shown that the employer cannot obtain in the Commonwealth a worker of at least equal skill and ability.

In 1911 the shortage of labour became so pronounced in both New South Wales and Victoria that inquiries were held to ascertain the exact amount and to make suggestions for a remedy. A Royal Commission in the former State concluded that there was a provable need at the time for 3,000 skilled workmen, and that generally there was a great and permanent need for the introduction from abroad of trained and competent workers for most of the skilled trades and for the manufacturing industries. Simultaneously, in Victoria, there had arisen a demand for skilled labour, a shortage being revealed of almost a thousand male artisans. Other evidence concerning the quantity of labour offering and the changes in its nature and direction may be found in the following table of comparison between the occupations of the working population of Australia at the censuses of 1901 and 1911. After excluding from the return of the whole population all who were classified as having no specific occupation, all who were dependent, and all unspecified, the results shown on page 138 were obtained.

In this table several significant tendencies in the movement of the supply of labour manifest themselves. While the general increase in the population was only 18.05 per cent, and in the total working population less than 20 per cent, certain occupational groups have increased much more. Noticeably is this so in the case of those engaged mainly in manufactures. The supply of labour is moving towards this form of industry in an unmistakable fashion. Among the notable increases is that in the professional group. The spread of education and the increase in governmental and administrative functions have produced this relatively undesirable increase. On the other hand, two startling decreases in the supply of labour are revealed. Though the

COMPARISON OF OCCUPATIONS AT THE CENSUSES OF 1901 AND 1911

Occupational Group	Number Employed 1901	Number Employed 1911	Percentage of Total Working Population 1901	Percentage of Total Working Population 1911	Percentage increase in number employed 1901–1911
Professional	111,134	144,611	6.87	7.46	30.12
Domestic	201,036	201,366	12.44	10.38	.16
Commercial	222,658	286,687	13.78	14.79	28.75
Transport & Communication	122,159	157,391	7.56	8.12	28.84
Industrial	426,166	562,337	26.37	29.01	31.95
Primary producers	533,107	586,148	32.98	30.24	9.94
Total Working Population	1,616,260	1,938,549	100.00	100.00	19.94

This table is compiled from figures supplied for 1901 in the *Commonwealth Year Book*, vol. ii, p. 184, and for 1911 in vol. iii, p. 121. For the purpose of comparison, the figures for New South Wales during the same intercensal period are supplied. "During the inter-censal period 1901–1911, the food-producing class, that is, persons engaged in agricultural and pastoral industries, increased at the rate of 19.9%, as compared with commercial and industrial classes 36.8% and 41.8%, total working population 23.4%, and total population of the state 21.7%" (*New South Wales Year Book*, 1913, p. 965).

primary producers have increased in number, the total working population has increased twice as fast. Again, the domestic group, defined as "embracing all persons engaged in the supply of board and lodging, and in rendering personal services for which remuneration is usually paid," [1] has remained at a standstill in numbers, and declined relatively to the population. In this case the commercial and industrial groups have benefited at the expense of the domestic. Women have gone into factories and offices, and as a result personal service is scarce and inefficient.

This movement of female labour is illustrated more strikingly by the figures concerning sex distribution in factories.

[1] *Commonwealth Year Book*, vol. viii, p. 126.

In New South Wales there was employed in factories, in 1886, one woman to seven men, in 1891 one to six, in 1903 one to four, and in 1914 two to seven. In Victoria the ratio has ranged from one woman to five men in 1886 to one woman for two men at the present time. In the whole Commonwealth there were, in 1914, 81,084 women employed in manufacturing interests and 250,495 men.[1] For several years there was a relatively larger increase in the number of female employees in factories than in that of males. Since 1911, however, this has altered. Not only has the number of females per hundred males decreased, but of the increase in the number of employees each year since 1901 a decreasing number are women. Of the increase from 1910 to 1911, 21.66 per cent were women; in 1911-12 the proportion had decreased to 9.75 per cent. Later figures for the two larger manufacturing states are equally emphatic. The corresponding increases in New South Wales were in 1911-12, 16.5 per cent; 1912-13, 8.1 per cent. In Victoria, where females form a larger proportion of the factory population than in any other state, being 65.2 per cent of the total, the percentages of increase of females to the total increase during the years 1909-1913 were as shown in the table on the following page. It is clear that the steady increase in the percentage of females since 1903 has been overtaken, and the ratio of 1914 is almost identical with that of 1905.[1]

This restriction of the labour supply, with its inevitable corollaries, seems to have no principle, either social or economic, behind it, by which it can be substantiated or justified. At first sight its governing principle would seem to be pure selfishness, its purpose apparently being to create an organized aristocracy of labour, whose position and remuneration would be safe during the lifetime of the mem-

[1] *Commonwealth Year Book*, vol. ix, p. 451. [2] *Ibid.*, p. 480.

PERCENTAGE WHICH INCREASE IN FEMALE WORKING POPULATION BEARS
TO TOTAL INCREASE IN FACTORY POPULATION VICTORIA, 1909-1913

Year	Factory Population		Increase on previous year		Percentage of increase of females to total increase
	Total	Females	Total	Females	
1909	97,355	34,533	3,547	1,598	45.05
1910	102,176	35,867	4,821	1,334	27.67
1911	111,948	38,375	9,772	2,408	25.66
1912	116,108	38,543	4,160	168	.04
1913	118,744	38,690	2,636	147	.05

The figures concerning the proportion of females employees were compiled from (1) the *Commonwealth Year Book*, vol. viii, pp. 462-463, (2) *Report of Chief Inspector of Factories* (N. S. Wales, 1912-13), (3) *Victorian Year Book*, 1913-1914, pp. 759, 760.

bers. To impeach it on these grounds, as is sometimes done, is to mistake a possible result for an implicit purpose. The aim may be faulty, from many standpoints; the methods by which it is sought to be realized are often crude and clumsy, but the purpose is definite. It is to secure a better distribution of work, and fundamentally a juster distribution of wealth.

A typical example of both the aim and the method is afforded by the subject-matter of a strike in the early days of the year 1915. On the outbreak of war in August, 1914, the staff of the wire-netting factory of Lysaghts (Abbotsford, Sydney) was reduced, single men especially being dismissed in the shortening of hands. Becoming dissatisfied, they approached the Wireworkers' Union, of which they were members, and induced that union to pass a resolution by which married men, who were in full employment on piece work, agreed to restrict their earnings to the very reasonable wage of thirteen shillings per shift for day work, and a shilling more for night work. All extra work required by the firm was to go to the single men who were then idle. Subsequently, four married men were found to be earning more than the maximum agreed to, and the single men objected, the result being a strike.[1] In this example, which is typical of the whole position, we see the two immediate and related results aimed at by the restriction of the labour supply.

(1) That, as far as possible, no man shall be unemployed.

(2) That no man shall earn excessive wages or profits at the expense of his fellows who cannot obtain a decent subsistence.

The latter of these aims has direct reference to the principle which leads to the demand for a living wage. Every man has a right to a living wage, but no individual's right is to infringe upon that of another. He is free to earn what will suffice to enable him to maintain himself and family in health and strength and to realize his full value as an efficient and useful citizen. But he has no right to do so at the expense of his fellowmen. This conception of economic justice applies not only to wage-earners but to all who obtain other forms of remuneration, such as profits, dividends, *etc.* To the Australian mind an inordinately large dividend has been earned, in part at least, at the expense of some social group or of the whole of society. If a large share of the profits had been distributed among the people in the shape of increased wages or diminished prices, then, *ipso facto*, a greater economic justice and a wider social harmony would have been realized.

Besides undertaking to secure equitable and reasonable conditions of labour, Australian democracy recognizes its obligation to secure work for the unemployed and to prevent unemployment as far as possible. Apart from war conditions, the percentage of unemployment in Australia is

[1] See *N. S. W. Industrial Gazette*, Jan., 1915, p. 237.

generally small. For those who cannot find work, there exist two avenues of social assistance: (1) Trade-union secretaries keep a list of members who are looking for work, and, in accordance with that effective form of preference which in practice is accepted, though denied in theory, these men have first chance for any work which may be offering in their trade. (2) In several of the states, government agencies are provided to assist in finding employment. Victoria has a Labour Bureau where applicants are registered for temporary or casual employment on government works, or for private employment, and where deserving persons who have themselves obtained country employment, which they cannot reach without financial assistance, are advanced railway tickets.[1] In addition, this State maintains a labour colony to afford temporary relief at sustenance wages to able-bodied destitute men. When a man has earned £2 he is required to go in search of work.[2] This colony is useful in relieving destitution and in restoring that measure of physical health, strength and independence of character, the loss of which is the most baneful effect of unemployment and the most serious detriment to the obtaining of further work.

New South Wales has a more extended scheme of social assistance. A State labour bureau exercises wide powers of relief, investigation and distribution of manual labour. For relief, there is provided food for destitute families which have an adult male at the head, in return for three days' work at a labour farm close to the city. Destitute men, unable to maintain themselves, are received at this farm for a

[1] In the year 1915, work was found for 7,884 applicants, of whom possibly one-half represent distinct individuals. During the same period railway tickets were issued to the number of 5,369, valued at £3,273, of which £1,210 has been refunded. Of a total advance of £19,474 during the past fifteen years, £10,882 has been refunded. (*Victorian Year Book*, 1915-1916, pp. 553, 554.)

[2] See *Victorian Year Book*, 1915-1916, p. 586.

period not exceeding three months, are trained to be useful citizens and efficient workers, and then sent to private employment. City and oversea youths are prevented from becoming social derelicts by being sent to an agricultural training farm for a three months' course of instruction. But the main work of the bureau is to obtain accurate information concerning industrial conditions and the needs of the labour market throughout the State, and to assist in placing workers where their work is required. To do this, a free registry office is maintained in Sydney and in each of 43 principal centers of population throughout the State. Here men requiring work and employers desiring certain classes of labour may register their requirements. A women's employment agency, performing a similar function for women, was opened in 1914. Railway and steamer fares are advanced, subject as in Victoria, to the condition of repayment, and materials and tools necessary for individual employment in such industries as rabbit-trapping and fossicking for gold are provided on the same conditions.[1]

In regard to unemployment, there are no delusions cherished in Australia. It is not expected that unemployment will be entirely done away with. Faults of character are recognized as too powerful in their incidence in the industrial sphere for this result to be obtained. But, at least, society can guarantee the recognition of a man's right to earn a living, and can insist upon such measures being taken as will actualize that right. If unemployment is the result of an organization of industry that neglects the human factor, then Australian unionism considers that the correct remedy is to require the industry to bear the burden and to divide the work it has to offer among the men who are attached to

[1] During the year ending 30th June, 1913, the N. S. W. Labour Bureau assisted and sent to work 3,165 persons, of whom 2,315 went to private work, and only 33 to Government work. The smallness of the latter figure is explained by the fact that the government works of the State have each its own employment bureau.

that industry. In order to facilitate this process of giving employment to more men, such measures as the limitation of hours and the restriction of apprentices have been accepted and extended. Whatever effects they may have had upon the health of the people, the desire to share the opportunities of employment and to ease the burden of unemployment has become increasingly their economic motive. The restriction of labour referred to above springs from the same cause, while more recently there have been signs of a restriction of output, actuated by the same motive. Thus a tendency for social principles that contain the germ of justice appears to develop into injustice and inefficiency.

The facts adduced in this chapter reveal a very distinct clash of economic interests. Strikes are numerous, costly and irritating. Through their number and their cost they come to constitute a public burden and a social menace. By irritating employers and alienating many of the leaders of public opinion, they have produced a widening and deepening of the line of cleavage between classes. Men sympathetic with the legitimate demands, even all reasonable demands, of trade-unionists raise strong objections to the means employed by the unions. These objections are given point through the liberal measures taken to avert disputes and to assist those in need. These measures have had a pronounced effect in increasing rates of wages, but a rise in prices has produced, latterly, a decline in effective wages. Part of the cause of this is to be found in the operation of economic forces. But the criticism is made that another cause of this decline is to be found in the restriction of the quantity of labour offering and in the failure to increase productivity so as to supply the economic means whereby capital expansion and increased wages alike are provided. In so far as this is true, justice has been repaid with injustice, and measures taken to develop the opportunities of life have led to inefficiency.

CHAPTER VII

THE CONFLICT IN POLITICS

SOCIOLOGICAL analysis of the political activity of a country or epoch resolves itself into a study of the conflict of groups or parties. Government is conditioned by the social pressure which these groups exert. The function and the sphere of government are shaped by the interests which they seek to realize. The exercise of political activity for the first time, therefore, by such a group as the labouring class, demands explanation through a contrast between the predominant interests prior to its rise, and those which succeeded, through a study of leadership within the group, of its solidarity and organization, and, finally, of the political aims sought and measures achieved. Out of the aims which the governing class sought to realize prior to 1890 came the stimulus and reaction which thenceforward made a struggle for a juster distribution of wealth the chief force in shaping political activity. The nature of the leadership of the new group, its methods of organization, its political philosophy and social ideals display great contrasts to those of previously existing groups, and mark the rise of the people to political self-consciousness in opposition to interests which had previously held political power.

No definite party creeds existed in Australia before 1890. The two leading party questions were the agrarian and the fiscal questions. In connection with the former, comprehensive but unsuccesful efforts had been made to break up the land monopolies which were congesting cities and hindering agricultural progress. The landed pastoralists held at least the balance of power. If a reaction was to arise against this position, it was bound to come from the cities where manufactures had begun.[1] But here the fiscal question alone was important. It was not the city dweller who wanted to break up large estates, it was the small settler and the immigrant. The artisan wanted employment. His industrial and political interests were considered to coincide with those of his employer. Would protection or free trade provide more employment and create greater wealth? As these were the predominant questions of political thought, there was no division politically between employer and employed. Unionism had no political program. It was conservative in action because of its vast benefit funds. At its congresses during the eighties it devoted much attention to the question of co-operation. At the congress of 1884, co-operation was declared to be " the ideal of the wage-earner's life . . . for co-operation in its true sense meant the recognition of labour as the employer of capital." [2] Though before the close of the decade some demands arose premonitory of the order which was to dawn in 1890, nevertheless, the trade unionism of that day had no definite party creed. It was not a fighting organization, seeking for shorter hours and increased wages. Nor had it become an instrument in the creation of an industrial democracy.

[1] In 1890, the numbers of persons employed in factories in the Commonwealth was estimated at 133,000, (Coghlan, *Seven Colonies of Australasia*, 1901-1902, p. 658). In 1914, the numbers had reached over 330,000. (*Commonwealth Year Book*, vol. ix, p. 472.) The increase in these numbers bears a significant relation to the growth of the Labour party.

[2] *Trade Unionism in Australia,* ed. M. Atkinson, p. 59.

That a new force had entered politics after 1890 was evident in the type of men who became the leaders of the new party. Elected by industrial centres, they were in almost every case toilers from the ranks. Coal-miners, gold-miners, compositors, and boilermakers (to choose four well-known instances), by vocation, they were self-educated men, whose chief qualification was a knowledge of human nature and of its needs, coupled with some insight into the springs of human action. In the trade-union world, they had received training in organization and administration. They were the more militant spirits of the "new unionism," the men who saw the future that awaited an organized proletariat, and had the courage and the vision to seek to realize that ideal. In this regard, they burst upon the complacent political order of that day like revolutionaries.

The contrast between the present leaders of the opposing parties, though distinct, is less acute. The Liberal members are representative of the commercial and professional classes, or, in a few cases, of the agricultural class. They are men of public spirit and sincerity of conviction, and enter into politics often from a sense of duty, rarely as a profession. They bring to the task of government the special qualifications peculiar to their own calling, but are not equipped with any general principles of social welfare, and are influenced by the prejudices of the conservative classes they represent. The Labour leaders are almost always self-educated, unremoved by training or mental culture from the opinions and prejudices of the average citizen, who has a dim perception of the social ideal and is a firm believer in the efficacy of legislation. Their leaders are like unto them. They are strong in that type of personality which marks the man who has risen from the ranks, but they are limited in intellectual strength and breadth. They are not statesmen but are diligent students of the science of politics, thoroughly honest, eager to do loyal service for their country and the class they represent, and capable in proportion to their experience of life, their shrewdness and common sense, and their public spirit. In the majority of cases, they are men of greater ability than the rank and file. But, because of the organization and discipline of the party, because of the mode of their selection, there is a tendency to put loyalty before personality. Their concept of loyalty inhibits impartiality and breadth of judgment. Thus, an employee's representative on a New South Wales Wages Board declared that he was there to do the best for the class he represented. In political matters, the Labour party prefers " a government of laws and not of men." Leaders exist to carry out the " platform." Hence, any type of man, provided he will be loyal to the party's platform, will suffice as representative, and the more subservient, the nearer he comes to the ideal. Further, the man of initiative, the leader, even, of experience, who declines to put into effect the more extreme demands of the party's platform, has to face hostile criticism and expulsion. This is but the logical conclusion of the method of organization adopted by the new party in 1890.

Coming into existence as a third party, it saw that its only chance of success lay in formulating a definite, coherent political creed, and in binding every Labour representative, before and after election, to that platform. The platform is drawn up, not by duly elected parliamentary representatives of the party, but by representatives from electoral leagues and trade unions. These leagues and unions are hot-beds of political discussion. Not only is every aspect of the wide areas of democratic politics discussed, and a political platform based upon the conclusions reached, but every member of the party, male or female, has a firm grasp of, and an intelligent belief in, the principles which the leaders of the party are fairly consciously seeking to erect as national ideals. Whatever judgment may be passed on the social validity of these principles, and of the fairness of conclusions arrived at on partisan lines, the unions are obviously training-schools in citizenship and in the modes of social control. They select the local Labour candidate, who before entering the selection must subscribe to the following pledge:—

I hereby pledge myself not to oppose the candidate selected by the recognized political labour organization, and, if elected, to do my utmost to carry out the principles embodied in the Australian Labour Party's platform, and on all questions affecting the platform to vote as a majority of the parliamentary party may decide at a duly constituted Caucus meeting.[1]

When Parliament assembles, the members of the Labour party meet together and thus constitute the caucus. The chairman they elect becomes the leader of the party in parliament, and, in case they have a parliamentary majority, he is the premier. They determine the personnel of the ministry, and remove ministers from office. Their decisions in caucus, whether carried unanimously or by the barest of majorities, control the vote of every member of the party. A Labour minister of state has to defend his projected legislation and his administration before the caucus and before annual conferences of labour organizations. Thus the Labour party has tended to make its leaders delegates rather than representatives. There is nothing intrinsically inexpedient in the system of drawing up party platforms in political organizations; on the contrary, it is a method politically educative and productive of an enlightened opinion. Neither is the caucus system intrinsically inimical to political liberty. Since " its functions are rigidly confined to determining the

[1] Hughes, *Case for Labour*, p. 66.

most effective way of placing the planks of the platform upon the statute book," [1] it has the same functions as the cabinet itself, or even any ordinary public meeting, whatever innovations it may have led to in parliamentary procedure. But a method by which a premier or a minister of state is compelled to answer for his actions, not to the people as a whole, but to those who have, in their own phrase, "put him in a well-paid position," is one which degrades the leaders of democracy to the status of delegates. It tends to make them timid, conservative and unstatesmanlike. It checks initiative and personality, and thus is contrary to the general trend of Australian social development.

The unmistakable success of this method of political organization compelled the Liberal leaders, in self-defence to adopt the same device, but their use of it was less logical and less consistent. The method of local selection was adopted, but the selected candidate was not required to sign any pledge or to adopt any definite platform, though he would not be acceptable to the party leaders if he departed from certain fairly well-recognized points of Liberal policy. The caucus method of party government has not been adopted, either, though again, in the interests of party solidarity, the same obligation is imposed upon Liberal politicians to vote for party measures. The great difference, however, is that the whole action of the Labour party, both in and out of office, is determined by the majority of Labour members and ultimately by the various Federal State conferences of representatives from Labour leagues and trade unions, while in the Liberal party the leader is the main factor. In short, the Labour member is bound to act in accordance with a definite form of party government, the Liberal

---

[1] Hughes, *op. cit.*, p. 76.

member is ostensibly freer, both in regard to his party platform and his political actions.

It was not the organization of the Labour party, however, but its aims, that enabled it to disrupt the old political order. These aims were expressed in a definite, systematic creed. In both its conception and its content this was an innovation. The personal and sectional quarrels which had formed the substance of political activity in earlier days gave place, as political stimuli, to a philosophy of social reform. Though not so significant historically as some of the modes of administration adopted in securing its aim, the social philosophy of the Labour movement arrests attention.

The philosophy of the Labour party is absolute in its humanitarianism and complete in its methods of reform . . . Labour's policy is "new and comprehensive" in that it stands for the abolition of monopoly, and demands that the exploitation of labour shall cease so that the workers may obtain the full results of their industry. Labour's educational ideal is to give every person the freest opportunity to become educated in the widest sense of the word. Labour teaches the fact that the world's production of wealth has now become so great that the problem of poverty would almost disappear if the distribution of wealth were as scientifically controlled as is the production of it. . . . Labour insists on the right of society —the State—to interfere with any person or persons who are by monopoly conditions injurious to themselves and the nation. In short, it recognizes that State interference must increase as society becomes more and more complex, and that the interference is absolutely necessary in the interests of individual freedom. . . . It stands for the destruction of charity and patronage by the classes, and all such relics of feudalism; it stands for true education, and, above all, for economic freedom. Economic freedom is the goal of Labour, and it will be won just as surely as our forefathers won political freedom. . . .

The fundamental principle of Labour philosophy is to improve the economic environment of people, so that some chance of moral and intellectual improvement may result. . . . The sweating conditions and intermittent employment that exist are incentives to ignorance and immorality. Root out the curse of the commercial instinct, and a better type of humanity will necessarily result.[1]

This philosophy, founded upon the support of an increasingly solidified working class, and obtaining a large amount of endorsement in public opinion, has been the chief impulse in quickening the pace of social reform in Australia. Assimilated by large sections of the people, whom class consciousness kept from active political association with the Labour party, it has been responsible for the progressive nature of Australian legislation. Liberal premiers have passed measures through the legislatures, the demand for which arose out of this new view of political activity. To state the chief political measures of the last twenty-five years is, therefore, to set forth the results of this leavening of public opinion.

The first characteristic movement of the new leavening forces was in the direction of a more popular franchise. In several of the States there existed plural voting and electorates represented by two or more members. Thus in 1890, New South Wales had 147 members of the legislative assembly, representing 74 electoral districts. At the same time, Victoria, where plural voting existed, had 95 members for 84 electoral districts. Queensland had 72 members representing 61 electorates, eleven returning two members each. The same State had a property qualification for the exercise of the franchise. South Australia used

---

[1] *The Worker* (Sydney, August 18, 1910), editorial article, "Labour Philosophy."

and still retains the system of electoral districts, sending from two to five representatives each. Tasmania had a property qualification similar to that of Queensland. Western Australia had just commenced its career of responsible government, with single electoral districts, and adult suffrage, but with a small property qualification.[1]

Reform has been along the line of the establishment of equal electoral districts and universal suffrage. New South Wales set up equal electoral districts in 1893, and in 1902 the franchise was extended to women. Victoria abolished plural voting in 1899, establishing equal electoral districts in 1903, while at the same time giving two special representatives to railway officers and one to the State public servants. This latter provision was repealed in 1906, and in 1909 the franchise was extended to women. Queensland has retained the property qualification, but in 1905 extended the franchise to women, in 1910 established single electoral districts, and in 1915 introduced compulsory voting. Of the total number of electors enrolled, over 88 per cent went to the poll under pressure. South Australia was the first of the Australian States to grant woman's suffrage, passing an act to that end in 1903. Tasmania granted the franchise to women in 1903. Its property franchise has been removed, and an endeavor made to give minorities proportional representation.[2] Thus, in the period since 1890, political democracy has been made real as far as the lower legislative chamber of each state is concerned. The legislative councils remain, however, either as nominee houses or houses elected on a property qualification for membership and for the franchise. These the Labour party aims to abolish, replacing them by the

[1] Coghlan, *Seven Colonies of Australasia*, pp. 307, 315, 319-320, 323, 325.

[2] *Commonwealth Year Book*, no. 9, pp. 878-883.

initiative and referendum. Public sentiment is opposed rather strongly to the former purpose, and is lukewarm to any other use of the referendum than that which the system of constitutional government permits.

On the matter of land monopoly, a definite opinion, based on clearly understood principles, has come to exist. Land-monopoly is considered to be inherently unjust. The right of access to the land on the part of all who desire to acquire it, and the right to acquire "a living area," are held to be vitally associated with national welfare. The right of a single individual to large holdings which carry sheep and cattle with few attendants, is contested on the ground that society is depriving a large number of men of their rights and is being deprived of its own just dues, in order to make a few men rich. Given ordinary seasons, no industry is so productive as the pastoral industry. In the census year (1911) while the average value of production, in the primary industries of Australia, per head of the persons employed, was £243, the value in the pastoral industry was £840. In Queensland, where a large proportion of very rich country is devoted to sheep and cattle stations, the returns of the income tax (1913-1914) levied on incomes over £200 a year, tell the same tale. Pastoralists, numering 2,152 out of a total of 19,976 taxpayers paid taxes amounting to £105,647 or 44.81 per cent of the gross assessment. In the previous year, for which more detailed figures are available, 41 pastoral companies, out of a total of 840 taxpaying companies paid 20 per cent of the total tax paid.[1] In the Commonwealth, 127 individual taxpayers under the Federal Land Tax owned land (in 1914) ranging in unimproved value from £100,000 to £1,120,000 and paid 38.9 per cent of the land tax. Half of the tax assessed to resident tax-

[1] *12th Annual Report of the Commissioner of Income Tax*, Queensland.

payers was paid by 247 out of 12,150 owners, while 34 absentees, out of a total of 2,260 absentee owners, owning land over £40,000 unimproved value, paid one-half of the more highly graded absentee tax.[1]

Against the economic and social position revealed in these figures, the national sense rebels. Men are of more value than sheep and cattle. The settling of fifty families upon an area owned and used by one individual is held to be justified by every axiom of national welfare and to justify measures which in essence seek to recover for society its communal rights and thereby produce a more equitable distribution of wealth. This is the principle behind several measures taken, in the various states and in the Commonwealth itself, to break up large estates and cause them to be thrown open for settlement. Within the last decade each state has made provision for the repurchase of alienated land for the purpose of dividing it into smaller blocks, to be offered to settlers on reasonable terms of repayment. Settlers are assisted to improve and pay for their holdings by financial aid from the State governments. Further, the Commonwealth has imposed a land tax graduated in proportion to the value of the land, intended to break up land monopoly, and to ensure that the land shall be put to such use as will best benefit the nation. Above an unimproved value of £5,000 (except in the case of land owned by absentees, non-resident in Australia, in which case there is no exemption), a tax of one penny per pound is imposed, rising with the value of the land until at an improved land value of £75,000 the rate reaches a maximum of 6d in the £. In the case of absentees, the rate is higher throughout, culminating in a tax of 7d in the £ on estates valued at over £80,000. As a result of these various measures, the number of large holdings has been diminished, and there has

[1] *Cf. Report of the Federal Land Tax Commissioner*, 1913-14.

been a gratifying increase in the area of land available for settlement and use. From 1901-1913 the area of unoccupied land decreased 25 per cent, while that in process of alienation increased 54 per cent.[1]

The same conflict of policies is manifest in regard to the utilization of tropical Australia, though here the pressure is in the opposite direction. Those who seek to destroy land monopoly aim to replace it by a more effective occupation of the soil and a wider distribution of the wealth won therefrom. In regard to tropical Australia, the position is different. The productive possibilities of this rich area are recognized: the necessity of peopling it with a people ready to defend it is admitted. In addition to its use as pastoral land and for growing sugar-cane, a large part might be profitably put under cotton and tobacco. But in order to raise these crops to advantage, colored labour would need to be employed. For many years, Kanakas from South Sea Islands were used on Queensland sugar plantations. But strong opposition arose, not merely from the labouring classes, and the first Federal Parliament deported these black men, and affirmed the policy of a White Australia. The economic basis of the opposition to the employment of colored labour is easily appreciated. Colored labour would be servile and ill-paid. It would be contradictory to the principle of a fair return, alike to the colored alien and to the white man whose wages, through competition, would sink. Hence, till some method has been found of overcoming the climatic terrors of tropical Australia, which medical skill and knowledge are minimising, and till white men can be found ready to undertake the task of settling this territory, Australians are ready to leave this part of the continent almost unoccupied rather than introduce

[1] *Commonwealth Year Book*, no. 9, p. 278.

economic conditions which would controvert the fundamental principles of their national life. The pressure of the social interests of the wage earner, who desires a richer national and individual life, has herein triumphed over the motive of economic exploitation, even at the price of the restricted development of a rich and extensive portion of the country.

The principle which lies behind the position just described is that of the White Australia policy. This involves restriction of the immigration of colored races, and of persons of other nationalities considered undesirable on other grounds than those of race. The Immigration Act (1901-1911) prohibits the entrance into the Commonwealth of any person failing to pass a specified dictation test or unable to produce a certificate of health, suffering from disease or any mental or physical defect or disability, or having been convicted of crime or of living by immoral means. No mention is made in this list of racial objections and no races are specifically named, because, on the advice of the late Mr. Joseph Chamberlain, the dictation test was substituted as less invidious and less derogatory to national pride. The dictation test consists of not less than fifty words of a European language. In general practice it is not, and never has been, imposed upon persons of European descent, so that no white person has ever been refused admission to the Commonwealth on any other grounds than those of health or character. On the other hand, the dictation test operates in the direction of excluding all races other than European, though the proviso exists that subjects or citizens of a country, with which arrangements have been made for regulating the admission of its citizens to the Commonwealth, shall be exempted from the dictation test. The number of persons refused admission to the Commonwealth during the period 1905-1913 was 858, while those admitted during the same period totalled 874,478, of whom only five passed (on being required to do so), the dictation test.

This legislation which, being federal, superseded that of various States specifically directed against the Chinese, was aimed mainly at Asiatic races, which were beginning to flow into the Commonwealth, or had already, as in the case of the Chinese, established themselves there, with results that were patent to all, and gave the White Australia policy a national sanction. At the census of 1911 there were 42,230 persons of non-European race in the Commonwealth, of whom 25,772 were Chinese, 3,698 Hindus, 3,576 Japanese and 2,423 Syrians.[1] The total persons of Asiatic race, numbering 38,690 in all, included half-castes to the number of 3,852. Their present numbers do not constitute a danger, but the proximity of the dense populations from which they sprang, and the serious social, economic and political results that threatened to follow their entrance in large numbers, have caused the White Australia policy to be accepted as a national principle.

The resolve to put social considerations above economic exploitation is seen when we examine the grounds on which this policy is supported. The principle behind it is that Australians shall preserve, for the benefit of their descendants and equals, the social and economic heritage that they enjoy to-day. They desire that what they have done to develop personality shall not be stultified by racial adulteration, and that what they have done to establish social efficiency shall not be destroyed by the competition within their own borders of races with lower economic and social standards. They are guarding a land that offers the last opportunity for the development of the higher races and the higher civilization. They have room

---

[1] *Victorian Year Book*, 1915-16, p. 242.

therein for every person whose standard of living, and whose moral and physical health are equal to those of the British stock from which they sprang. But they refuse to receive any race or classes of persons "whom" (in the words of Sir Henry Parkes) "we are not prepared to advance to all our franchise, to all our privileges of citizenship, and all our social rights, including the rights of marriage."[1] Two further quotations will show the principle on which the policy is based. The first is from Mr. J. C. Watson, the first Labour prime minister of the Commonwealth. Speaking in the Federal Parliament on the Immigration Act of 1901, Mr. Watson said:

The objection I have to the mixing of these coloured people with the white people of Australia, although I admit that it is to a large extent tinged with considerations of an industrial nature,—lies in the main in the possibility and probability of racial contamination. If those people are not such as we can meet upon an equality, and not such as we can feel that it is no disgrace to intermarry with, and not such as we can expect to give us an infusion of blood that will tend to the raising of our standard of life and to the improvement of the race, we should be foolish in the extreme if we did not exhaust every means of preventing them from coming to this land which we have made our own. If we are to maintain the standard of living we think necessary in order that our people may be brought up in the degree of comfort and with the scholastic advantages which will conduce to the improvement and general advantage of the nation, some pause must be made in regard to the extension of the competition of coloured aliens generally.

In a later article Mr. Watson puts his objections more concisely:

[1] Sir Henry Parkes, in moving the Chinese Restriction Act, N. S. W. 1888, quoted from *Nineteenth Century and After*, Jan., 1904.

The original objection to coloured immigrants was purely an economic one, but as experience was gained of their habits and standard of living, it was realized that they could not be absorbed into the community without risk of serious deterioration socially. The abhorrence of racial admixture added force to the original objection.[1]

The other quotation is from *The Bulletin*, the cleverest and most consistent advocate of a " White Australia " :

Australia objects to the whole Asiatic, African and Kanaka tribe, because they work for wages on which only a person far lower in the scale of civilization than the white Australian man live: because, where they are numerous, the white man, in order to work, has to come down to their wage level, and, in consequence, to their civilization level. It objects to them because they introduce a lower civilization. It objects because they intermarry with white women, and thereby lower the white type, and because they have already created the beginnings of a mongrel race that has many of the vices of both its parents and few of the virtues of either.[2]

To the Australian mind the incontrovertible differences in racial temperaments, and social and economic standards between the British stock and their colored neighbors are so great that nothing but exclusion of the latter will preserve intact their own ideals of social justice and social efficiency.[3]

In precisely the same way is the question of immigration regarded. On the one hand, we have the labouring classes who are, on the whole, strenuously opposed to immigration.

[1] " The Labour Movement " in *N. S. W. Handbook, B. A. A. S.*, 1914.
[2] *The Bulletin*, Jan. 22, 1901.
[3] Compare the Canadian attitude on the matter. Mr. Mackenzie King, then deputy minister for Labour in Canada, writing in the *Westminster Review*, June, 1910, said: " That Canada should remain a white man's country is believed to be not only desirable for economic and social reasons, but also highly necessary on political and national grounds."

On the other, we have the employers and all the holders of political opinions opposed to labour, who desire a constant influx of immigrants. Those who are opposed to immigration offer various grounds of objection. They insist that Australia has no easily accessible land to offer to settlers, even those of its own Commonwealth. Unless immigrants, therefore, have sufficient capital to enable them to acquire land without help, they are likely to gravitate towards the cities, to increase the congestion and economic pressure prevailing there. They would compete with their fellows for a living and, if introduced in any considerable numbers, while employment is regulated by supply and demand, would diminish the labourer's power to achieve the standard of living he has set up as a national ideal, and would stultify all that has been done by means of higher wages to create better social conditions and a juster distribution of wealth.

Those who urge the encouragement of immigration regard the immigrant, not as an industrial competitor, but as a producer and consumer of wealth. They adduce the demonstrated need of an adequate supply of labour, for "in every part of the country, in all producing industries, the producer is hampered by this difficulty, and is deterred from extending the operations."[1] The immigrant, they maintain, would thus be a producer of wealth, and a country which, while in a position to employ further labour power productively, declines to do so, is deliberately restricting its economic development. Further, it is pointed out that the consuming power of the immigrant is of great economic importance. In Australia the primary products are more than sufficient for the nation's needs. The manufactures, however, have not reached that stage. Nevertheless, at the rate at which they are advancing, both in productivity and

[1] Cf. *Royal Commission on Food Supply and Prices*, N. S. W., 1912.

number of persons employed in comparison with the general increase in population, the time must soon come when Australia will become a self-sufficient manufacturing nation, and will need to export its surplus. Competition in the world's market would create a demand for a reduction in Australian wages, in order that manufacturers might be on equal footing with those who have abundance of low-paid labour at their disposal. To avoid this disaster, it is argued, Australia must produce by natural increase or immigration an increasing population, to buy its increasing products.

So evenly balanced are these conflicting interests, and so much force is there in each of these opposing arguments, that political action on the subject has oscillated between the two extremes. In the economic crises of the nineties, state-aided immigration almost ceased. On the establishment of federation, the Contract Immigrants Act of 1905 was passed, the only statute which openly restricts the immigration of white men into Australia. This had the avowed object of guarding the Australian worker against competition that would destroy his standard of living. When, however, the need of farm labourers and of skilled artisans became urgent and manifest, Federal and State governments alike proceeded to give attention to immigration, and a vigorous campaign to that end existed in the United Kingdom from 1911 till the opening of the European War. Slowly, almost grudgingly, the Australian worker is learning that it is eminently desirable to meet the needs of Australian industries and to fill up the empty spaces of the continent by a carefully regulated system of immigration. He will not be convinced, however, of the wisdom of such a policy till measures have been taken to make agricultural land available for settlement on scientific and financially feasible lines.

On the question of the limits, the nature and the effects

of State interference, two contrary views are held. The Liberal party is impelled to governmental regulation of economic activities only by political policy or the pressure of some great social demand. That party has no definite principle beyond one of expediency and compromise. It believes that a too paternalistic government amounts to an "under-coddling of the lazy, the thriftless and the idle," and will prove detrimental to self-reliance, justice and equity. On the other hand, the Labour party has a definite theory of the increasing necessity for State interference in the interest of social welfare. Such a view receives wide endorsement by public opinion. The working philosophy of the majority of Australians is a "belief in the right of every citizen to claim state aid (both with money and with legislation), towards his efforts to develop the state's resources, and a vague idea that state aid to some extent justifies state control."[1] The more thoughtful of them feel that social welfare can be the only valid purpose, and therefore the only valid justification of a democratic government. In collective ownership they realize their personality as fully as in private ownership, which the present social system makes impossible for so many of them. Their individuality is strengthened by the sense that they have the right to demand the services which a democratic government, aiming at social welfare, offers them. Those charged with the administration of affairs are the servants of the people, who in return have a responsibility for the efficiency, honesty and thoroughness of their administration, the nature and character of their actions, and the maintenance, under conditions of prudent economy, of these services. Frequent extensions of the sphere of social control prevent public opinion from stagnating and

[1] *Quarterly Review*, October, 1911, article, "The Australian Commonwealth."

from causing society to lose the benefit of an extended sphere of personality. The need for new adjustments between social and private interests is conditioned by the adance of democracy. Hence larger and wider excursions into the sphere of private interests have come to mark the progress of democratic government in Australia during recent years.

Concerning that use of the State's resources which is represented by the larger part of the public debt of the country, there is no difference of opinion. The State has supervened in Australia to aid and direct productive activity. The greater proportion of the loan expenditure has been for railways, harbors, roads, land purchases and settlement.[1] A large part of it is productive of interest, either

[1] The following table will reveal the objects for which the public debt has been expended, as well as their relative importance. (See *Commonwealth Year Book*, no. 8, pp. 724, 725.

RELATIVE IMPORTANCE OF LOAN ITEMS IN STATES OF AUSTRALIAN COMMONWEALTH TO JUNE 30, 1914

Heads of Expenditure	Aggregate Loan Expenditure	Percentage of Aggregate Loan Expenditure
Railways and Tramways	192,188,206	60.70
Telegraph and Telephones	4,224,733	1.33
Water Supply and Sewerage	42,511,856	13.46
Harbours, rivers, roads and bridges	29,738,314	9.39
Defence	2,389,782	0.75
Public Buildings	13,229,339	4.18
Immigration	3,935,851	1.24
Development of Mines and Advances to Settlers	1,658,709	0.52
Land Purchases for Settlement, Loans to Local Bodies, Rabbit-proof Fences	16,849,203	5.32
Other Public works and Purposes	7,913,391	2.50
Total	316,605,552*	100.00 *

* Included in these totals are £1,866,168 for loans in aid of revenue, equivalent to 0.61 per cent of the aggregate loan expenditure.

fully or in part, and is balanced by tangible assets. In New South Wales, 82 per cent of the State's indebtedness has been incurred on directly reproductive works, 9 per cent for indirectly reproductive works for the facilitation of traffic, and only another 9 per cent on unproductive works.[1] In Victoria it is estimated that over 95 per cent of the loans outstanding have been allotted to revenue-producing works.[2] Throughout all the States but Tasmania, from 50 to 70 per cent of the loan expenditure has been on railways. This satisfies those who measure the wisdom of public expenditure by its interest-bearing power.

But a more recent extension of the economic and industrial activity of the State has not been so favorably received. This extension has taken the form of industrial enterprises which aim to increase the scope of public utilities and give the state the advantages which are associated with their control. These enterprises, which have been inaugurated wherever the Labour party has obtained political power for any length of time, are in accordance with that party's objective, "the extension of the industrial and economic functions of the State and municipality." Some of them are associated with the supply of raw material for roads, bridges and railways. Others are for the manufacture of goods used in government establishments, while some supply goods directly to the public. All are run on the basis of a "sufficient" price, which is sometimes above and sometimes below the cost of production. The result is that some of the undertakings show a financial gain, others a loss. Balancing losses and gains, there is generally a slight deficit, against which must be put the saving effected in price both by the *entrepreneur* government and the individual buyer. Thus, in the financial year ending June 30, 1915,

[1] *New South Wales Year Book*, 1914, p. 742.
[2] *Victorian Year Book*, 1915-1916, p. 178.

the state works of Victoria, covering 29 institutions in all, and including a coal mine, had a total debit balance of £640. New South Wales, which has brick-works, quarries, joinery works, clothing factory, timber-yard, pipe-works, bakery, butchery, motor garage and power house, had a deficit of £727 on operations during the same year. The Western Australian government has undertaken several such enterprises, including the control of some interstate shipping. The Federal Government has five factories under the control of its defence department, two being clothing factories. In addition, it has a remount depot for the breeding of horses. Thus, a practical, undogmatic state socialism, operated in the interests of the people, is slowly invading the sphere of capitalistic enterprise.

Our survey of the political aspect of Australian development, when taken in conjunction with many of the economic activities described, justifies the view that Australia is divided politically between the employer and the employed. Historically, the radical and democratic element therein has sprung from the nucleus of an enfranchised labouring class. The philosophy of this party is one of protest against the monopolies which the landed and manufacturing classes were tending to fasten upon Australia, coupled with a demand for a juster distribution of wealth, better conditions and greater opportunities of education and of economic freedom. Its organization is that of men, rendered distrustful of leaders and fellows in the economic struggle of life, who are unwilling to give power, prestige and security to any individual without subjecting him to group pressure. Its attitude on the franchise is that of men who appreciate the value of democracy in contrast to the autocracy of industrialism. On questions of land monopoly and immigration, its members fear the power of large landed interests to rob them, by the employment of low-priced labour from Europe, of their high standard of living. In the extension of the State, which is their own creation and subject to their own direction, they see the functioning of what they believe to be the chief instrument in the realization of that large social ideal that inspires their clumsiest movements and their most short-sighted activities.

To the employing and professional classes, politics has become a struggle against the growing power of organized unionism. The political influence of unionism during the last quarter of a century, and its recent predominance have seriously affected the prestige of wealth and management. Even if the total wealth of the country has not been relatively altered thereby, even if business enterprises have not seriously declined, yet industrial leadership no longer rests solely with the employer. His plans and schemes are subject to regulation, to the competition, in many cases, of state-aided enterprises, and to the inconvenience and loss caused by frequent strikes. The power of the manager of a factory is restricted in many ways by union organization, arbitration judgments and legislative enactments. In short, an entrepreneur may find in organized unionism at best a lukewarm friend, but more often a critical, self-interested partner whose co-operation is to be bought only on specific terms. As a result, the employers of the country present a solid front to the Labour party. To them are attached a large section of the professional classes, whom the rise of the workers threatens with a certain loss of prestige, whether the prestige be measured by intellectual leadership or in economic terms of remuneration received. Thus political division in Australia is between employers and employed.

One result of this division is a certain measure of conservatism. Conservatism in general is a mental attitude that varies with circumstances. It is always associated with a slowing-down of the process of reform, but is proportionate to the measure of reform proposed. In Australia it exists side by side with a general sympathy for democratic ideals. It is not a general principle, but is conditioned by the specific instance. The apparent paradox is enhanced by the name which the conservative party has hitherto borne, the so-called Liberal party. To deny that it has been relatively liberal is to betray a lack of historical perspective, but just as truly is it the conservative party in Australian politics. Its members are liberal in principles, but on specific proposals tend towards the conservative position. Thus, few persons could be found to support land monopoly, but many to oppose a land tax. Few would oppose the supplying of the necessaries of life to urban populations at a cost lower than that of monopolistic enterprise, but many will maintain that the state has no right to interfere with private enterprise, which, they hold, can perform its function more efficiently than the state. So the opposition to the industrial enterprises recently undertaken has been factional rather than based on profound principles of social development. In short, both the function and the sphere of government in Australia tend to be shaped by the pressure of opposing groups, which, in turn, are conditioned in composition and outlook by industrial considerations.

CHAPTER VIII

Social Phases of Australian Life

The trend of social development in Australia has been in the direction of the realization of definite aims. Certain standards of social action have been set up, and have shaped the direction of group pressures. Men have sought by economic and industrial change, and through political activity, the development of personality in a way that would be realized in the life of the community. To further that development, all conditions had to be removed which would restrict the fulness of participation in the life of society, and all capacities and desires fostered which would enable men to find their welfare in the service of their fellowmen. Every agency had to be promoted which would give greater moral independence, strengthen self-respect and give to human life, as a whole, greater meaning and significance. To that end it was necessary to secure for each individual a standard of living that would ensure a richer and fuller moral life. Those things which make life worth living are to be brought increasingly within the reach of all.

It is the social aspect of this ideal which is supreme. Measures which seek to establish economic justice by a wider distribution of wealth are more social than economic. They are to be measured less by their economic productivity than by their influence in furthering a social ideal. Political extensions of democracy are only instruments for the development of personality. They are means whereby the individual secures respect for his feelings, consideration for his views, the weighing of his claims for a fuller life on their own merits, and an advance towards a real equality of opportunity. To this concept of personality there is a reciprocal side. The individual has to secure a similar opportunity for development to his fellows. He has to organize society so as to remedy the defects of his fellows and lift the burden of its maladjustment off their shoulders. Herein lies the social phase of the struggle for a higher ideal.

A prominent element in this social ideal is the care of life and health from childhood to the grave. It is a fundamental part of the national aspiration that Australians shall themselves be healthy citizens rearing healthy families. The building-up of a nation with stamina and a reserve of physical strength adequate to the task of settling an almost unpeopled continent, with no mean supply of climatic difficulties, has been definitely accepted as a conscious ideal. On the basis of a healthy childhood in home and school, the Australian people desire to create a social order that will prevent disease from impairing their social efficiency and will give them power and strength to realize their destiny. "All Australia in its waste places is waiting for live men, with the fire of life in them, and a power of hand and brain, to translate what is barren and unlovely into something that shall be of use to man and beautiful as his desire."[1] To people the Northern Territory with white settlers, to wrest from the virgin fastnesses of tropical Australia its enormous wealth, to rule its heritage of tropical isles in the Pacific Ocean, to make the fertile but arid regions of Central Australia yield up their wealth, and in shop and factory to drive the humming wheels of industry, will require a strong and healthy people with no racial poisons in their blood. Such a people the Australians aspire to be.

[1] Buley, *Australian Life in Town and Country*, p. 50.

The recognition of motherhood as a social function is the first step in the realization of this purpose. When the problem of a sparsely settled continent was made more urgent by the declining birth-rate, frequent proposals were made to increase the population by immigration. Pronounced economic objections to immigration, coupled with a more thoughtful discussion of the national significance of the birth-rate, created a distinct change in public sentiment. Apart from a rise in the birth-rate, for which improved economic conditions are largely responsible, the most distinctive feature in this changed public sentiment is the recognition of the responsibility of the whole community for its child-life. " The baby is the best immigrant . . . the State wants every baby born to live and thrive, and grow up under enlightened conditions. The State will help the mothers in every possible way." [1] These words, backed up as they are by practical efforts, express the social purpose of the Australian people.

First among the methods of helping the mothers stands what is known as the Commonwealth Maternity Bonus, provided for by the Maternity Allowances Act, passed in October, 1912. An allowance of £5 is paid to the mother of a viable child immediately on satisfactory proof of its birth. More than 95 per cent of the mothers who have borne children since the passing of the act have applied for and received the allowance. These applications are invariably made promptly within a fortnight after the birth of the child, and the bonus is used in payment for better medical and nursing attendance than could have been obtained otherwise. The mothers of the future are being helped

[1] Preface to pamphlet issued to mothers by the N. S. W. department of public health. Thousands of these pamphlets, containing clearly-expressed directions to expectant mothers and mothers of children, are issued free.

towards the fulfilment of their function, by lectures given to the senior girls in the public schools. As yet, the subject of sex instruction has not been introduced, but it is probable that lectures on sex hygiene will soon be added to those on allied topics already given. These cover the questions of the care of babies in health and disease, their feeding and clothing, sick nursing, home and personal hygiene. The course is most highly appreciated both by the girls and the parents. There is a distinct demand for the most complete nursing facilities in the interests of motherhood. Provision for a maternity annex to every hospital, for the free services of a thoroughly qualified and registered mid-wife where desired, with medical attendance under government contract, and for the full instructions of expectant mothers by clearly-written pamphlet literature, has been made in New South Wales and is in line with the Australian purpose of "assisting motherhood in her hour of trial."

For the protection of child life, strict measures have been taken to prevent adulteration of foods, as described below, and to reduce the great waste of child-life through infantile mortality. Of the latter measures, the chief are those which aim to secure a pure, clean milk supply. In all States special laws and regulations have been passed for the supervision of dairy farms and dairies, for the notification of infectious diseases among either the employees or the herd of the dairyman, and for the prevention of the sale of milk which is not fresh or wholesome, or which has been watered, adulterated, reduced, or changed in any respect by the addition of any substance or by the removal of cream. Local authorities have in addition the power to secure samples for the purpose of analysis. In metropolitan districts, in Sydney, for example, nurses are appointed by the health authorities to visit mothers and infants, to encourage breast-feeding and proper care for the children's diet and health.

These measures have been very successful in effecting their aim. The infant mortality rate for the Commonwealth has been reduced from 103 per 1,000 in 1901 to 68 per 1,000 in 1911.[1] In 1914 it stood at 71 per 1,000.[2] Within the metropolitan area of Sydney the rate has been reduced from 119 per 1,000 in 1902 to 73 per 1,000 in 1915, while it fell as low as 71 in 1911. (In the year 1915 the infant death rate in Melbourne was 80, Brisbane 70, Adelaide 75, Perth 78, Hobart 82, and Wellington (N. Z.) 63.)[3] A great part of this success is due to a local visitation of every new-born child and its mother by one of three special nurses, who carry on an education campaign in the feeding and nurture of infants. Within New South Wales it is proposed to systematize this care of the infant during the dangerous years of infancy. The work carried out in years past by private and public institutions, the Benevolent Society, for example, is to be made a more definite part of the social purpose of the community by state action. Under the direction of a specially chosen board, baby clinics are to be established in all thickly-peopled towns, where mothers may take their babies for help and advice. Sick babies will be taken to special hospitals for infants. Mothers will be advised in regard to the feeding of infants; those outside of the area served by the clinics will be instructed by pamphlets dealing with each year of the child's life. Nurses will go from the clinics to teach the mothers in their own homes, and by their intimate contact with the home life will not only know when extra medical attention is required, but in cases of poverty, desertion or unemployment will be able to advise other government departments in the interests

[1] *Commonwealth Year Book*, no. 6, p. 211.
[2] *Ibid.*, no. 9, p. 174.
[3] *Victorian Year Book*, 1915-16, p. 382.

of the children and the home. Where special circumstances warrant it, arrangements will be made for recently-confined mothers to go with their babies for a week's rest to a convalescent home. In the interval the home will be cared for by the voluntary services of women willing and qualified to act *in loco matris*, of whom a roster will be kept by the State department.

Care of the child is carried on into school life by a system of medical inspection. In the various States, medical officers, oculists, dentists and trained nurses are engaged, as officers of the respective education departments, in this task. Parents are informed of defects which are likely to prove detrimental to the physical and mental development of their children. The chief defects are in vision, hearing, adenoids, post-nasal growths, and the teeth, dental defects being most frequent. The need for this care has been abundantly proven. The Queensland Medical Inspector reported that, on an examination of 5,027 children, she found 25 per cent to be " suffering from physical defects which required immediate attention if physical and mental development were not to be interfered with." [1] In South Australia during the same year 4,490 children were examined by a medical officer, who found 20 per cent with defects interfering with their educational progress at the time, or likely to in the near future.[2] Each parent is notified of the child's condition and is urged, by circular or through public meetings, to have the defect remedied. The public interest does not cease with notification. Nurses are sent to the houses to second the doctor's words. Nor is the inability of the parent to meet his child's needs allowed to be an insuperable obstacle to the child's development. In New South Wales eye-glasses are supplied by the State at a minimum

[1] *Report of Queensland Department of Education*, 1913.
[2] *Report of South Australian Department of Education*, 1913.

quotation, dentists are sent to fill defective teeth, and in the more remote regions, where medical attention is difficult to procure, a traveling school hospital has been established. Better conditions in regard to the lighting and ventilation of schools are being provided in every State, and the whole policy secures the almost unanimous endorsement of the parents.

The social interest in health manifests itself further in a crusade against consumption and in a growing feeling that the foolish silence concerning syphilis should give way to wise action for its prevention and for the alleviation of its evil effects upon the race. The crusade against consumption has so far been largely preventive and educational. Further measures, more restrictive of "the liberty of the subject" than any yet proposed, seem called for, and the general sentiment of the community is in the direction of endorsing any measures which aim to benefit unborn generations. Public attention has been drawn to syphilis by a knowledge of its evil effect upon child-life and by the very absence of reliable data as to the extent to which it may have undermined the stamina of the race.[1] Little definite

[1] Evidence adduced recently before the Venereal Diseases Select Committee (Sydney), gives more definite information than has hitherto been available. A night clinic established at Royal Prince Alfred Hospital, Sydney, treated 1320 cases of venereal disease in a few days less than six months. Of these cases 1009 were males. During the year 1914, 317 cases of syphilis were treated at Sydney Hospital, a large proportion of the patients being married. Few, however, showed signs of hereditary syphilis. At the former hospital as many as 25 children suffering from venereal diseases were presented daily for treatment. A medical witness gave it as his belief that 33 per cent of men between the ages of 18 and 35 had contracted one or other of two venereal diseases at one time or another. *Daily Telegraph*, (Sydney, Aug. 18, 1915). A medical contributor to the *Intercollegiate Medical Journal of Australia* gives data in support of his statement that 10 per cent of Australian children are infected by a syphilitic taint, and that for these the chances of death before arriving at adult age are seven times as great as in the case of normally healthy children, *Daily Telegraph* (Sydney, December 28, 1914).

effort has been made so far to deal with the matter, but, as with consumption, the desire for such action is widespread and based upon the motive of care for child-life.

Somewhat apart from the desire to protect the growing generation is the interest in an extended medical organization. A demand has arisen that the nation as a whole should undertake the stamping-out of disease and the providing of medical attention as far as possible for all. The ultimate and logical conclusion from this attitude is the nationalization of health. So far, the public interest in health has authorized no more than a wider extension of hospital facilities, the organization of a scheme for providing nurses and resident medical men in sparsely populated districts. The organization of a scientific system of health insurance has not become a pressing problem.

In Australia the problem of the habitually underfed and ill-nourished child or adult seldom arises, except in connection with unemployment or the loss of the breadwinner. In the former case, if unemployment is general, the State is logically bound by its economic policy to do what it can to provide sufficient work to keep men and their families from starving at least.[1] If it is casual, arrangements exist whereby no family with a male at its head need starve.[2] In the latter case, the mother and children will be provided for by state relief. This freedom from starvation is due, not only to ready and adequate state relief, but to the ease with which abundant nutritious food can be procured in a country of primary producers. The high standard of living prevalent may be measured by the meat consumption, which is estimated at 40 lbs. per week for a family of two adults and four children, or about 330 lbs.

---

[1] *Cf.* the action of the various States during the European War.
[2] *Cf.* report of State Labour Bureau of N. S. W. 1913-14 (in *N. S. W. Industrial Gazette,* July, 1914.)

per head per annum; on this basis statisticians consider Australians to be the greatest meat-eaters in the world.[1] Further evidence concerning the consumption per head of the population is available in a report tendered by the minister of customs to the house of representatives (June 4, 1915). It showed the following consumption per head per week: sugar 2 lbs., meat 4 lbs., butter ½ lb., with one four-pound loaf of bread. These latter figures are for a period when meat was at a high price.

The social interest in an adequate supply of nutritious food reveals itself in two ways: (1) in measures to restrict any economic movements that would make the price of food dearer and thus limit the quantity available to the average family; (2) in measures ensuring the purity of the food supplied. The former class of measures is not yet systematized throughout Australia, but the public sentiment against trusts, monopolies and combines, especially such as are likely to affect the price of necessary commodities, is undoubted. This was proved when, on the outbreak of the European War (1914), practically every State in the Commonwealth passed legislation giving the government power to regulate the prices of such articles as were necessary commodities. The agitation for anti-trust legislation is another indication of the same interest, especially as the alleged existence of a meat trust is one of the impelling factors in the agitation.

Measures requiring the protection of food from contamination and ensuring its purity are more numerous and more systematic. The Commonwealth has passed two acts that enable it to control the quality of all articles of food or drink or which are used in the preparation of food or drink by man, as well as in medicines or medical preparations. Another act gives power to inspect as well as to regulate the conditions of preparation or manufacture of any

[1] *Cf. N. S. W. Report on Food Supplies and Price,* 1912.

article of food or drink to be exported, and to ensure its purity, soundness and freedom from disease. In every State there are pure-food acts and health acts. Under the former, all food and drugs are subject to inspection and regulation, so as to provide for their purity, wholesomeness, cleanliness and freedom from adulteration. All receptacles, places and vehicles used for the manufacture, storage or carriage of articles of food and drink must be kept clean. Duly qualified inspectors, of whom each State has, unfortunately, an insufficient supply, have power to inspect any article at any time or place, or in any stage of its manufacture or carriage, and take samples for examination and analysis. They have power also to confiscate and destroy articles the sale of which would be detrimental to health. Precautions are taken also that an undue quantity of preservatives is not placed in articles of food and drink, without regard to the effect upon health and well-being. To arrange for a standard by which the purity and nutritive value of food, drugs and drink shall be tested, advising committees meet regularly, and, as a result of their work, common standards will soon be enforced throughout the Commonwealth.

In all States of the Commonwealth there exist both central and local authorities whose function is to collect and disseminate information, to initiate and regulate action for the conservation of the health of the community and the prevention of diseases. Local authorities have to regulate all arrangements for private and public sanitation, with reference to buildings, streets, factories, offensive trades, hospitals, cemeteries, abattoirs, and dairies. In addition, they are charged with the administration of the Pure Food Acts and with the control of infectious diseases.[1] To pre-

[1] Under this provision, Queensland has sought to limit venereal disease by compulsory notification, free treatment, and compulsory segregation, if deemed desirable.

vent the spread of infectious diseases precautions of three kinds are taken, (1) quarantine, (2) notification, (3) vaccination. Vessels arriving from over sea on which smallpox, plague, cholera, yellow fever, typhus fever or leprosy has manifested itself, are quarantined for a specified period, fumigated and disinfected, while passengers are kept under surveillance. Certain other infectious diseases have to be reported to the local central health authorities by some responsible person, generally the medical practitioner attending the patient. Action is then taken to find the source of the infection and to prevent its spread. The more dangerous infectious diseases are specially provided for, and special measures for the treatment of consumption are being devised throughout Australia. In all the States but New South Wales vaccination is compulsory, though Victoria alone enforces the legislative measures stringently. South Australia and Western Australia allow exceptions upon a "conscientious objection" by parents. In Queensland and the Northern Territory, where there exist tropical diseases that are carried by parasites, some slight effort has been made to destroy mosquitoes, while a Bureau of Tropical Medicine has been established at Townsville (Queensland) for further research work.

Social interest in labour and industry centers around three demands of the labourer: (1) By his toil he must be able to secure an economic reward that will enable him to renew his strength from day to day and thus conserve his health. (2) If in the industrial battle he loses health or life, he demands that the industry wherein he suffered, and the community in whose industrial service he fell, shall compensate him or his dependents. He has endorsed "the new and already almost world-wide theory that industrial risks shall be perceived by society to be the inseparable accompaniments of industrial enterprises."[1] As a result

[1] *Harvard Law Review,* December, 1911, p. 132, quoted by Mr. Justice Higgins in 7 C. A. R., p. 231.

of this demand there have been passed in several States workmen's compensation acts providing for certain payments in the case of death or of partial or total disablement. The Commonwealth Workmen's Compensation Act of 1912 provides for compensation to workmen in the employ of the Commonwealth for personal injuries by accidents arising out of or in the course of their employment. In the case of death, an amount is granted varying from £200 to £500, in proportion to the number of dependents.[1] In the case of disablement, a weekly payment is made of one-half of the average wages for the previous twelve months up to a maximum of £2 per week. Should a person become permanently incapacitated by accident or be rendered blind, he is entitled to the Commonwealth Invalid Pension, which is limited to £26 per year. (3) He demands, further, that the hours and conditions of labour shall be regulated in the interest of health. For this he has fought so long and so successfully that a vast body of legislation and of industrial regulations exists to express this social purpose. Hours of labour are limited by law in the case of factories and shops, the general working week being forty-eight hours, spread over five and a half days, one half-day per week being a holiday. The long agitation for eight hours per day was based primarily on the health plea. Further measures were found necessary on the success of this agitation to restrict injurious over-time. In this connection, the main object was to guard the health of women, girls and boys. Over-time may not be extended beyond three hours a day, nor over twenty-four to forty days per year, varying in the different states. Employees may not be compelled to

---

[1] For 62 cases of accidents resulting in death in N. S. Wales in 1913 where the range is from £200 to £400, compensation was paid to the extent of £14,797-9-5, an average of over £238 each. Minor accidents, numbering 6061, were compensated for with less than £5 each. More serious cases, 156 in number, received an average of £58-4-0 each.

work over-time on more than three consecutive days. Females and males under sixteen years may not be employed before 6 a. m. nor after 6 p. m. The hours in shops for males under sixteen, and for females under eighteen, are limited to forty-eight per week. An interval of at least one-half hour must be allowed for lunch, and no person may be employed for more than five hours continuously. Some factories and a few shops allow a short break of a few minutes in the forenoon to their female employees. No female is to be employed in shop or factory during the four weeks following her confinement.

The conditions under which factory work is carried on are similarly guarded. To protect them at the most critical period of their growth, girls and boys are not allowed to enter factory life before the completion of the fourteenth year, except with special permission and under certain restrictions. Stringent regulations exist to safeguard life and limb, providing for adequate air-space, healthy conditions in regard to effluvia and sanitation, adequate lighting, sufficient and separate lavatory accommodation for the sexes, luncheon rooms, accident safeguards, and seating and dressing room accommodation for females. Unhealthy and dangerous occupations are carefully supervised and regulated so as to minimize the danger to health. For instance, the working week for rock-choppers and sewer-workers is limited to thirty-six hours,[1] special regulations governing the working of wet and dry rocks. All females and boys under sixteen are prohibited from having charge of lifts[2] and from the cleaning of machinery in motion. Dangerous trades, in which a minimum age is fixed, are

[1] *N. S. W. Year Book*, 1915, p. 717.

[2] This provision, so far as it affects women, has been amended in New South Wales since the beginning of the war. A large proportion of the licenses recently issued to lift attendants are for women.

specified. Adequate protection has to be made against fire, and effective fire-escapes provided. The same care for health is extended to mines, where a minimum age is fixed for various employments, and elaborate scientific precautions adapted to protect life and health among the miners.

A social conscience upon the connection between housing and health is only just awaking. In the large urban centers, despite the general desire to prevent the creation of slums, there have grown up conditions of housing that are obnoxious to the average Australian. Building acts have been passed to impose restrictions upon the building of unhealthy houses upon inadequate land, but these regulations have been subject to the interpretations of so many various bodies that no uniformity exists. Hence in every large city there are crowded areas where dilapidated and unhealthy houses are to be found built upon very small areas of land, devoid of every convenience necessary for the health of child and adult. The slum conditions manifest in the nature of the buildings are accentuated by an over-crowding in the dwellings. Thus, out of 732 mothers visited by district nurses in Sydney during 1914, 125 lived in one room.[1]

The general public attitude on this housing question is woven of two separate strands: (1) There is a widespread anxiety lest Australia should reproduce the conditions of misery and over-crowding prevalent in old-world cities. (2) There is a growing feeling that, even if, on the authority of those who can compare the two, the crowded city areas are not slums, still they exhibit conditions that are detrimental to the health and morality of the growing generation, if not of the adults. Without the destruction and demolition of the unsanitary and unsightly tenements that disfigure certain parts of the principal cities, centers of disease will remain in the large urban areas, as well as con-

[1] *Report of the Director of Public Health*, N. S. W., 1915, p. 86.

ditions that will stultify the efforts made along other lines to improve the health of the community.

Out of a recent recognition of the sinister significance of these conditions, and the greatness of the need, has arisen a demand for a more far-sighted method of town-planning and a better system of housing workmen. Town-planning associations have been formed in several of the States, and New South Wales has appointed a commission to report on the housing of workmen in Europe and America, and to propose measures for adoption in New South Wales. Little legislative provision has yet been made either for housing reform or for the town-planning on which it depends. In New South Wales, a suburb of Sydney has been built under the direction of a Housing Board appointed in terms of the Housing Act (1910), an experiment that has been successful, but has not led to an extension of the system either in New South Wales or in any of the other States. Sydney has also striven by municipal regulation to obviate some of the evils of injudicious and unregulated town-planning of old, and has replanned several areas on a large scale. It should be said, further, that the new Australian Federal capital, Canberra, is being scientifically planned.

Education occupies a prominent place in the national life. From a neglected opportunity, thought to be the perquisite of wealth, it has recently come to be regarded as the right and privilege of every individual, and one of the most potent forces in democracy. The mode of development of the national life explains the recency of this conception, as well as the form that it has taken. The pioneers of Australia came from the masses of the mother country where illiteracy was prevalent. The new country offered the immigrant few opportunities for the education of his children. The life of toil and adventure he led was not favorable to intellectual advance. Education was won in the school of life, a life of toil, of practical effort of hand and foot, without leisure and with few interests. Communication was difficult, papers and books scarce; life's chief aim was to conquer nature and win some monetary recompense for the long years of isolation and labour. To this end, book-learning, the formal work of the schools, was of little value. From the commencement of the settlement, schools were established, but parents were content if they taught merely "the three Rs," reading, writing, and arithmetic. Parents and children alike longed for the age when the latter could leave school to give their labour on the farm or in the workshop, and regulations of the education departments, allowing pupils to leave school on proof of satisfactory completion of the primary curriculum, were eagerly welcomed. Neither in the school nor on the part of the parents was there any recognition of the social value of education. The interest in knowledge was inchoate and incomplete. The power of knowledge and the scope of its influence were dwarfed by an unsocial manifestation of the economic interest.

Then almost suddenly there was made manifest an intimate connection between education on the one hand and preparation for vocational life and citizenship. In the main, two factors produced this enlightenment of public opinion. The leaders of educational thought, influenced by the teachings of American educationalists and inspired by their practical work, clamored for a reconstruction of curricula, and a systematization and co-ordination of educational effort. On the other hand, the leaders of the democratic masses of the nation, aware of their own handicap, and blindly seeking after a social ideal, came to recognize in education " the one reform that will strike at the root of the injustice from which the masses now suffer," and the only force that would produce " an active enlightened democracy."[1] This excellent combination of forces, of guidance from above and pressure from beneath, has made education an integral part of the social purpose of the Australian people. "Australians never grudge money for educational purposes, it being a tenet of their creed that every child should be given an equal chance in the race of life. None, therefore, must be handicapped by lack of knowledge."[2]

Australian education seeks to create an educated democracy, the best brains of which have been selected and trained for its services, and in so doing to prevent, as far as possible, the congealing of the social strata, and the crystallization of class feeling. This twofold aim is to be realized by the method of giving a free and equal opportunity to every boy and girl to receive the fullest intellectual, vocational and civic training. Along one line, the road is open from the kindergarten to the university, where the best brains, selected step by step in the educational ladder, will be trained in large numbers to be the leaders of democracy. Along another line, the pupil may proceed through trade schools and technical colleges, even to the science schools of the university, where the highest industrial and vocational training may be secured. These pathways separate only when pupils have obtained a wide general education that has made a social life possible and given some measure of guidance for citizenship, morality and the enjoyment of leisure.

Primary education, which is entirely free throughout Australia, commences in infant or kindergarten schools, often as early as four years of age. Herein the Montessori system, adapted to the Australian environment and graded to the higher ages at which retarded children are found in

[1] Spence, *Australia's Awakening*, p. 585.
[2] Wise, *Australian Commonwealth*, p. 78.

the infant schools, has been recently adopted. What is technically termed primary education commences at the age of eight, and during the next six years instruction is given in elementary subjects. The work is graded, and educational progress co-ordinated with age-differentiation. The adoption of this principle, more scientific and more valuable than any external test of progress, is complicated by the problem of retardation, arising from the commencement of school education at too late an age or from irregular attendance. To counteract these two influences, the law makes attendance at school compulsory between the ages of six and fourteen, and on all or a large proportion of the days on which school is open during the year.[1] Through reasons of laxity of home control, indifference to the need of education and the desire to use the services of children, the proportion of average attendance seldom exceeds 80 per cent of those enrolled, while in all States a large number of children fail to fulfil the minimum attendance required. In the more compact and closely settled States there are few children whose instruction is neglected, but in the larger and more sparsely populated States the spread of settlement over widely separated areas makes the matter of affording a reasonable primary education to all children of school age one of great and increasing difficulty.[2] New South Wales,

[1] New South Wales, Victoria, Queensland, Tasmania, and Western Australia, require attendance on every day on which school is open: South Australia for a minimum of 140 days in the year. Western Australia has the highest proportional attendance, New South Wales the lowest.

[2] The Victorian Statistician estimates that out of 218,430 children of school age on 30th June 1915, the number not being instructed in schools was 2,395 and " if allowance be made for those being taught at home, for others who having obtained certificates of exemption, have left school, and for those bodily or mentally afflicted, it would appear that the number of children whose education is being wholly neglected is not great." (*Victorian Year Book*, 1915-1916, p. 501. On the other hand,

Queensland and Western Australia have devised various methods for meeting this difficulty. Traveling schools in the former state, itinerant teachers and Saturday schools in Queensland, and government aid in the conveyance of children to school, in the formation of provisional and half-time schools for groups of ten pupils, and in the subsidizing of teachers for smaller groups, represent the efforts of the State to prevent any child suffering from the handicap of lack of elementary knowledge.

Though the public schools of Australia are secular, provision is made in the curriculum for religious instruction by the regular teachers within school hours. This instruction differs in the various States both in quality and amount. In New South Wales it enters into the ordinary school course, provision being made in the Public Instruction Act of 1880 that " teaching in all Public Schools shall be strictly non-sectarian, but the words secular instruction shall be held to include general religious teaching as distinguished from dogmatical or polemical theology." Scripture lesson books are regularly read, and lessons given, along the lines laid down, by teachers, irrespective of creed, though children are exempt from such lessons on the written request of their parents. Queensland, Western Australia and Tasmania make similar provision for religious instruction. South Australia allows a portion of scripture to be read " without note or comment " if the parents so desire, but Victoria has eliminated religious instruction from the school curriculum. Provision is made in Victoria for one-half hour, and in New South Wales for one hour daily to be

the N. S. W. Statistician, after giving figures showing an increase at each decennial census since 1901, in the proportion of children not receiving instruction, proceeds to show that outside of the metropolis there was a decrease in the numbers receiving instruction, while in the metropolis there was a corresponding increase. (*N. S. W. Year Book*, 1913, p. 204.)

allotted to special religious instruction by visiting clergymen, a right of which only limited use is made. In addition to this modicum of formal religious instruction, systematic training is given in the principles of morality and good citizenship.

During recent years the fuller preparation of the child for the demands made upon him by modern life, in industry and in citizenship, has become a part of the educational aim. As a result the educational systems of the various States have been co-ordinated, so that it is possible for the poorest child to climb the ladder from the kindergarten to the university. The only thoroughly co-ordinated system is to be found in New South Wales. It is the ideal towards which other States are moving, and therefore gives the keynote to the fairly considerable interest in education manifest in the Commonwealth. In that State free high schools are provided, though many secondary schools that are not under government control and were the earliest providers of secondary education, charge fees reaching twenty guineas per year. These, however, are co-ordinated with the State system in regard to courses of study, and are subject to inspection as a condition to participation of their pupils in the advantages of free university education. The course of study provides for (a) a general course leading more directly to the university and to the professions, (b) a commercial course, (c) a technical course, or (d) a domestic course. The general course is intended to cover four years, and embraces studies that give a wide general education, the satisfactory completion of which admits to the higher studies of the university. On the results of the "leaving certificate" examination, at the close of the course, the University of Sydney is required to allot one "exhibition" for every 500 of the population of New South Wales between the ages of seventeen and twenty, or in such other rate as Parliament may determine. These exhibitions carry exemption from all fees, and are tenable under any faculty of the university. A number of "bursaries," carrying the same privileges with the addition of a money grant, are also given.

The commercial, technical and domestic courses, which cover only two years, are vocational primarily, being concerned with the preparation fundamental to various groups of industry, but embrace studies designed for training in citizenship. The schools in which they are given are known as day continuation schools, as distinguished from evening continuation schools. The latter give the same courses, within shorter time limits, to persons in employment who have failed to receive the full advantage of primary education. The technical course in these schools is the only road to the trades schools, which in their turn are preparatory to the studies carried on in the technical college.

The various States have advanced along somewhat parallel lines. Victoria has established evening continuation schools and district high schools, charging a fee of £5 per year to the pupils of the latter. A large number of scholarships tenable at high schools and registered secondary schools, and exhibitions tenable in any faculty of the University of Melbourne or in technical colleges, are also available.[1] Queensland has a system of free State high schools, whose nature and curriculum resemble those of New South Wales. In addition there are ten grammar schools, endowed and inspected by the State. Each of these educates five State scholars. Twenty scholarships, carrying with them a monetary allowance, are available yearly from these secondary schools to the University of Queensland. Some slight provision has been made in Queensland for voca-

[1] *Victorian Year Book*, 1915-1916, pp. 506-8.

tional training. South Australia has established evening continuation schools, and has a series of high schools, at which "exhibitions" granted by the State are tenable, while other exhibitions are tenable at approved secondary colleges. For pupils proceeding to the university there is a limited amount of assistance. In Western Australia evening continuation schools are in existence, but technical, commercial, and domestic courses are being added to the work of the primary schools. High schools have been provided and their "leaving certificates" are accepted by the University of Western Australia. The educational system of Tasmania is being remodeled on the New South Wales type, but the financial resources of the State do not yet permit of extended State help.[1]

The educational systems above described have one common weakness. Between the primary and the secondary school there is a gap which threatens injury to the individual and the nation. Boys may leave primary school at fourteen years of age, and are at once eligible for apprenticeship. Nevertheless they are seldom indentured as apprentices till they are sixteen, since employers prefer the five years of apprenticeship to end at, not before, the attainment of the legal majority. These two years, when the mind is singularly plastic and receptive, are spent either in idleness or in a variety of unskilled occupations that develop bad habits and give no stimulus to the mental powers. The primary education the children have received has been good of its kind, but in the case of those who drift out of school "to go to work," it has neither quickened the imagination nor implanted interests which will give content and meaning to leisure hours, nor fostered habits and ideals which will make the pupils sympathetic and useful units in the social

---

[1] *Commonwealth Year Book*, no. 9, p. 805.

life of the community. Whatever value there is in the primary system is quickly lost in such cases, since nothing enters in to conserve the past values, to feed and discipline the growing mind and cultivate and direct the awakening social conscience. The moral mischief, the social waste, the danger to social efficiency involved in this position are clearly recognized. Two remedies have been proposed. In the first place, it is suggested that the school age should be raised to sixteen years.[1] The two additional years could be occupied in manual training, to cultivate the constructive instinct and to train hand and eye for work requiring skill, and in cultural training which would satisfy the social instincts that arise in the mind at this age. A second proposal is that all persons under the age of eighteen, who are not undertaking any other course of education, should be compelled to attend continuation and trade schools during their hours of employment, to receive further cultural training and to be taught the theoretical and scientific aspects of their trade or vocation.[2] In Sydney alone more than 13,000 boys from fourteen to eighteen are apprenticed to trades. It was computed in 1912 that New South Wales had 116,000 children between these ages who were getting no education whatever.[3] In the interests of the efficiency of the nation it is seen to be desirable to enforce the continued education of this large section of the population. No definite legislative measures have yet been taken, but the proposal is freely and sympathetically discussed.

On the matter of vocational training, a much clearer social conscience has been evolved. The complexity of the sub-

[1] *Cf. Report of Royal Commission of Inquiry* (N. S. W.) as to Shortage of Labour, 1911-12.
[2] Cf. the reports of the Education Departments of New South Wales, Queensland, South Australia and Western Australia.
[3] *Report of the Minister of Public Instruction* (N. S. W.), 1912, p. 8.

ject and its relation to future economic conditions has made it a subject of frequent discussion among the industrial classes. The genesis of the interest of the workers in this matter lies in the change which has come over modern industry. In the agricultural stage of Australian life, work itself was education. All the preparation needed was a healthy body and an observant mind. But better and more scientific methods became necessary when the virgin soil lost its primitive fertility, and the man trained in science and agriculture was found, first, in the experience of other countries, and then in contiguous localities, to be more capable. The growth of towns, too, accompanied the introduction of manufacturers, and the organization of modern industry soon showed how suicidal was the prevalent indifference to vocational training. Boys without such training found themselves in blind-alley occupations, with the cramped economic and social future of the unskilled labourer facing them. Boys and girls who entered factories were found to have the hand and eye untrained, and such was the chasm between school and factory life that for the first six months at least the juvenile's services were of little value. With no idea of the use of tools, no adaptability and little executive capacity, these young men and women were severely handicapped by the failure of the school to train them for their vocation. The failure of apprenticeship as a mode of industrial education has only intensified the need of vocational training. If the future supply of efficient tradesmen is not to fail utterly, if the irresponsible and inefficient juvenile is to be made into a useful artisan and citizen, education must be enlarged to include industrial and vocational training.

Interesting and significant evidence concerning the need of vocational training is afforded by statistics collected in New South Wales during the last four years. Teachers have submitted statements of the careers and occupations sought by those who leave school. During 1914, 9,705 boys were recorded as leaving the primary schools. Of these, 2,467 proceeded to some form of secondary or advanced education. Of 8,163 girls in the same category no less than 2,164 entered some higher school. Of the 7,238 boys who went directly from school to some occupation, 1,940 took up pastoral and agricultural occupations, 1,836 entered into commercial work, 1,185 into trades, 1,559 became labourers, messengers or entered into some unskilled occupation, 229 became miners, 332 entered the post-office and railway service, while 113 entered upon professional careers requiring neither technical nor university training. Among the girls, 4,840 left the primary schools to enter upon home duties, 190 became shop assistants, 157 clerks, 109 went into the factories, 27 took up professions, while 269 became domestic servants.[1]

To supply this needed vocational training, technical education is provided in most of the States, but has not yet assumed its rightful place in the educational process. The expenditure and equipment are insignificant in comparison with what is available for other forms of education. The courses offered were until recently unorganized, consisting of a miscellaneous group of subjects out of which students might select only that which was related to their daily occupations. The student's work was consequently aimless, and he failed to attend regularly or to sit for examination in his subject. During the last year or two these defects have been remedied in New South Wales by a reorganization of the course of studies, by the establishment of entrance standards and by the delimitation of the aims of technical training. Junior technical schools or classes in primary schools will in

[1] Interview with minister for education, *Sydney Morning Herald,* May 12, 1915.

future give a thorough preparation and a practical training for higher work, and will admit only apprentices or those actually engaged, or about to be engaged, in a trade. The completion of the junior technical course, or the possession of equivalent knowledge, will be the condition of entrance upon a higher technological course, which will train men to be foremen or managers, and will be equivalent to a university science course. By this means it is hoped to train efficient artisans, fitted to meet the needs of modern industrial society.

The care for child life, manifested in regard for health and in an extensive and co-ordinated educational curriculum, extends to dependent and delinquent children. No more interesting experiment in social reform has ever been attempted in Australia than the endeavor to take the orphans, the waifs and strays, and convert them into decent, useful citizens. Every state in the Commonwealth has made more or less provision for the care of neglected children, or those who, because of their parentage or domestic disabilities, are in danger of becoming neglected and delinquent. This work is not carried out in state-controlled institutions alone. Widows and deserted wives are subsidized by the State to rear their own destitute children under the protection of the home, advice and assistance being rendered and efficiency guaranteed by the frequent visits of government inspectors and other men and women who have voluntarily and gratuitously undertaken this task. Motherly women, too, whose capacity and suitability are tested beforehand, are paid to act as foster-mothers, and perform their duty with rare fidelity and true motherly tenderness.[1]

[1] The report of the South Australian Council furnishes two striking testimonials to the value of such work. " The State Children's Council has lost two valuable homes during the past year through the death of the foster-mothers. One of these . . . proudly boasted that she had had 40 State Children, some of them as sickly babies, and

The system differs in most of the States, but more in scope and method than in principles. We shall describe that of New South Wales as the most thorough, advanced and logical, and as that which is admitted to be the model for the Commonwealth. It must not, however, be regarded as typical, but rather as the ideal to which all social interests converge, and from which political exigencies, rather than deeply-rooted objections, cause the various States to diverge.

Care for the dependent child commences in New South Wales before its birth and is continued thence forth in stages proportionate to the needs and development of the child. A Children's Protection Act (1902) compels the registration and supervision of all nursing homes and the registration of the custodianship of infants under three years of age. Every effort is made to rear every child born in these homes, and to do so by educating the mother, who is very often young and unmarried, in the responsibilities and possibilities of her position. In infants' homes, provision is made for the girl-mothers to stay with their children for some months, while foster-mothers, who undertake guardianship, are required within the metropolitan area to take their infant wards to a children's hospital for consultation and advice every fortnight. By the Infants' Protection Act (1904) provision is made for the supervision of the maintenance, education and care of children, up to seven years of age, who have been placed in private homes or religious establishments apart from their parents. No pri-

only one had died.—The other foster-mother . . . had 17 boys, whom she brought up wisely and lovingly. When she died, one of the lads, who was just over 18, came all the way from Crystal Brook to attend her funeral, and when he reached "home" too late to see her, he threw himself on the grass and sobbed like a child. This testimony shows to whom the percentage of success is really due, i. e. to the good, kind, great-hearted women who bring the children up—who give of their heart's love and their life's toil." (*Report of the State Children's Council, S. A., 1914*).

vate house may take more than five foster children, and these children are often those taken as babies under the Children's Protection Act. The children must be fed, clothed and educated to the satisfaction of competent inspectors who show themselves the friends and advisers of the dependent child. The principle of the intervention of the State as the over-parent is carried farther in the State Children's Relief Act of 1901. This act provides for the boarding out of the dependent children with approved guardians or with their own mothers, when the latter are deserving widows or deserted wives with children under twelve years for whom they cannot provide. By a later regulation the payments made to mothers and foster-mothers are continued till the child is fourteen. In the year 1915 there were 12,391 of these wards boarded out amid the civilizing influences of home life. On their behalf the State spent a total sum of £156,631–6s, equivalent to an actual cost to the State, after deducting parents' contributions, of £17–0–11 per head for children boarded at home with the mother.[1] Inspectors and honorary lady visitors keep in touch with the home and see that the children attend school regularly, and that their moral interests are being cared for.

The most important piece of social legislation introduced into New South Wales for the protection of children was the Neglected Children and Juvenile Offenders' Act (1905). This act provides for the remedial treatment of all children under sixteen who are delinquent, neglected, or uncontrolable. They are not treated as criminals, and everything is eliminated from the proceedings that would suggest a

[1] The amounts paid are: 12/- per week for ailing infants: 10/- per week for children up to 1 year: 7/6 per week up to 2 years: 6/- per week up to 3 years, and, thereafter, 5/- per week until 14 years, or till the child is physically fit for service. (*Report of State Children's Relief Board*, N. S. W., 1916, p. 15).

court of justice. A court is provided, presided over by a special magistrate possessed of unique gifts in the handling of children. The policeman, though present, is not in uniform. The child whose conduct has brought him under the notice of the police is taken to a shelter, the superintendent of which uses his opportunity, during the week or two the child may be there, to give instruction on rules of conduct, *etc.* The children, of whom over 90 per cent are boys, often have never previously received advice of a proper kind, or encouragement to lead honest lives. This instruction from the superintendent has a marked influence on every boy, even if he has been only a week in the shelter. When the child comes before the special magistrate, the latter seeks to find what forces are at work to produce delinquency, and an officer is despatched to make inquiry into the home life. If, in the opinion of the officer, the conditions of the home are not satisfactory, the parents are summoned to the court. The magistrate impresses on them their duty to keep the house clean, to clothe the children properly and to send the child to school regularly. The family tie is so strong that the threat to remove the child from the home is sufficient sometimes to lead the parents to give up indulgence in alcoholic liquors, to which cause an experienced probation officer attributes 80 per cent of the delinquency.[1]

The main feature of the law is the release of the delinquent child on probation, either to his own parents, other families or certain institutions. Regulations provide that the guardian to whom the child is released shall supply adequate and suitable clothes, food and sleeping accommodation, give reasonable opportunities for amusement and healthy recreation, supply medical attendance and nursing

[1] *Cf.* also an article on "The Feeble Minded" in *Daily Telegraph* (Sydney, August 21, 1915), by Sir Chas. Mackellar.

in cases of sickness, send the child to school regularly and to church and Sunday school, and care for its moral and religious training. In this sense, both children and homes are under supervision. The probation is an incentive to good conduct, strengthened by the parental oversight of voluntary probation officers, who safeguard the child as far as possible. Less than 10 per cent of the children released on probation behave unsatisfactorily. Even these are not abandoned to the cruel mercies of the law, but in farm houses and industrial training schools further efforts are made to secure their reformation. The question of street trading, so closely related to delinquency, also falls within the scope of this law. Boys under fourteen are not granted regular licenses for street trading, and no license is granted except under conditions which conserve the lad's moral and material welfare. When it is reported that boys are falling into idle, mischievous and disorderly habits, efforts are made to induce them to seek some other avenue of employment and not allow street-selling to become a continuous avocation. In extreme cases the licenses are withdrawn.

This desire to prevent social wastage and to give every person an opportunity to live a useful life is carried forward from delinquent children into the ranks of the criminal and the defaulter against law and order. Within the last decade or so the gaol system of Australia has become reformative rather than punitive. Prisoners are classified scientifically and restricted in their association. They are treated to a more liberal dietary and one which is no longer punitive. They have special educational privileges extended to them: a paper is circulated among them, lectures are given to them, a large library is available in most of the States and the use of the electric light makes it possible for prisoners to read until a stated hour each night. The grading of offenders is logical and complete. In the first grade come "first offenders," men who on their first lapse into crime are, at the discretion of the judge, allowed to go free on recognizance being entered into for their good behavior for a specified period of time. In the second grade come persons under twenty-five, with sentences of less than twelve months. The reformative treatment provided for these consists of useful employment (often out-door, such as vegetable farming and afforestation), educational and religious facilities, physical drill and the strict segregation of all prisoners of vicious tendencies. In another grade stand prisoners with longer sentences and a worse criminal record. A fourth grade consists of habitual criminals who, in accordance with acts in force in most of the States, may be subjected to an indeterminate sentence, during the service of which they are usefully employed at work for which they receive half value till a consultative committee considers them fit for freedom. This system acts as a powerful deterrent on the professional criminal and lessens the psychological effect of frequently repeated acts of gross criminality. Lastly, come the inebriates, for whom remedial measures are proposed, consisting of detention, healthy out-door occupations and medical attention and care.

The result of this social effort has been a large decrease in serious crimes and a small decrease in the prison population. More important still has been its influence in checking the individual impulses and incentives towards crime, and in making into orderly and fairly efficient citizens those who otherwise would be constant inmates of penal establishments. The humane treatment of first offenders results, in a large majority of cases, in their being saved from a career of crime. Few of them are found to relapse. Of those receiving their first sentence, during service of which they are given beneficial forms of disciplinary, moral and industrial training, only a small number relapse. Further, in consequence of the medical attention paid to all, especially to alcoholics and those suffering from venereal diseases, the released prisoner returns to society more fit, physically and mentally, to win his way back to self-respect. Auxiliary agencies, like the prisoners' aid associations, assist him in his task so successfully that only about 11 per cent of the persons assisted are reconvicted. The indeterminate sentence, together with various modifications of the treatment of debtors and wife-deserters, results in a penal system that fulfils the dual purpose of protecting the community and reforming the offender.

One of the most characteristic instances of social legislation in Australia is that of old-age and invalidity pensions. These, especially the former, arise out of the idea that the state, as organized society, owes a duty to those who have borne its burdens and contributed to its upbuilding. The preamble of the original New Zealand act, which was the foundation for Australian legislation, enunciated the principle that "it is just and right that every person who has for a number of years assisted by his (or her) work in the development of the country, and has also by payment of taxes contributed to its good government, should be protected against want in his, or her, old age." This principle is very generally accepted throughout Australia, and has put the pension on the basis of a right, not a charity. The Commonwealth Invalid and Old-age Pensions Act, 1908-1912, establishes this position, and shows due regard for the applicants' self-respect, by requiring the magistrate investigating the pension claim to "make his recommendation according to equity, good conscience, and the substantial merits of the case, without regard to technicalities or legal forms."

The system of old-age pensions in vogue in Australia is one which provides a small payment per week to persons above a certain age, deduction being made from the pension for any property or income from any other source. The recipient must be at least sixty-five, if male, and sixty years if female. A man permanently incapacitated for work may claim the pension at sixty. Continuous residence in Australia for twenty years prior to the application, and during the currency of the pension, together with good character, are fundamental conditions. Instalments of the pension may be forfeited for drunken, intemperate or disreputable habits, and the pension certificate will be cancelled in the case of two convictions for short sentences of less than a month, or one conviction for a longer period than a year. Pensions are limited to £26 per year, or to an amount that will not raise the pensioner's income from all sources above £52 per year. In order to reduce the costliness of the scheme and to ensure the restriction of the pensions to those who are actually in need of them, provision is made for a reduction of the grant where the applicant has other property. Accumulated property to the value of £310 or over disqualifies for the receipt of a pension, while the pension is subject to a reduction of £1 for every £10 of value of any accumulated capital the pensioner may have. In the estimate of the old-age pensioner's income, the following payments are excluded: any benefit from friendly societies, any sick benefits from trade unions or other provident society, any allowance made under the Miners' Accident Relief Fund, any gift or allowance from children; while the value of the home in which the pensioner resides is not to be counted in with the capital value of property for which deductions may be made.[1]

[1] *Commonwealth Acts,* vol. xii (1913).

Invalid pensions, not exceeding ten shillings per week in any individual case, may be granted to any person between sixteen and sixty who is permanently incapacitated for work by reason of accident or of his being an invalid, or who is permanently blind. The conditions are somewhat similar in principle to those regulating the grant of old-age pensions, except that the residence qualification is five years.[1] In these schemes Australia makes more liberal pension provisions than any other country in the world. In the period of their currency[2] there has been a much greater increase in the number of pensioners than in the population generally, due to the diminution of the feeling that the receipt of a pension carries with it the stigma of pauperization. However, although approximately 5¼ per cent of the population have the requisite age qualification, only 34½ per cent of that number (that is, about 1¾ per cent of the total population) are in receipt of old-age pensions, while the proportion of invalid pensioners is less than three per 1000 of the total population. The actual liability on 30th June, 1916, for the old-age and invalid pensions then in force was £2,900,352 per year, or an average per individual pensioner of £25-3-5 per annum.[3]

In relation to the position, powers and rights of women, Australians are both generous and just. They are free from sex-prejudice. They recognize that no arguments for a fuller life for mankind can logically exclude woman from

[1] *Cf. ut supra.*

[2] Old age pensions were first provided by Victoria early in 1901. Later in the same year a pension scheme came into force in New South Wales. Queensland undertook to pay pensions from 1st July, 1908. The Commonwealth Parliament next made provision for the payment of pensions throughout Australia from 1st July 1909, superseding the state acts thereby. Invalid pensions were first paid by the Commonwealth on 15th Dec. 1910. (*Commonwealth Year Book*, no. 8, p. 1068).

[3] *Victorian Year Book*, 1915-16, pp. 596, 597.

the same advantages and rights. They have admitted her to equality at the ballot-box. They demand for her, as for themselves, a living wage. In the larger opportunities for civic and social usefulness, women play an important part. In addition to the right of the franchise which they exercise in some of the more compact States even more fully than men, they are eligible for election to either house of the Commonwealth parliament and to the legislative assemblies of Queensland and South Australia. They are not excluded, provided they have the property qualification, from the exercise of the municipal franchise, and there is a strong feeling that their services as councilors would be of benefit to municipalities in those matters of hygiene and of town-planning and decoration that are coming increasingly into the municipal sphere. In political conferences and on public committees dealing with charity and social reform they are given a large and important place. A considerable number have obtained university degrees in medicine and are engaged in general hospital practice. They are found especially in children's and maternity institutions, as well as, to a minor extent, in private practice. In factory administration, female inspectors are a necessity, and several of them have left their mark upon methods to be used and purposes to be attained in this sphere of administration. In the report on the year's work for 1913, one of the New South Wales inspectors (Miss Duncan) lays down the following important principle which sums up the attitude of Australia on the matter of the position of women:

I am quite sure that, as time goes on, the public conscience will be roused to insist that the conditions of women's work shall, in every avenue of public life, be established on a basis better fitted to their own natural constitution, instead of being fitted into gaps left in the pattern originally cut out for men.[1]

[1] *N. S. W. Industrial Gazette*, October 1914.

That women shall have free and equal opportunity to work out their lives and develop along the line of their own initiative and temperament, so as to further the social good, is a definite part of the Australian interest in personality.

A characteristic development of this freedom and equality of opportunity afforded to women is seen in the movement of female labour away from domestic service into factory and office life.[1] The explanation of this seems to be found in the irksomeness of domestic service. It is not that the work is intrinsically dull or unpleasant, but there is a closeness in the relation that inhibits initiative, and is felt to bind and restrict the personality. Bright young girls cannot be induced to accept the position of a general servant. They object to the loneliness which their position in the household entails upon them, the absence of spontaneous association and of the opportunity for sharing in any real family life. They have an instinctive desire to count, somewhere in the social process, as an integer. They give, also, as another reason for not entering upon domestic service, their objection to such activities as waiting upon the table. At bottom, this is a particular instance of a general reluctance to enter upon any relationship which is not free, in which they cannot stand upon a basis of economic and personal independence. They express a preference for boarding-houses and hotels, because their economic independence is guaranteed, in terms of wages and hours of labour, by awards of wages boards, and they have therein greater freedom and fulness of associational life. On account of the same objections, the great majority of girls refuse to enter domestic service at all, and find, in offices and factories, the social and personal satisfactions they fail to find in the service of the home.[2]

[1] *Cf. supra*, p. 138.
[2] See the interesting reports of the New South Wales Women's Employment Agency in *N. S. W. Industrial Gazette*, June, July, 1914.

In regard also to the remuneration of women wage-earners, a position has been reached that is increasingly in accordance with this social estimate of women. Their entrance into industrial life in Australia was associated with the "sweating" against which the Victorian system of wages boards was aimed. When this had been abolished, men began to fear that women would reduce their wages and displace them. It has been discovered, however, that women have not dispossessed men from trades where the latter were formerly numerous. On the other hand, they have made certain industries, especially those concerned with the preparation of clothing, food and drink, peculiarly their own. In regard to wages, there was a distinct tendency for female labour, where it came into competition with male labour, to reduce the scale of remuneration for the latter. But in all organized industries, where the arbitration machinery operates, that danger has passed, with the fixing of a standard rate for each, and the establishment of a principle upon which their competition is to be adjusted. One sex is not to be protected against the other in fields of industry that are common to both.[1] The suggestion that women should receive equal pay for equal work has been defeated by the assertions of a more valid social principle. An approach is being made to a wage sufficient to enable a woman to support herself. The most recent shop assistants' award in New South Wales provides that girls of twenty-three and over shall receive thirty-five shillings per week, and if engaged in departments which have until recently been exclusively men's, shall be paid the rates for male assistants, less 20 per cent. But more cheering and significant than the increased remuneration is the diminishing proportion of female labour. One fundamental cause operated to drive women into the labour market. In com-

[1] *Cf. supra*, p. 110.

mon with their fathers and brothers they desired to realize a standard of comfort and decency. Where the earnings of the bread-winner were insufficient, they went to work to supplement those earnings. When, however, the breadwinners' wage came to be based upon the needs of a family, the necessity which drove women to work lost its urgency. Hence the decrease in the proportion of females to males in industry which has manifested itself since 1911. While at the same time making possible a reasonable sustenance to the women who have to work, Australian legislation has achieved for others the opportunity for the development in the family circle of a normal life.

It will be convenient here to summarize the social effects of the vast body of legislation and regulation which, whether described as economic or political, has had a social bearing. The operation of economic forces has come to be associated with a desire for a fuller life and a more adequate expression of personality. The standard by which the living wage is measured is one which allows a man to develop himself as a worker, a father and a citizen. He is held to have a right to what he earns, to the full produce of his labour. His remuneration is based rather on his social value and the needs of his personality than on the economic value of his work. The whole industrial legislation of Australia is social in character rather than economic. It is not even merely "humanitarian," as its opponents call it; it is always based upon a certain ideal of the personal worth of men. The arguments against it are usually economic; those in favor of it are social. Whatever restrictions have been imposed upon economic expansion are attempts to give to all, workmen and employers alike, more opportunities of comfort and leisure and a higher standard of living. The limitation of hours was the first and most important of these restrictions. Men and women who worked hard and incessantly for eighty and (in the case of waitresses) one hundred hours per week, had no opportunity for mental and moral development. While health lasted they lived an animal existence. Now hours are strictly limited and a weekly half-holiday is given. Practically every person has his evenings free for home life, recreation or amusement. The weekly half-holiday affords a better opportunity for recreation. Sunday labour is penalized in most industries by the enforcement of double wages, while in occupations where Sunday work is necessary, arrangements are made for giving the Sunday itself as a rest-day as frequently as possible, and for substituting another day of the same week when the employee has to work on Sunday. By this, which has been called one of the cardinal industrial laws, there has been secured that leisure which is the prime essential to the development of personality.

The whole machinery of arbitration operates to foster the development of personality. It restricts the arbitrary power which one man possesses of giving or refusing the employment necessary to the maintenance not only of physical well-being but of personal dignity and integrity. It destroys that artificial weight which the present economic system gives to the will of one man and sets up in opposition a court that offers a full, fair hearing on economic matters, wherein the employee may meet his master without fear or favor. The employer is no longer the sole arbiter of the conditions under which his workers shall toil and live. He must now take into account their feelings, ideals, desires, and needs. He must allow them a voice in matters affecting their own welfare, for if he should refuse, they have a court created by legislation, not only to remove inequalities, but to protect the weak against the strong. The result has been increased intelligence and self-respect on the part of the worker, and his establishment on a higher social status. The sense of his relationship to his fellow-workers, the recognition of the solidarity of their interests, and the mental effort needed and given to grasp all their economic, industrial and social interactions, have made the average Australian worker more intelligent and independent.

Our survey has shown how in the realization of the social ideal which has dominated Australian life during the last quarter of a century there has been woven together a complex of social values. They have not been in any direct way the result of the economic or political conflicts that have raged. Most of them have received general endorsement, and a far larger measure of support than many of the social activities discussed in the two preceding chapters. Thus, for instance, the Pure Foods Act (1908) of New South Wales was passed without any actual opposition to the principle, while on the subject of education the two political parties were divided not so much by diverse views of the place of education in the State as on the principle of the use of taxation and the need of a financial surplus. The exponents alike of progressive and more radical views have been able all along to endorse that social valuation which is the basis and the rationale of Australian social legislation. Hence the student of society will see in this fact a confirmation of the thesis of this volume, that Australia is a land intolerant of special privileges, resolved to give human values their full meaning and significance, and divided on those matters of economics and politics where difference concerning methods and the weight and value of conflicting interests becomes an actual principle of social organization. A country united in regard to methods of organization for the realization of such social values in every sphere of collective life would not fail to effect its purpose. But with serious differences in economic and political interests there has come economic and social disorganization that, in its turn, is hindering the full realization of those social values which are the ultimate end of such a democracy as Australia constitutes.

CHAPTER IX

Struggle and Failure

The struggle in Australia to create a social democracy where social justice would be realized has advanced far enough for its success and failure to be evaluated. The social ideal which inspired the political activities of the last quarter of a century has almost reached its full fruition. What it has achieved has been stated in previous chapters. Its deficiencies and failures are many. Instead of realizing the national purpose with a minimum of loss in time and social energy, it has produced a wasteful and bitter class struggle, wherein social energy and political activity are consumed, and whereby economic advance is hindered. Faced with the problem of land monopoly, the nation has done much by political measures to wrest the land from the hands of the monopoliser, but has not given scientific attention to the questions of irrigation, soil survey and the form and nature of the farming which will most effectively develop the natural resources. In the organization of its labour power, the tendency of unionism has been to work for a substantial equality among apprentices, unskilled and skilled workers alike, instead of a grading conformable to industrial efficiency. In the matter of the reward of labour, stress has been laid rather on the distribution of employment and of the wage-remuneration than on an increase of productive efficiency. In the political system, with its tendency to distrust leaders and its failure to base political activity upon prior sociological and economic investigation, a similar tendency to prefer democratic equality to scientific efficiency is manifest. Finally, in social life, inability to realize the national purposes without waste of time or energy is seen in the restriction of the population, in the deficient linking of the interests of the individual to productive tasks, and in the class consciousness which hinders social harmony.

The inefficiency of the primary industries has consisted largely in their inability in the period of settlement to overcome all their difficulties. Their development has been a praiseworthy struggle against many obstacles that arise from the environment. The pastoral industry is conditioned mainly by the quantity of rain which falls. Sheep thrive best where the rainfall is between ten and twenty inches a year, and where the temperature does not exceed an average of 75° Fahrenheit. In regions of higher rainfall, they are subject to several diseases. Hence the hilly portions of the coastal districts are unprofitable for sheep raising. In those districts where the average rainfall is below ten inches, as for instance, the Lake Eyre Basin with an area of 150,000 square miles, sheep could be reared in good seasons, but the inevitably recurring droughts, the prohibitive cost in such regions of water conservation and of facilities for transporting the sheep to wetter regions, measure the obstacles which have to be met.

Praiseworthy efforts to overcome this handicap of unsuitable natural conditions mark the economic development of Australia. (1) The scanty rainfall has been supplemented by a certain amount of water conservation, mainly by tapping the vast reservoir of artesian water which underlies 576,000 square miles of the arid regions of New South Wales, Queensland and South Australia, where the pastoral industry is supreme. Because of the presence of alkalis, the water is not generally suitable for irrigation, but may be used for watering stock. Government bores and artesian water trusts have made the water available for a small payment per acre, with the result that pastoral areas are being occupied by small settlers, where previously only large and wealthy companies could operate, and the closer settlement has meant more sheep and cattle. (2) The adverse conditions have called for improvement in the breed of sheep so as to fit them to their environment, to make them hardier and more profitable; both for wool and mutton, this has been achieved. Merino sheep do best in New South Wales where they form 83 per cent of the whole. In order to suit other climates, to obtain a hardier sheep which would be more useful for mixed farming, and one with a bigger frame to meet the demands of the export market, the merino has been crossed with other sheep, without loss to its wool-bearing powers. The fleece cut from each sheep has risen from an average of four pounds when the merino was first introduced, to an average of eight pounds at the present day.[1] In addition, the quality of the wool has improved, and the weight of the original sheep nearly doubled. (3) The State has pursued a railway and land policy which has led to an increase of productivity. The large areas, as a result, are being replaced by small holdings which, because of the greater care bestowed upon water, fodder, and the breed of the sheep, do not diminish the yield of pastoral products even in districts where wheat is grown as well. The presence of these small holdings gives rise further to railway construction for the transport of stock and the carriage of wool.

Yet all these efforts have not fully succeeded in putting the pastoral industry in a condition of continuous increase.

In 1910 a South Australian wool crop averaged 13 lbs. 7¾ ounces of wool for each grown sheep. (*Federal Hand Book to the British Science Meeting*, Australia, p. 393).

The number of sheep in Australia has declined in recent years. It must be admitted that the pastoral industry is limited, through climatic conditions as explained, to about 28 per cent of the country, though an area embracing another 19½ per cent would be available, if provision could be made for the transport of stock to wetter areas in dry seasons. Advance in pastoral productivity must come along the line of more effective use of these areas by conserving water, preventing over-stocking and providing artificial food crops for sheep. The fuller use of the more temperate parts of Queensland and the Northern Territory for the grazing of horses and cattle is also required.

As in the case of the pastoral industry, the progress of agriculture has involved the overcoming of great difficulties. The land laws favored large estates, and thus restricted settlement. A scanty rainfall led men to consider large areas of land in New South Wales, Victoria and South Australia unsuitable for wheat growing. Scarcity of labour threatened to make the cost of production too high for the average yield of wheat to repay the farmer. Most of these obstacles are being overcome. Legislation combating land monopoly has diminished the number of large holdings, while at the same time increasing the number of settlers. The use of scientific methods of cultivation has tended to overcome the other difficulties. In a country where labour is scarce and dear and can soon pass into the employer's grade, the Australian farmer has had to devise economical methods for putting in and taking off his crops. These he found in the use of machinery. His ploughing is done by multiple ploughs, which throw six to eight furrows at one time. His harvesting is done by the combined stripper and harvester, an Australian invention. As a result of this economy so low an average production as ten bushels of wheat per acre is profitable. Again, he has had to guard against insufficient rainfall, and, as dry farming in its real sense has not yet been attempted, the precautions taken have been those of fallowing and a rotation of crops. The fallowing is so conducted as to conserve in the soil two winters' rainfall and thus to obviate the evils of a dry harvest season. An experiment conducted by a government expert in New South Wales upon two blocks, one of which received a normal rainfall, the other getting very little, showed that in this method of fallowing, the Australian farmer has found the means to make wheat growing a sure and profitable industry. The rotation of crops, together with a liberal use of manures, is intended to guard against the exhaustion of the soil. Most of the wheat areas are on very rich soil, but nature will not replenish herself. Lastly, to obtain a more intensive culture, the system of mixed farming has been adopted. Agriculture, sheep-raising, and in some better-watered districts, dairying, go hand in hand. Share-farming, in which the man who works the land has seed and implements found for him in return for his labour and shares the produce with the owner, has overcome the difficulty of scarcity of labour and has led to greater productivity, and to a distribution which is gradually producing a race of yeomanry. Lastly, almost unknown workers in the field of science, notably Farrar, have been at work producing new varieties of wheat which will resist drought, wind and diseases and retain their fertility and milling qualities. In this latter respect, great success has crowned the efforts of the scientists. Federation wheat, a variety produced by Farrar's experiments, has led to a great extension of the wheat belt westward into the drier regions, and is estimated to be producing an annual increase in the value of the wheat production of New South Wales and Victoria equivalent to at least £600,000.[1]

---

[1] *N. S. W. Handbook to the B. A. A. S.*, 1914, p. 223.

Yet all that has been done but points the way to a more effective use of the national resources of the country. The soil of the drier areas is rich in nitrogenous materials, and needs irrigation chiefly to enable it to produce various agricultural products, as well as root crops for sheep. A start has been made, but no national sense of the potentialities and the need of irrigation has been aroused. Experiments made on areas where closer settlement is possible have shown the fruitfulness of this method. New South Wales has built a large reservoir at Burrinjuck, on the Murrumbridge River, which can irrigate over 3,000 square miles of territory. At present it is used to furnish water to a section about 40 miles in length, where 881 farms have been established, and a population of 5000 persons brought together.[1] In Victoria, the state irrigation works are capable of irrigating 6000 square miles, though their area of irrigation in 1915 was only about 423 square miles. Some of these works are situated in closer settlement areas where, as in New South Wales, land but sparsely populated and used mainly for pasture, has been set apart for agriculture. As a result, the land purchased and subdivided by the State consists now of 1881 separate blocks in place of the 172 original properties, and supports 1,477 families instead of the 118 who occupied it when purchased.[2] The success of the settlements at Mildura, Victoria, and Renmark, South Australia, is further evidence of the potentialities of irrigation. Yet the full capacities of even these experiments have not been taxed. Estimates of irrigable land in the various states assign five million acres to New South Wales, a million and a half to Victoria and a million to South Australia. Only a small fraction of this area is

[1] *Commonwealth Year Book*, no. 9, pp. 526-531.
[2] *Victorian Year Book*, 1915-1916, pp. 686-689.

now being irrigated, and existing works could supply only one-twelfth of the quantity of water required. In the case of artesian water, though many bores have been put down, the formation of artesian districts, in which the water is distributed by wide, open drains available for watering stock, has not been greatly developed.

The same failure to realize and adequately use the available agricultural land is shown by a comparison of the land suitable for wheat with that which is actually tilled for that crop. In considering the potentialities of land for wheat, it must be remembered that different regions have distinct periods of rainfall to which agricultural operations must be fitted. On the whole, Mediterranean climates, that is, those with a winter rainfall, are best suited for wheat. Regions where the bulk of the rain falls in summer and evaporates rapidly, or which do not receive sufficient rain during the growth of the crop, though suited by temperature and soil, must be excluded from the available area. Wheat can be grown in areas which have ten inches of rain during the months, April to October, when the wheat is growing. Areas whose average rainfall is from thirteen to seventeen inches per year produce good crops in favorable seasons. In New South Wales the wheat belt coincides roughly with the twenty-inch isohyet, in South Australia it follows the thirteen-inch isohyet, the winter rainfall being so opportune. In 1907 the rainfall in one of the wheat districts of South Australia was seventeen inches, twelve of which fell during the growth of the wheat. It follows that if twelve or thirteen inches of rain can be conserved in the soil by scientific methods of dry-farming, wheat can be grown on most areas where that rainfall is found. Weighing all the conditioning circumstances, the Commonwealth Meteorologist estimates that 500,000 square miles are suitable for wheat growing, from which the possible output would be 900 to 1000 million bushels.[1] Yet out of this possible area, only 14,511 square miles were cultivated in 1913-1914, while in 1915, when the needs of the world prompted to the largest possible planting, the area under wheat reached only 19,578 square miles. The production in the former year was over 103,000,000 bushels, and in the latter was estimated to yield, under normal conditions, 179,000,000 bushels.[2]

When we pass to the organization of the labour force of the country, we find a tendency to prefer equality in industrial grading to efficiency. This is manifest first in the matter of unskilled labour. It must be recognized that the conditions of the national development have operated to regulate the proportion and value of unskilled labour. In the opening up of a new country, the class of labour most required is what is technically called "unskilled." A premium is placed upon physical strength and endurance, which comes to be regarded as a form of skill. This sentiment is especially noticeable in Australia, where the trend of thought among the labourers is against this division of labour into skilled and unskilled. There is a distinct sentiment among them that the division is only partly justified. Thus *The Worker*, the official organ of the Australian Workers' Union, and of the labour movement in general, writes:—" There is hardly any such thing as unskilled labour where human beings are employed. Unskilled labour means physical strength in its prime."[3] Mr. W. G. Spence, president of that union, which is the biggest in Australia, stated the views of a large number of unionists in a speech in the federal parliament:—" I repudiate the idea that in some classes of employment no skill is re-

---

[1] See *Federal Handbook*, p. 149.
[2] *Commonwealth Year Book*, no. 8, p. 310; no. 9, p. 315.
[3] Feb. 13, 1908.

quired. Skill is necessary in connection with everything that a man has to do."[1] With the industries and activities of an undeveloped country preponderating, and with this sentiment prevailing, unskilled labour has been able, by its very weight of numbers, to affect industrial organization, and subtly determine the quality of labour offering.

In the first connection, there has resulted a movement in favor of industrial unions, based on the industry, and including all employees engaged therein, replacing craft unions based on the tools of trade. Large unions, embracing thousands of members, are being formed, and are giving to the labouring class greater solidarity of sentiment and a keener class consciousness. The unions themselves, by reason of the preponderance therein of the unskilled, are becoming more militant. The organized craft unions of 1890, which set out to establish their industrial and political power by organizing the unskilled, have found themselves swallowed up entirely, or, in a few happier cases, engaged in an uneven struggle for those differences of wages that are held to be the chief marks of superior skill. For Australia illustrates the axiom that, in a new country with vast natural resources, unskilled labour is relatively well rewarded in comparison with special skill. The Commonwealth Statistician has estimated that in the census year (1911) each person employed in the primary industries where unskilled labour predominates, produced wealth to the value of £243 per annum, while the value produced by each worker in the manufacturing industry was £175. As a result, there is a very scant appreciation of any difference between the artisan and the unskilled labourer. There is no "aristocracy of labour" in Australia. There is an artisan class, but its standard of comfort differs little from that of the unskilled labourer.

[1] *Federal Hansard*, July 29, 1910.

Evidence of the failure to appreciate and, in consequence, to encourage the efficiency which comes from skill may be gathered under three heads.

(1) Little stress is laid in the industrial world of Australia upon the grading of labour in proportion to skill. Few trade unions impose any test of competency before admitting a member. Once unions were craft unions and required their members to be skilled artisans, some demanding proof of thorough training. Now the only form of test is that a member must be employed for a certain period in a reputable shop or factory and receive not less than the minimum wage.[1] Slow workers are not encouraged, and, on the whole, the unions are suspicious of, or indifferent to, any proposal to grade tradesmen. The tendency, as explained above, is in the direction of replacing craft unions, which consist generally of skilled artisans, by industrial unions, in which the unskilled predominate. As a result, few, if any, even of the craft unions give any attention to any other question affecting their skill and status save that of apprentices.

(2) The training of youths by apprenticeship to be the skilled artisans of the future is chaotic and futile. The attitude of the unions, representing the body of workers, is clear, if unsatisfactory. They began by obtaining a restriction of the number of apprentices who might be employed in each trade, and followed this by a general disinclination on the part of journeymen to teach apprentices. By admitting apprentices to the unions, by thereby interfering with disciplinary control on the part of their employers, and by forcing up their wages, the workers have seriously restricted the supply of new mechanics. Neither

[1] See evidence of Mr. E. J. Kavanagh, M. L. C., Secretary of the Sydney Labour Council, before the New South Wales Commission on the Decline of Apprenticeship, 1911.

is it any part of their program to foster or develop, within the scope of their trade-union activities, a system of industrial training.

The employers, on the other hand, are even more negligent in regard to a future supply of efficient skilled labour. They protest that the apprentice is now economically unprofitable, that he is too difficult to control, and too careless of diligence and efficiency. They are unwilling to train a boy in all branches of his trade. The division of labour resulting from the use of machinery has so specialized industry that the attainment of thorough knowledge of all its branches is impossible without definite and systematic teaching. The employers fail to give that teaching. They, themselves, are generally only organizing heads, and cannot give the personal attention that is necessary for the careful education of apprentices, and foremen and journeymen have no interest in the task.

To make matters worse, industrial boards, under the pressure of one of the mistaken ideals of trade unionism, are restricting the number of apprentices. Further, no complete and all-inclusive system of trade-education has yet been devised. Even with good technical schools provided, few employers are wise enough to link their workshops with the school classrooms, preferring to encourage or compel their apprentices to attend the technical school after hours. Life is too easy and unskilled labour too well paid in Australia for such a short-sighted policy to be generally effective. The industrious youths who, under any circumstances, would become skilled artisans, are made efficient, while the large body of average youths are neglected. In general, it may be added, apprenticeship is not attractive. Of the boys going out from the public schools of New South Wales into employment, the greatest number go into unskilled occupations, the next greatest number into commercial careers, including such positions as clerks and shop assistants, while the skilled trades receive only from one-seventh to one-sixth of them. As a result, there is being trained in Australia a number of apprentices quite disproportionate to the increase of production and of population, and the consequent scarcity of skilled labour has to be met by immigration.

(3) The methods of industrial remuneration give no definite preference to skill. It must be admitted that the arbitration courts, in fixing wages, maintain that after the living wage has been secured there shall be added something for skill. This increment is measured, however, by the custom of the employers, and is regulated by the supply of labourers rather than by added value produced by the skilled worker. In general, no method of payment by results finds great favor in the industrial world. Employers in the past have caused piecework, a just and logical mode of rewarding superior skill, to be associated with "speeding up," and with an unjust reduction of rates, in order to keep wages within a conventional minimum established in their own minds. They have thereby set the fashion in divorcing wages from any measure of productivity. Now the trade unionists have copied the fashion. They raise three objections to piecework. They hold that it is inimical to health, because of the pressure that is put upon the worker, either unconsciously, or by organized team-work. They assert that a man of character is worth as much, and will give as much labour, on time wages as on piecework. The advantages of piecework are thus held to be offset by the demoralization of the labourer. Lastly, they fear that by the piecework system the slow worker, whose needs are as great as those of his fellows, will be penalized. There are none of these objections that cannot be overcome, and the maintenance of a minimum

wage, below which no piecework rate shall fall, suffices to meet the two most serious of them. This provision is written into every award where piecework rates are provided, yet few trades avail themselves of the system, while others seek to prohibit it absolutely. Thus, in 1914 the Iron and Shipbuilding Trades of New South Wales sought to persuade the Chairman of the Wages Boards in their group of trades to forbid piecework. In this they were unsuccessful.[1] On the contrary, the Stove and Piano Frame Makers, a section of the iron trades, consisting of highly skilled workers, obtained an award in which piecework was allowed under three conditions:

(1) The rate was to be such as would enable an average competent man to earn at least 10 per cent above the minimum wage.

(2) No piecework was to be done outside the regular hours of the shop, except in case of a breakdown.

(3) No apprentices were to do piecework during the first two years of their apprenticeship.[2]

Though this trade has a large measure of piecework, its example, even under the satisfactory conditions outlined above, is not widely copied.

The result is a tendency to a " flat " rate of wages. Piecework encourages efficiency, brings out a large measure of potential productive energy, and increases the economic resources of the community. In the matter of wages it introduces a greater elasticity, a greater range. In their graphical representation, it brings in a second " peak," which is characterized by its height and its distance from the "peak" of the average unskilled labourers. The absence of any large differentation between skilled and unskilled

[1] *N. S. W. Industrial Gazette,* August and December, 1914.
[2] *N. S. W. Industrial Gazette,* vol. vi, p. 541.

labourers is demonstrated by a study of the distribution of wages among groups of employees. The following table, with the accompanying graph, depicts the situation in Australia.[a] Though these figures are for November 1912, when a special investigation was made to ascertain the distribution of wages paid to employees, both male and female, there is no reason to doubt their representative character up to at least the outbreak of the European War. Because the element of skill, in the sense of long and special training or apprenticeship, scarcely enters into the industries wherein females are employed, figures concerning the distribution of their wages are not included.

DISTRIBUTION OF MALE EMPLOYEES IN WAGE GROUPS IN MANUFACTURING INDUSTRIES OF AUSTRALIA, NOV., 1912

EMPLOYEES IN THOUSANDS

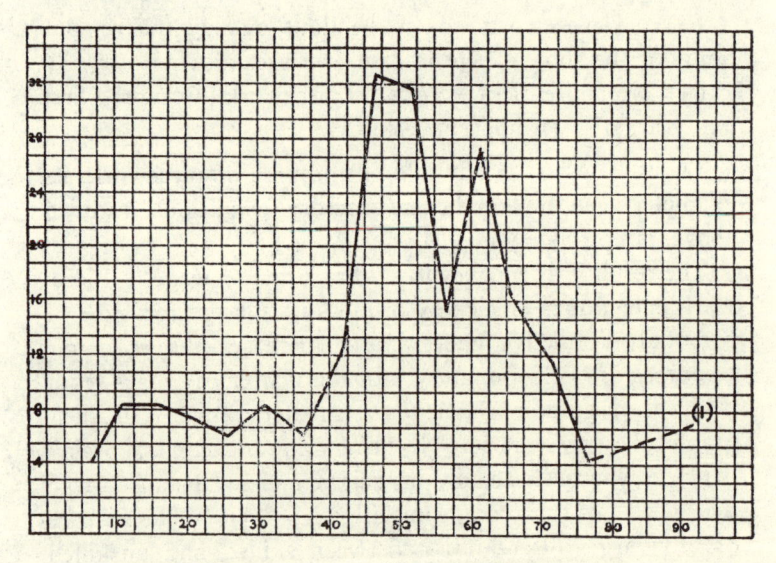

WEEKLY RATES OF WAGES IN SHILLINGS

[1] The upward trend of the curve marked thus — — — is due to the form of tabulation of those whose wages were 80s and over, and has no statistical relevance.

Commonwealth Labour Report, No. 3, pp. 9-11.

DISTRIBUTION OF MALE EMPLOYEES IN WAGE GROUPS IN MANUFACTURES
OF AUSTRALIA, NOVEMBER, 1912

Rate of Weekly Wage	Total Number of Employees	Average Weekly Wage s d	Percentage of Total Employees %
Under 10s.	4,090	7 0	1.9
10s. and under 15s.	8,481	11 5	4.0
15s. and under 20s.	8,284	16 3	4.0
20s. and under 25s.	7,241	21 1	3.5
25s. and under 30s.	6,149	25 11	2.9
30s. and under 35s.	8,183	30 9	3.9
35s. and under 40s.	6,303	36 2	3.0
40s. and under 45s.	12,202	41 6	6.0
45s. and under 50s.	32,781	47 0	15.7
50s. and under 55s.	31,757	52 2	15.2
55s. and under 60s.	15,247	56 6	7.3
60s. and under 65s.	27,470	60 10	13.1
65s. and under 70s.	17,606	66 4	8.4
70s. and under 75s.	11,386	71 1	5.4
75s. and under 80s.	4,205	76 3	2.0
80s. and over	7,743	92 0	3.7
	209,128	49 3	100.0

The graph reveals four peaks which correspond fairly closely to the grades of labour known as boy labour, apprentices, unskilled and skilled labour respectively. The most noteworthy fact illustrated by the graph is the certainty and speed with which the wages of adult men rise towards the average wage, which centres round 50 shillings. This is a statistical demonstration of the effect of arbitration in making a minimum wage available to all adult men. But the next significant fact is the proportion of male employees who belong to the grade of unskilled labour. About 36.7 per cent of all male workers fall in the wage group ranging between 40 and 55 shillings. Of the workers of both grades who receive more than 40 shillings, this group forms 47.8 per cent. These figures suggest that the greater volume of employment in Australian industry, when boy labour and apprentices are considered, is unskilled. Further, the graph shows a short range of wage separating the skilled from the unskilled. The median wage is about 51s. 8d., and the "peak" of the wages of skilled men stands at a point a little above 60 shillings. If it be admitted that trade unionism and arbitration have raised the level of the wages of unskilled labourers, it must also be admitted that Australian industry has not succeeded in effecting a corresponding increase in the degree, the quantity and the reward of skill.

For confirmation of this point, one turns to the statistics of added value.[1] Added value connotes the contribution made by labour and machinery in the process of manufacture, and is measured by the difference between the value of the raw material and that of the finished product. Out of this added value, wages, among other things, have to be paid. In 1912 the average wage of males was £128 per year, the average added value per employee was £193. Now in the industries in which the added value per employee was less than £200, (the average in the last class being only £182), there were employed 139,367 males, or 66.6 per cent of the total males, and 66,104 females, or 89 per cent of the total females. In industries where the added value ranges from £150 to less than £200 per annum, 54.7 per cent of the total number of males are found, but less than 9 per cent of the females. These industries included sawmills and joinery, engineering, railway workshops, furniture and cabinet making, coachbuilding, agricultural implements, tinsmithing, sugar factory, biscuits, confectionery, cycles, and twenty-four other industries each employing less than 2500 employees. Industries in which the average net production per employee was less than £150 per annum comprised a considerable part of the clothing and textile manufactures, and are chiefly associated with female labour. Among those in which

[1] *Commonwealth Labour Report*, no. 3.

earnings were between £200 and £300 per employee per annum, the most considerable were the printing and publishing trade, bricks and pottery, meat preserving, aerated waters, tanneries and fellmongery. Those which show an average annual added value of over £300 include smelting, the making of butter and cheese, and gas and coke, brewing and flour-milling. The eight leading industries in 1912, in order of the number of employees of both sexes, were (1) clothing and textile fabrics, (2) metal work and machinery, (3) the preparation of food and drink, (4) working in wood, (5) books and printing, (6) vehicles and saddlery (7) the preparation of stone, clay, and glass, and lastly, (8) furniture, bedding and upholstery. The added value in the case of the first was less than £150 per annum per employee, of the second, third, fourth, sixth, and eighth, between £150 and £200, and of the fifth, and seventh between £200 and £300. The skilled trades are not distinguished from the unskilled trades by any striking difference in the net value of production. In so far, skilled labour is not being employed to its highest efficiency.

Two factors often found influential in preventing higher wages for skill and in destroying the differentiation between skilled and unskilled do not seem to be operative in Australia. The results established above are not due to a restricted employment of machinery nor to the influence of wage-determinations in putting a premium upon unskilled labour. The extensive and profitable use of machinery is reflected in the statistics of industrial development. Employers, on the whole, are quick to appreciate the value of new labour-saving devices, and ready to cast out obsolete machinery. Though the belief in the advantages of machine production is not so general nor so powerful as in America, it is spreading among those who have control of production, including the pastoralist and the agriculturalist.

Shears driven by power have replaced the old hand shears in the woolsheds. The multiple furrow plough, the driller which sows the wheat and distributes the artificial manure evenly, and the combined harvester, have been of inestimable benefit to the wheat farmer. They have enabled him to cultivate relatively large areas, to achieve a higher production per man, and to effect such economy of time and labour as to make a limited production per acre economically profitable. In the dairying industry, the milking machine, an Australian invention, and the home separator, have enlarged the scale and productivity of the industry.[1] In the mining industry, coal-cutting machines are slowly winning their way against the opposition of the miners, while improved methods of treating low grade ore are making gold, silver. and copper mining more profitable. In manufactures there has been a great increase in plant and machinery, each year showing an increase approaching ten per cent over the previous year. In the period 1908 to 1913, the value of plant and machinery increased 43.7 per cent. The significance of this is seen when the relations between capital invested in the industry, rates of wages and added value are examined. In general, as the capital investment increases, so do rates of wages and added value.[2]

Nor does the relatively small difference between wages of skilled and unskilled workers seem to be due to the influence of wage determinations which, by adding to the cost of production, increase the cost of living, and thus involve a cycle of readjustments of the minimum wage of the unskilled worker, with which neither the increase in

[1] Figures concerning machinery used in other than the manufacturing industry are available only for New South Wales. In that State, during the decade ending 1911, the value of the machinery used in the rural industries, (agricultural, pastoral and dairying) more than doubled. (*Official Year Book of N. S. W.*, 1912, p. 577.)

[2] Cf. *Commonwealth Labour Report*, no. 3 *ut supra*.

the wages of skilled labour, nor the added value from which wages are paid, can keep pace. One has to admit the fact that the adoption in a period of rising prices of the principle of the needs of the worker, as measured by a social standard that is ethically sound and economically justifiable, has involved this vicious circle of increased wages, followed by increased prices, leading in turn to agitation for an increase to meet the new cost of living. Despite the prevalent public opinion, the student of society finds no adequate proof that the full onus for this increase in price lies upon the worker. Increased wages are neither solely nor primarily the cause of the increased prices. In his report on Food Supplies and Prices in New South Wales (1911), Mr. T. R. Bavin quoted the verdict of the United States Senate Commission in 1910 and a New Zealand Report on Prices, to the general effect that trade unions were not serious factors in advancing prices. He proceeds:—" My own general conclusion is that, except in increasing demand through higher spending power, and except perhaps in the milk trade, increases in wages in the particular trades investigated have not had any very considerable effect in causing any increase in the price of commodities in question." In the case of meat, Mr. Bavin held that the increased cost due to the rise in wages would have been covered by a rise of one-twelfth of a penny in the wholesale trade, and from one-tenth to one-fifth of a penny in the retail prices. In the milk trade, where the wage cost is relatively high, the increased cost per gallon since 1900 amounted to only 1.3 pence. More recently (September 20, 1916), Mr. Justice Higgins, in giving his award in the Meat Industry Case (No. 8 of 1913, and No. 19 of 1914) was able to trace the operation of wages on the price of the product in the case of mutton. The slaughterers were being paid at the rate of 27s. 6d. per 100 sheep, a rate equivalent to less than one-twelfth of a penny per pound for a sheep of 40 lbs. weight. They asked an increase of 2s. 6d., bringing the rate to 30s. per hundred. This increase would advance the price per lb., only $\frac{1}{137}$d., bringing the total cost of slaughtering to less than one-eleventh of a penny per pound. The argument referred to, that increased wages are the chief cause of the increased prices and the higher cost of living, is offset by the fact that while cost of production has increased, there has been a greater increase in added value of production. The Inter-State Commission, in their first report to the Minister for Customs (April, 1915), pointed out that during the period of their investigation, (1908-1913) the increased return to manufacturers had aggregated £62,031,132, the increased cost of production was estimated at £50,235,646, leaving a difference in added value of £11,795,486.[1] This total difference had been made so large by a rise in prices over which the increased cost of production had no influence, and which was out of all proportion to the quantity of goods manufactured. It seems clear, therefore, that the increase in the general rate of wages has not been such as to produce the tendency to increased prices. On the other hand, these increased prices have been a factor in increasing the wages of unskilled labour somewhat disproportionately to those of skilled labour. Nor have increased wages so diminished the net product of manufacture as to make it difficult to pay higher wages for skill. As the figures show, the manufacturing industry in the aggregate succeeded during the years 1908-1913 in realizing, over and above the increased cost of production, an increased gross profit of £11,795,486. Other reasons than the failure to apply new capital and machinery to industry, or the inability of Australian industry to earn profits must be advanced to account for the failure to bring skilled labour to its highest productivity.

[1] *Cf.* page 6 of the *Report*.

One reason may be found in the refusal to use the piece-work system of work and remuneration as a means of encouraging and rewarding skill. Piece-work under proper regulations of conditions and remuneration gives an opportunity for the fullest exercise of skill, the greatest quantity of production and the highest possible remuneration. The failure to use piece-work implies a loss in economic productivity and a restriction upon efficiency. In part, also, the small quantity of added value may be due to the scale of production in Australia. In comparison with older and more established centers, its production is carried on in a comparatively small way. In 1914 less than 4 per cent of the factories employed more than 100 hands each, but embraced 41 per cent of the total number of employees, having an average of 247 per factory. More than 79 per cent of the total number of factories employed less than twenty hands each.[1] There is a tendency for the larger factories to increase in numbers, though not in size. It would be almost correct to say that Australians have not learned, even if they desire, to organize industry on a large scale. Consequently, they suffer the loss of those economies in plant, supervision and distribution which are associated with the progressive methods of business enterprise on a large scale, and are less able to pay higher wages for greater skill.

Herein lies a suggestion of industrial inefficiency on the part of *entrepreneurs*. Of this, the Inter-State Commission, after a careful inquiry into the manufactures of the country, was reluctantly compelled to bear witness. After stating that these industries afford not a few examples of keen business enterprise and the most approved modern methods, the commissioners went on to point out defects which must be held responsible in part for the low net output of Australian factories. They suggested that a careful system of

[1] *Commonwealth Year Book*, no. 9, p. 475.

accurate " costing," so that the efficiency of each section of the plant might be rigorously and scientifically tested, was a prime requisite of manufacturing methods too often neglected. One might suggest that this defect is due to the general failure in Australia, outside of the professional circles of the civil service, to appreciate the importance and value of the statistical method. The commissioners proceeded to criticize the neglect of manufacturers to pay close attention to what is being done by rivals in other countries, as represented by importers. Under the plea of the " urgent necessity for a greater appreciation of industrial efficiency," they spoke of the waste of power, the unsuitable construction of buildings, not only involving the double handling of goods and material, but also interrupting the continuous process of manufacture, unsuitable sites for the location of industries, the non-utilization of by-products, and, above all, the want of knowledge or appreciation of the value of applied science to industry. Summing up the effects of these deficiencies with the question of the tariff in mind, they concluded: " These and the want of organization in other directions naturally enhance the cost of manufacture, lessen the quantity, variety and volume of the output, and render higher duties necessary than would be the case if their operations were accomplished by the most efficient modern means." [1]

To this industrial inefficiency the trade-unionists of Australia, by reason of their organization, their attitude towards capitalism, and the stress they lay on distribution rather than production, also contribute. Their general attitude towards superior skill we have explained as in part the result of their organization. The more powerful the industrialist section, that is, the unskilled labourers, becomes and the

[1] *Tariff Investigation Report of the Inter-State Commission of Australia*, 1914-1915, p. 5.

more the crafts are subordinated to unions covering industries, the less obvious will be the value and the significance of that skill which means efficient and large production. Along with this depreciation of skill goes distrust of capitalism and the present economic system. The majority of the workers live under the belief and fear that most of the new wealth, created by greater skill or more energy on their part, would go into the pockets of the capitalist. They claim that the present economic system is so fundamentally unjust that no power, industrial or political, can prevent the capitalist getting most of the increase. Hence, they will have nothing to do with any proposal which seems to support or conserve the present system. On these grounds they object to such methods of remuneration as piece-work, co-operation and profit-sharing. In a word, through fear of an unjust distribution of the wealth they produce, they would restrict its production till they have created institutions which will " kill exploitation and capture Capital in the interests of, and make it subserve the welfare and well-being of, humanity." [1] Herein lies the truth and the error of Australian unionism. A just distribution of wealth is a measure and a prerequisite of social welfare. It tends to secure for every man the opportunity of living a full and complete life as a member of a civilized community that looks to him to be a father and a citizen. It will make possible the education of his children, will guarantee him leisure to develop his own powers and give him security against old age and unemployment. Hence, provided the total wealth of the community, the social surplus, is more than adequate for its fundamental needs, the social welfare is conditioned rather by the distribution of wealth than by its increase. Social well-being depends more, under such circumstances,

[1] *The Worker* (Sydney, April 9, 1908).

on the relationship existing among the various social-economic classes than on the aggregate wealth of the community. The demand on the part of Australian trade-unionists for a living wage as the expression of social justice, and for an economic society in which wealth will be justly distributed and human values given first place, is ethically sound.

But any restriction of production is economic suicide. Quantity of production is of great sociological as well as economic significance. It is the fundamental condition of social efficiency. The primitive stages of society when nomadic tribes wandered without settled habitation, were distinguished by scanty and ineffective production. The introduction of agriculture marked a transition to a higher stage of civilization just because the increased production made such advanced civilization possible. Later on, the introduction and application of machinery to industry led to a vast increase in population and a great advance in the attainment by the masses of the people of what were formerly the luxuries of the few. Nor has the process whereby civilization advances relatively to increased production reached its end. Two considerations govern this advance: (1) First, the satisfaction of the primal wants leaves the individual free for the development of more ideal desires. Appetite grows by what it feeds on, and when once the material wants of food, clothing, shelter and fuel are supplied, the desires born of opportunities for leisure have room to develop. Even if any society existed to-day where the material wants of every individual were met, there is none where the desires for leisure, education and recreation have been very widely or effectively satisfied among the people. In most countries the economic condition is lacking for the realization of those desires, *viz.*, an adequate and efficient satisfaction of all necessary material wants.

STRUGGLE AND FAILURE

(2) This forms the second consideration which governs social progress. The world's productivity is not equal to its needs. The total wealth per capita is insignificant. Mr. Chiozza Money estimates that of the United Kingdom at £313 per head of the population.[1] The Victorian Statistician has computed the private wealth of Australia at £231 per head.[2] If the latter figure be applied to the average Australian family of two adults and three children, if it be assumed to be productive, and if its annual value be reckoned at five per cent, it gives the family an average income from capital of a little over £1 per week. Recent figures submitted by the Commonwealth Statistician, as the result of a wealth census in 1915, have placed the total private wealth of Australia at nearly £300 per head, which increases the annual value of the income.[3] Even with this higher rate there is no proof that the production of Australia is sufficient to meet the needs of all its own people. There need never be any fear of over-production while the total wealth of the world is so low. There is practically no limit to the consumptive power of human beings as they advance from the satisfaction of primal needs to those refinements and elaborations which gratify higher feelings.

The conclusion seems obvious that the welfare of a people depends in large part upon the quantity of the wealth annually produced, for only thus can the material for consumption be obtained. Any increase in consumption in consequence of increased purchasing power without a corresponding advance in the rate of production has three results worth attention. First, it curtails the creation of new capital available for increased production. Secondly, the proportion of wealth available for consumption to increased

---

[1] *Cf. Riches and Poverty*, 10th edition, p. 62.
[2] *Victorian Year Book*, 1915-16, p. 295.
[3] *Cf.* G. H. Knibbs, *Private Wealth of Australia*.

population is reduced, and, thirdly, there is no advance in economic well-being in such a society. The industrial situation in Australia shows that the workers, at least, do not understand how a juster distribution of wealth, having reacted upon social well-being, needs to be followed by increased efficiency and further production, in order that the cycle of economic activity may be complete.

Evidence in disproof of alleged restrictive tendencies of Australian trade-unionism is not large. The workers themselves, individually and through their official organs, strenuously deny that they are doing less than a fair day's work as measured by physical ability rather than by an artificial standard created in a period when competition and "speeding up" were dominant factors in determining the quantity of work done per day. If they be confronted with a demonstrated reduction in output, they justify the reduction on the ground that production should be for use, not for profit. As they are producing enough for the needs of their own continent, they seek to limit further production unless an increase can be made to subserve social welfare, by giving more employment and a juster return to labour. The Inter-State Commission of 1914, when confronted with the specific question of restriction of output, thought it likely that there had been a decrease in the amount of work done per employee, but held that the decrease might be due rather to the presence in large numbers of inefficient labourers, because the great manufacturing expansion had absorbed the more efficient. Further, it is pointed out, by the use of the figures compiled in the following table, that there has been an increase in the value of production in the manufacturing industries, both per employee and per head of the mean population, which, it is held, is not consistent with any charge of restriction of production.

VALUE OF PRODUCTION OF THE MANUFACTURING INDUSTRIES OF AUSTRALIA, 1909-1914

Year	Per head of mean population	Per employee	Index Number per employee (1911=1000)
	£	£	
1909	9.81	157	908
1910	11.01	168	971
1911	12.03	173	1000
1912	13.03	185	1069
1913	13.56	193	1116
1914	13.54	201	1162

For the figures in columns 1 and 2, cf. *Commonwealth Year Book*, no. 9, pp. 491, 492.

There is seen to have been a progressive increase in the value of production which is not seriously curtailed when the fluctuations of wholesale prices are taken into account. It is also possible to establish for the manufacturing industry the conclusion which is generally true of all production in Australia, that " the increase in productive activity per head has relatively been far greater than the increase in nominal wages and still greater than the increase in effective wages." [1]

But productive activity in industry is correlated with such factors as the quantity of raw material and the amount of plant and machinery available. With an increase in each of the latter, and more especially in machinery, there tends to follow a proportional increase in productivity. The same degree of energy applied through the medium of an increased amount of plant and machinery to an increased quantity of raw material should be reflected in a productivity greater in degree than the increase in either of the other factors. The following table shows the position in Australia, so far as statistics are available.

[1] *Commonwealth Labour Report*, No. 7, p. 438. Compare the figures given, *supra*, pp. 131, 133.

RELATIVE INCREASE IN THE VALUES OF RAW MATERIALS, PLANT AND MACHINERY, AND PRODUCTIVE ACTIVITY PER EMPLOYEE IN THE MANUFACTURING INDUSTRY, 1909-1914

Year	Raw Materials Index Number 1911=1000	Plant and Machinery Index Number 1911=1000	Productivity per Employee Index Number 1911=1000
1909	814	850	908
1910	921	910	971
1911	1000	1000	1000
1912	1117	1090	1069
1913	1220	1179	1116
1914	1263	1310	1162

For the figures on which this table is based cf. *Commonwealth Year Book*, no. 9, pp. 489, 495.

This table, with the accompanying graph, shows at least a decided tendency on the part of the productive activity in Australian industry to fall behind the increase in raw materials and plant and machinery used in manufacture.

Other evidence, more positive in character, is available. Some of it is symptomatic, some of it statistical. Thus, in giving evidence before the Inter-State Commission in 1914, Mr. E. L. McCray, managing director of a firm of engineers, Sydney, stated that when his firm installed a new pneumatic machine to do the work of two men, the union organizer insisted on two men being set to work it. The union held that the machine should be for the benefit of the men, and should not increase the efficiency of the factory at the expense of the employees. One infers that, in this case, as in all, the general principle of sharing work, not of increasing production, operated to shape the union organizer's judgment. Further, the unions, in their effort to divide work so as to increase the number of persons employed, force upon the employers, under the threat of a strike, conditions of work that are wasteful and inefficient.

RELATIVE INCREASE IN VALUES OF RAW MATERIALS, PLANT AND MACHINERY AND PRODUCTIVE ACTIVITY 1909-1914

INDEX NUMBERS

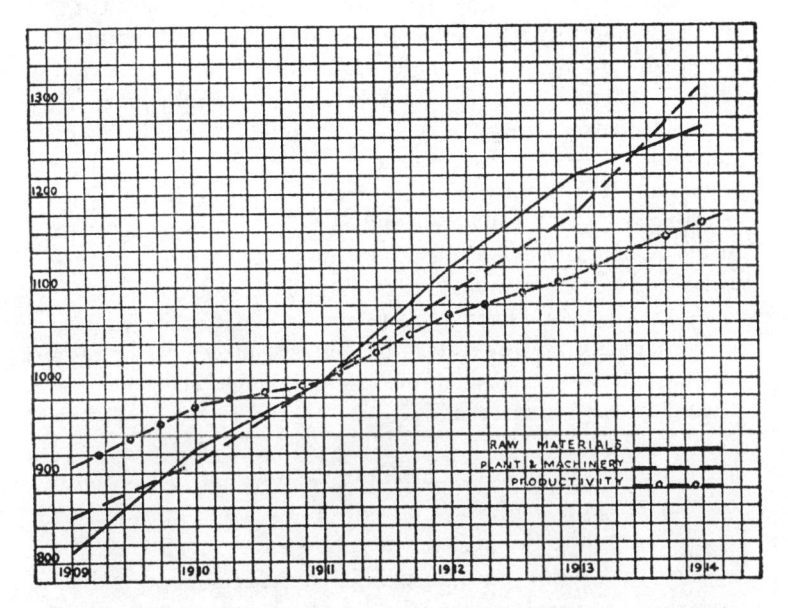

The shipping industry, one of the largest in Australia, is thus much at the mercy of the wharf labourers or longshoremen. In the award governing the conditions of employment in that industry Mr. Justice Higgins drew attention to some of these conditions forced upon the employers. They bear on their very face the proof of their tendency to inefficiency and waste.

The Melbourne Wharf Labourers' Union insists on a minimum of 14 cwt. in a sling: so that when, the other day, a White Star liner was discharging soda ash in barrels of 8 cwt. each, the men refused to land more than one barrel on the wharf at a time. The gear was fit to carry 3 tons. The rule of the coal lumpers in Melbourne, not to discharge a vessel on its first night of arrival, causes delay, inconvenience and loss: and at present I cannot see how it is reasonable. But a letter from the Sydney Wharf Labourers' Union to the Sydney Stevedoring Association and other employers (4th September, 1913) is astounding. In the letter the secretary coolly "notifies" the employers, without asking even for a conference, of a resolution "that the following rules *re* working conditions are to come into effect after to-day." Then follow thirteen resolutions, all of a substantial character, but they need not all be reviewed. The first is that there must be not less than six men trucking from each hatch, unless it be proved to the satisfaction of the vigilant officer (of the union) or to the secretary (of the union) that such a minimum is excessive: and truckers are to do nothing but trucking. The manager of the Stevedoring and Shipping Company states that, in consequence of the resolution, he has to employ ten men to each hatch where he used to employ only six or seven.[1]

Mr. Justice Higgins drew attention also to the fact that the Sydney union provides for 20 cwt. as the maximum weight of a sling, while the Melbourne union fixed 14 cwt. If the Sydney maximum was reasonable, the Melbourne restriction was irrational, and involved inefficient use of the gear.

Another instance is afforded by a case recently before the New South Wales Arbitration Court. It concerned men employed in discharging coal for the Sydney Gas Company. The award under which the men worked required a gang of five to unload ten tons of coal per hour, while the machinery at their disposal made a maximum output of twenty-five tons possible. The employees were induced to work up to the maximum rate of discharge by a bonus equivalent to overtime rates. That is, they were paid wages for twenty hours for eight hours' toil at the full rate of maximum discharge. After a while they wanted a sixth man

[1] 8 *C. A. R.*, p. 75.

added to the gang, who was to share in the work, but be paid the same wage as the other men were earning. This demand being refused, they struck, but were induced, under threat of action from the New South Wales Arbitration Court, to return to work. To mark their dissatisfaction, however, they reverted to their previous production of the ten tons per hour, whereupon the award was altered to provide a minimum discharge of twenty tons per hour.

Other instances of restriction of output might be quoted, but two more will suffice. In July, 1916, the Commonwealth minister of defence was compelled to deal promptly with a demonstrated restriction of output in the federal clothing factory, which was, at the time, chiefly engaged in the production of military clothing and accoutrements. In Sydney the State government erected new and up-to-date abattoirs, with sufficient machinery to do all the heavy work and to cope with an increased output. This business was a State enterprise, entered upon as a part of the program of the Labour party to use the resources of the State to make brighter the lot of the workers. The latter, however, have not shown any desire to serve the State as an employer any more efficiently than a private employer. In this case the men reduced their output to one-half of what was expected of them, and caused the costs of production of this new and well-equipped factory to be much greater than it was in the older abattoirs.

The New South Wales railways, which are owned by the State and whose employees comprise almost every grade of skilled and unskilled labour, reveal to what extent increased wages and better conditions fail to be met by increased efficiency. Economically, they are among the state's best assets, and until the financial year 1914-1915 had, under normal conditions, returned a surplus on their working. At about this time a considerable increase in wages was met by an increase in rates for both passenger and freight traffic. But along with the increased wages and better conditions have gone a serious increase in working cost, a decrease in efficiency per employee as measured by train miles in the railways or by car miles in the street tramways, and a falling-off in the amount of work produced in the repair shop. The figures are as follows:

The working cost of running trains per train mile was over 3s 9d in 1907-8; by June, 1915, it had reached 5s 3d. The net receipts decreased in the interval from 3s 6d to 2s 0d per train mile. The efficiency of the staff as measured in train miles was in 1905, 825, in 1907, 957, in 1915, 783. The average miles per car in service in the electric tramways were in 1908, 17,109, in 1915, 13,645. In car miles per employee a greater continuous reduction is shown, from 13,314 in 1908 to 9,635 in 1915. In the repair workshops the number of engines repaired from 424 in 1906 to 584 in 1915, while in the same period the fitting staff increased 152 per cent, the boilermakers 148, and the total staff 153 per cent.[1]

These figures demonstrate a restriction in output and a decline in efficiency.

It is obvious also that the numerous and costly strikes indulged in, seldom for any industrial principle of great moment, are a further check on efficiency. They do not repay, in better wages or conditions, their cost in loss of wages and industrial dislocation. With the legislative chambers open to the appeal of the worker, and with well-equipped and sympathetically responsive industrial machinery available for the settlement of those questions that lead to industrial disputes, practically every strike is to be condemned as a stupid and inefficient weapon for the attainment of ends realizable by other means.

[1] Statement of the New South Wales Railway Commissioners, quoted in *The Sun* (Sydney, July 18, 1916).

Practically the same verdict must be passed upon the restrictions typified above. They are crude and clumsy expedients for securing a better distribution of work among the workers. They do not produce more work; they do not make easier, more certain nor more extended the process of the application of labour and machinery to natural resources. They merely divide the work to be obtained so as to give more men the opportunity of being employed. In themselves, all measures for steadying employment and securing its distribution so that under-payment and excessive over-time are both avoided, are praiseworthy. But this method of securing more employment by restricting production is equivalent to securing the same wages for less output. Such action is economically fallacious in method and ethically unjustifiable in motive. As a method, it has succeeded in separate industries, because its economic burden is thrust upon the general public in the shape of higher prices. But as a universal principle the method fails. To it, not to the mere demand for a just wage, must be credited the vicious circle of increased wages and increased prices. It restricts the supply of new capital: it diminishes the social surplus and, as countries like Spain testify, where the method has been carried to its logical conclusion, produces an impoverished country. It produces the paradox of a society, in which human values are appraised highly, trending toward a position in which the economic foundation for that high valuation is being destroyed. It is all the more significant because, in her manufacturing industries, as the figures concerning added value show, Australian industry has no great margin upon which increased waste and decreased industrial efficiency can play. The burden of increased cost of production has to be passed on to the public, and, in the main, has to be met out of the wealth of the primary industries. It is possible that the burden could thus be carried for many years, but such a process is the reversal of that by which a nation attains economic strength. An efficient system of manufactures reared upon the basis of a wealth of natural resources fully developed and wisely exploited, carries a nation forward in wealth, population and strength. This is the program which Australia must substitute for that which has, by subtle and unconscious steps, become a fixed principle in the minds of trade-unionists.

An analysis of the political system reveals the same preference for equality rather than for efficiency. In the sphere of organized labour there is great distrust of leaders. Democracy, as a whole, tends to be distrustful of men whose abilities bring them to the front. Australians, generally, have no distrust, but rather the warmest welcome, for ability, provided it is associated with genuine sincerity and whole-hearted adoption of the ideals of the political group. But the position of the leaders of the Labour party, more especially, is that of delegates, rather than representatives. They are chosen by a cast-iron procedure which enforces rigid bonds of discipline and emphasizes party loyalty. When chosen, they are subject to constant calls to defend and explain their actions, and, if the more recent trend of the Labour movement is correctly interpreted, are treated with suspicion and mistrust. By a decision of the New South Wales Labour Conference in June, 1917, the parliamentary representatives, who have attained the local selection which made public election possible generally through years of service to the movement, are to be excluded from the central executive of the party. By this means, all that experience contributes of insight into motives, of knowledge of methods, and of clarity of judgment is lost to the movement, and the decisions concerning a large section of the industrial and political activities of the country are entrusted to men less tried in action and less stable in judgment. Positively, and negatively, this is the selection of the unfit. Its positive aspect is seen in the automatic exclusion from leadership and the involuntary ranking as delegates of those who have won their way to the front. The negative aspect is less apparent, but no less real. Men who can be delegates only, not representatives, will not offer themselves for selection. A person may be willing to endorse a party platform in loyalty and singleness of heart, but if entrusted with the task of carrying out the platform, will demand scope for his own original equipment for political decisions and general administrative duties. This natural demand is denied by the recent trend in the Labour movement, which tends to substitute the equality implied in common membership for the efficiency born of experience and expert knowledge. The political and industrial intelligence of the collective group is held to be superior to that of the elected leader, who, further, is not trusted either to obey or to guide the group. A democracy that distrusts its leaders, with or without cause, is on the road to inefficiency. While large sections of the Australian people do not fall under this condemnation, that considerable section which is associated with Labour politics does, and through their unguided and inconsequential activities social efficiency is seriously threatened.

In connection with the vast quantity of industrial legislation, one is struck with the small amount of attention paid to the social sciences. By the former, Australia has been made a "laboratory of political experiment." By reason of the absence till recently of any careful study of the social, economic and political results of such action, this legislation has tended to be either doctrinaire or at best a daring experiment. If it has succeeded, it has been because of the wisdom of its original sponsor, as in the case of the various

New South Wales Arbitration Acts, or because of the high level of intelligence among the people. Whether projected legislation is economically sound or likely to be socially beneficial is not a criterion in common use. Such standards occur only to the minds of those to whom the social sciences are familiar fields of study. While a good deal of attention is given to the pure sciences, and to scientific research therein, the social sciences, economics, political science and sociology (history excepted), are given little recognition. Among the six universities of Australia there are but two professors of economics. Other universities have lecturers on the subject. Political science is, in practice if not in theory, confined to those who are taking a law degree. Sociology is, as yet, untaught in any university. The presence of a demand for these sciences is evident in the progress of the Workers' Educational Association, which was introduced in 1913 with the object of bringing to the masses of the people the careful scientific teaching of the university. Tutorial classes in connection therewith have been formed in every State of the Commonwealth, and teach economics and industrial history mainly, though sociology, philosophy, psychology and biology are selected. In general, however, there is little endeavor made to appraise in scientific fashion the results of the various industrial and social experiments. Without such a process of evaluation the Australian people have no measure of social efficiency, and are without sane and careful guidance in their program of social reform.

In social life, inefficiency appears in the operations of a class consciousness which hinders social harmony. Class consciousness is the solidarity of sentiment which economic and industrial organization have brought about. It is symbolized on its better side by the pride which the average man has in the title and status of worker, and by his recognition of the fact that loyalty to his class is a surer means of self-advancement, under the conditions, than the following of his own interests. In the political life of the country he finds examples of the rise of men who have remained true to their class to positions of power and influence. As organized, class consciousness is reflected in the psychological reaction from industrial unions. They have made difficult the creation of an aristocracy of labour, and by the preponderance of the unskilled have themselves become far more democratic and socialistic than craft unions are. Their attitude, as reflected in the control of the labour movement by what is known as the industrial section, is becoming syndicalistic. Their aim, so far as consciously realized and openly expressed, is to set up an industrial commonwealth, and among their methods is that of fostering class consciousness to the breaking point.

The presence of class consciousness in Australia needs little other demonstration than is afforded by the various instances of social disharmony. The distrust by the workers of the whole capitalistic system in general, and of the employers more specifically, coupled with the readiness of the latter to lay upon the former the full blame for industrial upheavals, advancing prices, and industrial inefficiency; the inability of employers to understand and sympathize with the objections of the workers to competition and to the "law" of supply and demand in relation to wages, are but some of the more fundamental instances of the disharmony that prevails. More patent illustrations of the bitterness created by class feeling are found in the frequent breaches of agreements made between organizations. The history of voluntary conciliation, before the establishment of compulsory arbitration, reveals the fact that agreements made with their employees by various pastoral and mining associations were broken frequently. The recent history of industrial affairs shows a turning of the tables. Trade unions break the agreements they have made even more readily than did the employers. This fact becomes more significant when it is understood that industrial agreements are now made under the Arbitration Acts, are registered with the force and sanction of law, and that their violation is subject to penalty. Further, wages boards, though their method is that of judicial determination of wages rather than of conference, nevertheless consist of representatives of both classes, and represent a distinct extension of democracy into the vexed problem of wage determination. With all that, however, has come no sense of the social duty of the group to accept its responsibilities, recognize and endorse the acts of its representatives, and maintain the agreements they have made. Instances are found of trade unions which, having been denied by law what they have sought, have proceeded by sheer pressure upon employers to enforce conditions of employment judicially determined to be socially disadvantageous. While in the demands which lead to the breaking of the agreements a large measure of right is to be found on the side of the unions, this spirit of revolt is distinctly a menace to social efficiency, and involves a retrograde step in democracy.

In the sphere of education, as seen in its social perspective, there is one serious defect, namely, its failure to link the interests of the individual to productive tasks. Education and knowledge in general should stimulate the creative faculty. It must be admitted that constructive capacities which begin to manifest themselves as the boy enters upon adolescence, and are afterwards to remain the essential part of the interest in work, have been given opportunities for training in schools. Manual exercises of various kinds, experiments in the science laboratories, practical work for girls in domestic science, all supply the opportunity for satisfying the desire to do and make. But two considerations go to substantiate the conclusion that only a very partial success has been attained in this regard. First, the tendency to seek new inventions is not strong in Australia. In a country with vast natural resources and great scope for invention, applications for the issuing of patents are not relatively numerous, and are confined to small matters. Employees do not concern themselves with endeavors to make their work easier or more productive. Even if diversity of economic interests leads them to refuse to assist their employer in many cases, there are enough corporations willing to reward an inventive employee to prove that both the desire and ability to carry out original constructive work are absent. Secondly, the preponderating interest in recreational activities leaves no time for the stimulation and nourishing of productive activities. Not only is there a willingness to surrender to recreation any possible increase in productive efficiency, but pleasures and amusements displace the opportunities for advanced individual efficiency and for civic service. The "holiday spirit" is too prominent, there is too much preoccupation with the pleasures of the fleeting moment. Education, invention, reading, educational travel, the cultivation in various ways of intelligence, ability, industrial and scientific initiative—these are absent in any serious degree from the leisure moments of the Australian. The use made of his leisure reacts upon the national life. There is not enough seriousness, not enough thoroughness, and, to that extent, a loss of efficiency. "It is not that he is better than his fellows elsewhere that fills the Australian with pride, but that he has more of the comforts and luxuries of life." In a word, he values leisure for its own sake, and not for the part it might play in the attainment of social efficiency. He has yet to learn, by the extension of education and the cultivation and satisfaction of the aesthetic and moral interests, that leisure must be used for the generation of moral, intellectual and material power ere it can be a criterion of material efficiency. If the expressed ideal of the Australian Workers' Union,[1] of machinery making more leisure possible, is to be realized, the process must be reciprocal in the sense that the increased leisure that has been secured shall be employed in constructive as well as recreational activities. To this end a more widespread and systematic education will contribute by giving a broader general culture and a larger interest in life, and by furnishing, through vocational training, form and direction to the constructive instincts.

Two failures to put health before wealth must also be noted, one the scarcity of playing areas for children, the other the failure to adapt hours and conditions of employment to the physical strength of women. The rapid growth of cities, the overcrowding that exists, with the consequent scarcity of large areas of land, have deprived children of playing areas and sent them to the streets, where physical and moral dangers abound. Thus the preventive work of medical school inspection is undone. There is more infection in the crowded home and the filthy streets than in the school,[2] and more in the school than in a well-established

[1] *Cf. infra,* p. 90.

[2] *Cf.* Dr. Halley's investigation in *Report of Education Department of South Australia for 1913.* " Since my appointment 1,796 cases of infectious disease among school-going children have been reported to the Department. . . . It will be seen that the number of cases of infectious disease reported before the week before the midwinter holidays, June 28, was 39; then after July 12, 56; and the next week, July 19, 115. The greater number of these 115 cases were cases of measles and whooping cough,—diseases that vary from 21 days to incubate. Clearly the infection was begun in the holidays, not at school. After the Christmas vacation, when the schools have been closed for over four weeks, we find on December 20, 30 cases were reported: on Jan. 19, 120 cases. This clearly shows that infection was not due to the schools." (p. 38).

children's playground where, through the play so necessary to the growing organism, health is established. Yet the crowded and ill-arranged school grounds, where organized play is always difficult and, in many cases, quite impossible, remain the chief offering of the community to the play-spirit of the child. In several of the capital cities a little has been done to meet the need of children's playgrounds, but there is not enough public interest to provide what is fully necessary.

The conditions of factory life also leave much to be desired from the standpoint of health. The hours of work are arranged without adequate discrimination in regard to sex and age. Even if the lighter tasks of industry fall to women, they have to toil at them the same length of time as men. The pattern on which industry is built was originally designed for men. Gaps were left in it where woman could employ her distinctive industrial virtues with profit to her employer. But the conditions of toil remained as in the original pattern without regard to her constitutional peculiarities. So, too, in regard to youths. Boys over sixteen years, and girls over eighteen, have to do the work of adult males or rather to work the same length of time, and to submit to the same requirements concerning overtime. The results in both cases are detrimental to health. Striking evidence of this is furnished by a competent social worker who spent a fortnight as a factory hand in several workshops in Sydney.

Quite half a dozen times I was asked if I was an immigrant. I could not understand until I asked another girl the reason. She replied: "We thought you were an immigrant because we so rarely see a girl with a good color." I was normally healthy and physically fit, and our modern civilization denies these blessings to its girl and women workers.[1]

[1] *The Worker* (Sydney, Jan. 2, 1913), article "Our Factory Girls."

Some part at least of the evil results of the continued strain would be obviated by a few short breaks, especially in the forenoon. Some shops and factories give ten minutes at eleven o'clock. But the printers of New South Wales, who had allowed fifteen minutes to their female employees, were able soon after to alter the concession to six minutes at any time of the day. The reasons advanced were purely economic. To give a respite from toil for even a few minutes to one section of the employees is said to dislocate the work of others. Brief intervals of this sort, however, do not dislocate routine and production in the more carefully organized industrial processes, and there is no economic necessity in favor of unbroken production. But if the principle of short breaks is not endorsed, the other alternative is shorter hours for females and youths. This has become a persistent demand, which is backed up by the recommendation of Mr. A. B. Piddington, who was asked to report on the hours and conditions of employment in New South Wales. The grounds for his recommendation will be seen in the following extract:

The present working week permits of too great a strain on boys and women. . . . Remembering the physical traces of fatigue, and sometimes of downright exhaustion, seen amongst women workers at the end of a week's work, I am satisfied that if the object of factory legislation for the unprotected class of workers is not merely to strike a bargain between the rapacity whether of capitalists or parents, and the claims of national health, but to put a barrier between defenceless workers and the hindering of their development or the injuring of their health, then the present maximum working week has been left too high when it has been placed on the same level with that of the adult male in most occupations.

On these grounds Mr. Piddington recommends that the

working week for women and boys should be forty-four hours and that overtime should be forbidden for them.[1]

Finally, in the presence of an empty continent with tremendous potentialities, the restriction of the birth-rate in Australia must be considered a movement in the direction of social inefficiency. Until a quarter of a century ago the Australian rate was high.[2] Then, in common with other countries, it fell at a somewhat startling pace, till it reached its minimum in 1903, when the rate was 25.29 per thousand. Public attention was concentrated on the matter, and various proposals were made to make marriage economically more possible and to care for child life. With the return of better conditions the rate slowly rose, till it was 26.73 in 1910, 27.21 in 1911 and 28.05 in 1914. This puts Australia ahead of Germany, New Zealand and even Great Britain. The death rate in Australia is so low, however (10.51 per 1000), that, taking the average for the last five years, the Commonwealth stands third among the civilized nations of the world in the rate of natural increase. One of its states, New South Wales, stands second in the list, surpassing New Zealand, which is ahead of the Commonwealth as a whole.

What influence due to natural laws may be at work to restrict fertility in Australia cannot easily be ascertained. By some it has been explained as an instance of the correlation between restricted fecundity and increased consumption of food, especially of meat, which is a large element in the Australian diet. The fundamental thesis of this explanation has not itself been proved, hence it does not carry us far. Further, the age constitution of brides has risen in

[1] *Cf. N. S. W. Royal Commission on Conditions in Factories*, 1912.
[2] Between 1877 and 1890 it remained almost stationary, being 34.99 per 1000 in the former year and 34.98 in 1890, but had fallen to 27.15 in 1898 (*Commonwealth Year Book*, no. 6, p. 262).

Australia as in other countries. Marriages are later, and hence, by natural law, potentially less fertile. Later marriages are, however, only the correlate of the fundamental cause for the small families to be found in Australia. The rising standard of living causes men and women to postpone marriage till they are in an economic position to maintain a family up to the average standard; and the restriction in numbers, deliberate probably as elsewhere,[1] is the result of the desire of an emancipated and educated democracy to maintain a fairly high standard of health, comfort and decency. Parents desire to give every child his natural birthright, a fair share of the opportunities and privileges of the conditions into which he is born. For themselves, they seek relief from the burden, physical, financial and social, of rearing more than three or four children. There is nothing mysterious or recondite about their attitude. On the parents' side it is often selfish, as far as their own interests are concerned, but in relation to the child it is the result of the ideal of a good start in life and a free field of social opportunity.

This desire, however, to maintain a high standard of health, comfort and decency, and to hand these down as the heritage of each child born, though in itself valid and praiseworthy, is not its own justification. The quantity as well as the quality of a nation's life is important. "A large number of physically sound and happy human beings must be taken as a prime condition of social welfare."[2] A nation that deliberately over-restricts its numbers is unfitting itself for that struggle of race with race which the utmost progress of civilization has not yet found any means of avoiding, and by allowing certain sections to increase, where religious considerations or mere want of foresight

[1] *Cf.* Newsholme, *The Declining Birth Rate.*
[2] Hobson, *Work and Wealth*, p. 317.

operate in opposition to the prevalent view, may alter its very composition and change the national characteristics in a few generations.

Two principles overrule the economic considerations advanced in favor of the restriction of the birth-rate. First, whatever advantages may be conferred by the presence of natural opportunities, man is himself the chief factor in production. By mental and physical energy he transforms natural opportunities into raw or finished products. His efforts create an industrial system and a system of exchange, and react upon the nation in the growth of cities and the transformation of the social structure. Secondly, man is a market for man. He is a consumer as well as a producer, a customer, not merely a rival. Hence, where the lower classes, always the more prolific, increase more rapidly than the population, the catastrophe so much feared in Australia does not result. When there are more workers, and per-capita production increases, there is not less work for each, but more, since there are more consumers. On economic grounds the Australian attitude of over-restriction and exclusion stands condemned. This is not the place to deal with the biological objections; let it suffice to say that the policy is ethically unjustifiable and socially invalid, since it places present materialistic comfort before the wider welfare of the nation in relation to its present and its future. " It is not easy to defend the prosperity of a people who shall seem to purchase a fuller and even a more spiritually complex life for some or all of its members by a continuous reduction of their numbers." [1] This must be the verdict of the sociologist upon the Australian people in this matter.

Our analysis has served to show that amid much of promise and social potency in Australian life, there has

[1] Hobson, *op. cit.*, p. 317.

been a failure to realize the purposes and aims of a democratic community in such an environment. An attempt has been made to actualize in the social process ideals of social justice that, in themselves, are commendable. The forms of political administration have been such as to make possible their actualization in full agreement with the aims and spirit of democracy. The people themselves stand without a peer among the democracies of the world for humanitarian feeling, love of liberty, power of initiative and sound, good sense. One of the freest and most complete democracies of which the modern world knows, situated in the midst of an empty continent with great resources, has only inadequately developed its natural resources, and tends, by a restriction of production, to destroy the economic basis of social efficiency. In the political sphere, the distrust of leaders, the neglect of the finest minds of the community to devote themselves to the problems of social organization, and the absence of any adequate scientific study of society as a guide to political activity show that the path to social efficiency is yet uncharted. Australia has used the experimental method in the crudest fashion, without continual and effective criticism of her working principles, without thorough examination of her methods or sufficient evaluation of her results.

Further, the program of social reform which the country, under the impetus and, in part, through the guidance of the Labour movement, entered upon in 1890, has been almost exhausted. A cleansing and revivifying force has spent itself, and in its shallows and stagnant backwaters flourish growths that would have been uptorn in the full flood. A movement built up through solidarity of action and the fullest respect for democracy has become distrustful of leaders, intolerant of freedom of opinion, and has developed the caucus system into control by a series of cliques. The economic morass into which this situation has led the workers of the country has been pointed out; it is sufficient to say that its seriousness is greater than that of any political evils that threaten. The people of Australia can be trusted to express their disapproval at the ballot-box of that which is contrary to obvious social justice. But with the past history of capitalism in Australia, and its slowness in adjusting itself to the progressive demands and needs of the workers, with a bitter class sentiment existing, making modes of co-operation and methods of conciliation difficult, there is no considerable section of the people ready to direct social organization into a new channel.

Under such circumstances, the most pressing need of the country is a program of social efficiency that has arisen from an examination of the social process in its successes and failures. There can be no merit in such a program unless it springs from an attempt to examine scientifically the development of the country. Its value depends, first, upon the accuracy of the prior analysis and examination, and, secondly, upon the adequacy of the projected remedy. Nor can there be stability in the program. It must necessarily be subject to criticism and amendment in the process of its realization. For society is a form of co-operative association, and no living organization is rigid. Criticism should, however, be formulated in the light of first principles. A concept of what social efficiency means is necessary to the possibility of continuous adjustment of the program to the national needs. It remains for us, therefore, to set forth the concept of social efficiency before proceeding to a program.

CHAPTER X

The Meaning of Efficiency

Social efficiency is the idea of efficiency applied to the functioning of society. Efficiency implies both an ideal and a measure. As an ideal, it means carrying out fully certain purposes and functions. This is the primary meaning of the word. An action, a process, a mechanism is thoroughly efficient if it fulfils the purpose for which it was instituted. This fact, that efficiency implies complete functioning, in its turn leads to the idea of a measure. On the one hand are purposes and intentions, on the other is the accomplished result. It is the latter which is to be measured in terms of the former. The measure must, therefore, be a ratio between what has been achieved and what might reasonably be regarded as a maximum or standard performance. Ultimately, this is the real measure, but as other factors enter in to determine achievement, it is possible and feasible to express efficiency in terms of these latter factors. Thus increased effort and outlay are charges on the debit side of achievement. So with time and energy. Hence efficiency comes often to be equivalent to the concurrence of a relative maximum of achievement with a minimum of effort and outlay. It means that the same or an increased result is obtained by checking the misdirection and waste of time, energy and money. In short, efficiency implies the ability to carry out operations and realize results in the best way and in the quickest time.

In application to society, it means little more and nothing

less. Society is an organization whose functioning is open to waste of energy and effort. It passes through a continual process, which has a purpose implicit in its form and direction. If the nature of its organization is neglected or imperfectly understood, if the social purpose and goal are not consciously and clearly before the members of the social group, there will abound opportunities for waste and inefficiency. Examples of such misunderstanding have been concretely analyzed and weighed in the preceding chapter. Their significance will be more fully appreciated after an adequate analysis of the nature, purposes and functioning of society. As such a task, which is equivalent to the preparation of a text-book on sociology, is beyond the scope of this work, it must suffice to give a slight sketch instead of a full analysis, laying stress only on points significant for the development of the theme.[1]

Society is an organization of individuals who have come together in association and co-operation. The fundamental basis of their co-operation is their like reaction to the same or similar stimuli furnished by the physical and social environment. Differences of individual equipment and temperament make habits of toleration necessary to the existence and continuance of co-operation. As collective action becomes more and more necessary, social organization develops in internal complexity. The primitive group, compelled by the pressure of increasing numbers to conquer or emigrate, is divided into leaders and followers. Those men and women who are superior to their fellows in energy, persistence and readiness of response to a situation become a class of leaders, and attain political prestige and economic power. Within the group various forms of industrial and

[1] This analysis of the nature, purposes and functioning of society owes much of its form and content to the teaching of Professor Franklin H. Giddings, of Columbia University.

political co-operation arise. Civilization progresses in proportion as these types of co-operation lead to the stability of the population, its increase in numbers, and the furnishing of an economic surplus which makes it possible to meet the wants and needs of the people and to build up arts and sciences for the enlightenment of mankind. The quality of civilization comes to be measured by the security it affords, the economic abundance it supplies for the largest number of people, and by the emphasis laid on those habits of toleration and social restraint that create and strengthen social co-operation. Society is, therefore, an organization in which the power and strength of an increasingly complex group are made available for its own advance. To that end social harmony is desirable, along with an organization which is not entirely spontaneous but is, in large part, the deliberate creation of those sections of the people that have the insight, the readiness and the initiative to meet the needs of every altering situation.

The purpose of society is to realize in each individual personality certain qualities held to be socially valuable. The French formula, " liberty, equality, fraternity," though neither adequate nor comprehensive, is suggestive of what these social values imply. In its evolution, society produced fixed classes, of rulers and governed, of conquerors and conquered. The rigidity of these classes was disturbed by forces which liberated the individual in the interest of the whole group. Economic betterment lifted the servile class. A growing political consciousness, after defining rights and duties, led to a conflict concerning the limits of rights and duties that educated the group in the meaning and power of its form of organization. The physical and psychic dynamic of increased numbers and increased economic and political complexity furthered the process. All these forces tended to strengthen and exalt personality, that is, they tended to produce a valuation of men and women as entitled to respect, to the recognition of their selves in the process of social interaction, and to the opportunity of equal rights for the full expression of their views and ideals. To this end democracy as a form of social organization was evolved. Where it resulted in a real equality of political opportunity and a system of representative institutions, it achieved its political aim. While great advance has been made in this method of social organization, society moves forward to a better adjustment of the conflicting interests and privileges of classes and castes and to a fuller endowment of personality. Men's feelings must be respected, their views considered, their claims for a fuller life weighed on their own merits and not discarded because they do not serve other men's purposes. A real equality of opportunity is desired, so that no accident of birth, no sport of circumstances, no restriction of environment shall operate to prevent a man functioning in society for his own and every one else's benefit. To realize these and kindred social values is the purpose of society.

Society functions through a process of inter-stimulation and response. The individuals who compose it co-operate on this basis. The stimulation arises from the physical as well as the social environment. It comes in the needs of safety, food, and sex. It increases in complexity as society itself becomes more complex. The physical environment, especially in the temperate and colder regions, challenges man to meet the vicissitudes of life by setting up a surplus. With the advance in economic complexity and the establishment of the division of labour, this social surplus becomes both an end and a means. Along with it goes a demand for freedom, for the opportunity not merely to develop but to display personality. Society intervenes here to limit the stimulation in the interests of social order. Thus the whole machinery of social control, created at first as a restraint, becomes a stimulus in turn. But ultimately society functions under the stimulus of the need for attaining a socialized personality. Men work and keep at work when they receive the concrete expressions of a recognition of the development of personality as the social end. Among these are opportunities for the exercise of an effective citizenship, recognition and social esteem in proportion to services rendered to society, an economic reward adequate for the rearing of a family, and, in industry, conditions which make possible delight in skill and pride in occupation. Where these stimuli are present in largest quantity and fullest number, society may be expected to function more efficiently.

Social efficiency, then, connotes that form and degree of organization that makes the power of the whole people available in support of social ends. It includes the utilization of the physical environment in such form and quantity that the mass of the people is lifted into a reasonable degree of comfort. It implies a social ideal in which each individual is allowed the fullest opportunity to assert his powers and abilities, for which he is secured a just economic return and a valuation commensurate only to the value of his services to society. Lastly, it necessitates a type of social organization, a form of social machinery, in which every degree and variety of individual difference may have power and scope to stimulate to social ends. That is, it calls for the realization of the fullest and freest forms of political and social democracy.

For the realization of social efficiency, at least three social factors are necessary: (1) industrial competency,[1] (2) social harmony, (3) the organization of society in con-

[1] I borrow this phrase from Professor John Dewey's *Democracy and Education*.

formity with a concept of social progress. In the stress and strain of national warfare it has been demonstrated that these three are among the chief factors that contribute to a nation's strength. The nations that can hold their own against assault are the great manufacturing nations wherein individual technique and national industrial organization alike tend towards industrial competency. The present war, too, has become a war of nations, to be decided as much by the unity and essential harmony of the nation from within as by the military power from without. It has no better justification than the creation of an organized society that will leave room for progress. It also bids fair to demonstrate that a political and social democracy has within it the capacity for efficiency and progress. War is, however, not the ultimate nor only test of social efficiency. For the furtherance of the health, welfare and happiness of the individual citizens, and for the advance of civilization, these factors are as influential in peace. They are among the chief means whereby society realizes its purposes.

Industrial competency includes, first, a careful survey of the natural resources and the formulation of methods for their development. Industry builds on what nature supplies. Man may be ignorant or wasteful of these resources. In either case inefficiency is promoted, though the latter trait is more disastrous, since it involves the depletion of the capital fund. Waste is, however, best checked by full knowledge of potentialities and by a scientifically planned development of what is available. Thus, for instance, a community which was aware of the extreme limit of its resources in coal, iron, silver, and oil, would feel the necessity of conserving its supplies, and under this pressure would seek to eliminate waste in mining. So with the nation's forests. Where the people realize the value of foresting the hillsides and in maintaining the regular flow of rivers, there will be less waste and more concerted action to reclothe the hillsides with native timber. Nowhere, however, is there so much need of a careful survey of natural resources as in the case of the production of food. It does not seem to be true that there is always in the world a superabundance of food. It seems more true that, through wars, climatic pulsations and other forces less clearly understood, there have been recurrent periods of world-wide scarcity, if not of famine. With increased numbers and a corresponding diminution of new and hitherto unproductive areas whose rapid exploitation can be used as an offset, the possibility of such periods of scarcity increases. Any nation, therefore, that desires either to feed its own people or to produce a surplus of food to exchange for the manufactured products of other countries has to develop its pasture and agriculture to the fullest. To this end scientific knowledge must be applied to the nature of the soil, to the means by which its fullest productivity can be realized, and to the organization by which the farmer markets his products. The physical and social sciences are alike included. The soil chemist, the breeder of new seed varieties, the scientific irrigation engineer, the expert in rural economics and rural sociology must be put to work if the soil is to be made to produce all that is possible. A country with rich soil may be able for a while to do without any of them, but she is sowing a bitter harvest of inefficiency through soil depletion, rural depopulation, and decreased food productivity manifest in rising prices. Unless, therefore, a society is to be stunted in material development or subjected to great waste and injurious exploitation, it must survey its resources. It must formulate plans so that waste will be eliminated in mining, forests will be conserved, agriculture developed along scientific lines, the land put to its best use, and the full return of his labour assured to the farmer through efficient economic organization.

Second among the factors in the realization of industrial competency is the training of men to use industry to its highest productivity for social ends. This training involves employers and employed. The former are anxious to increase the productivity of industry, but their end is private profit. In their absorption in the pursuit of that end they have tended to forget that industry is a social function and that its human costs are more important than any other costs. Further, they are only beginning to learn that a more acute economic analysis has shown that profits arise from some advantage the credit for which is due more to organized society than to the individual. If a profit remains after raw material and labour are paid for, after the normal interest on capital has been met, and compensation for risk and management paid to the *entrepreneur*, it passes into private hands largely to the detriment of organized society. It is necessary, therefore, that employers desirous of realizing social efficiency should learn to direct industry within the limits of economic cost above defined and with full attention to human values. Even within these limits of economic cost, within which most competitive businesses work, there is scope for much efficiency, but there are grave risks of neglecting the human factor. Thus the so-called system of scientific management, as controlled by and worked in the interests of employers, is at present feudal in its organization, mechanical in its method, and alien to much that psychology and sociology have taught of the place and worth of human personality in the developing process of democracy. Industrial competency, which may be secured along the line of a scientific regulation of toil towards the highest productivity combined with a minimum of effort, cannot come till the employers have found the opportunities for the workers to become integral parts of industry.

On the part of the employees the stress must be laid on the fullest production. They have an idea of the social purpose of industry, but their method of realization tends to produce a poorer, not a richer, society. They need to learn the value of skill and the desirability of enhanced production. Their position, individually and collectively, is to be bettered only by giving industry and agriculture increased productive power. Without minimizing the value or need of a just distribution of the wealth produced, the student of social and economic changes must stress the desirability of a larger product. The justest distribution that human ingenuity could devise or social organization effect would leave much room for the satisfaction of the wants of civilized man. Increasing productivity is the resultant of an effective use of machinery combined with increasing individual excellence in work and skilful, economical management. In every one of these factors skill is a prerequisite. Machinery that will free the energies of men and deliver up in fuller measure the products of natural resources is the result of the inventions of skilled, trained minds. Individual excellence in work and economical management are alike proportionate to the degree of training and skill manifested.

But neither care on the part of the employer for the human and social values in production, nor desire on the employee's part for increased productivity will secure industrial competency without co-operation. Production is a partnership of society, the employer and the employee. Failure to make this co-operation is a striking phenomenon in the development of the industrial revolution. Nevertheless many signs of the recognition and realization of this partnership have already marked social development.

By legislation concerning the conditions of labour and the distribution of the product, society has maintained its rights in the association. With the advance of democracy there has come, mainly from the working class, a demand for a social as well as a political democracy. Their demands are often short-sighted, their methods blind and clumsy, sometimes stupid and disruptive, sometimes anarchical. But behind both demands and methods is a feeling after an organization on the lines of that co-operation and respect for personality that characterize democracy. Industry, as it is organized to-day, is autocratic. Conditions of work and hours of labour are determined by the employer, unless society has intervened. Higher rates of wages and all methods of rewarding efficiency and greater skill are optional with him. His foremen have such powers of dismissal that a man with a grievance has little chance for conciliation over it. The period of employment is controlled by forces over which the worker himself can have but little control, and the employer not much more.[1] Against all this, the workers generally are protesting so vehemently that the older order of co-operation, in which the worker co-operated through ready and even submissive obedience, has given place to one of conflict and disharmony. The student of society, appreciative of the rhythmic nature of its progress, hopes that this is but a transition period, the trough of a wave whose succeeding crest will reveal a type of co-operation in accord with the democratic spirit of the age. Social philosopher, economist and sociologist are alike convinced that industrial democracy is that form of co-operation towards which the social process is tending. Industry is the one conspicuous social institution that resists the influence of democracy. What changes it will undergo before it has attained relative

[1] *Cf.* article by Ordway Tead in *American Journal of Sociology*, vol. xxiii, pp. 31-37, entitled "Trade Unions and Efficiency."

stability again cannot be foretold by any one. The workers are demanding an equal voice with the employer in conditions of labour, hours of work, conditions of remuneration and the manners and practices of foremen.[1] Some reasonable degree of acquiescence in these demands is called for both practically and ideally ere peace will reign in industry.

Such co-operation will lay great demands upon the worker, both individually and collectively. Even in his advocacy of industrial democracy there is a strong undercurrent of class bitterness and the desire to set a triumphant proletariat over all other sections. He needs to learn the economic and social values of industrial democracy, to see that form of organization as the corollary of the democratic process. But even more does he need education in those qualities and capacities which are necessary for partnership in industry. The sense of responsibility, power of judgment, ability to organize work, to determine costs, and to recognize the conditions of profitable labour, are all necessary. They are not to be learned in a day. Through their distrust of the present economic system, and their obsession of what is at the best a far-distant ideal, the workers have been blind to the more obvious lines along which the present system is to be transcended and reformed. They have not used their collective organizations in such a way as to have gained by experience the requisite qualities. Co-operative production and distribution, one at least of the methods whereby the necessary training could have been acquired, has had relatively little support. The growth of large monopolies and trusts has deprived this form of economic organization of its value and significance as a training school in responsibility and judgment, and in the economics of production. No detailed plan for education in

[1] *Cf.* for example, the speech of the president of the English Trade Union Congress, September, 1916.

these qualities can be submitted; it can arise only from the slow and gradual evolution of business forms. But certain steps can be taken, all of which will react progressively upon industrial competency.

First, there can be given to the working classes, or at least to their leaders, a fairly adequate education in economics and sociology. Through the former they will get a theoretical acquaintance with the process and the problems of production. The latter will give them a clearer idea of the trend of human society, and of the place, significance and influence of each class therein.[1] Secondly, the more formal education of the schools, by an extension of its vocational and technical aspects, can be made a training in the organization of work. Technical schools can train foremen as well as skilled artisans, while the earlier vocational instruction can include a theoretical acquaintance with the forms and methods of business as well as of trades.

But training in responsibility and judgment can come only by experience. The workers, through their duly elected representatives, must have intimate acquaintance with the actual problems and difficulties of business before they will be ready for fruitful co-operation. The road to such experience is beset by the fears of individualists and the dreams of collectivists. The large numbers of state-controlled industries in every Western country to-day afford the desired opportunity. Attention has been drawn to the paradox of a state where a large number of enterprises are directed by the state, and yet where the workers give grudging and inefficient service. The paradox lies in the fact that one expects such a measure of state socialism to be the stimulus and the opportunity for the working

[1] For a method of making such instruction available to working men, see the explanation of the working of the English university tutorial classes, as described by Albert Mansbridge: *University Tutorial Classes*.

classes to adopt such enterprises as their own, study the methods, conditions and results of their operation, and by their interest therein acquire a sense of responsibility and the good judgment that comes only from practical experience. Without education in these qualities and capacities, demands for industrial democracy will be resisted as inimical to efficiency, and the industrial competency which waits on co-operation will be correspondingly delayed.

Lastly, industrial competency includes the securing of a social surplus, an excess of wealth. The presence of such a surplus means social energy, ability to meet new exigencies and trying situations. It implies the possibility of new experiments. Only a wealthy country can afford the experiments and changes through which social efficiency is realized. For efficiency is not measured by the presence in the national exchequer of a financial surplus. Efficiency is measured by the proportion in which the state realizes its own collective purposes, and by the readiness with which the social machinery can be adapted to changes in the purposes and methods of government. Taxation, by which the national exchequer is replenished, is one of the greatest aids to good government, but to increase or diminish its quantity is not one of the ends of government. Business-like and economical administration of funds provided is a mark of efficiency, but reduced taxation can only come from a restriction of the functions of government or from a general increase in wealth, so that the burden falls less heavily on each individual. As social efficiency implies an increase rather than a decrease in the functions of government, it follows that the cost of efficient government is to be met by increased productivity, increased and more justly distributed wealth, and these in their turn are the product of an industrial competency which puts a premium on skill, industry, responsibility and judgment.

Social harmony is probably more important than industrial competency. The unity and cohesion of a nation are more considerable factors in any success it achieves than is the efficiency of the individuals who compose it. Social power is the resultant of the organized competency of the various groups. This resultant is determined in direction and in magnitude by the degree to which the organized groups co-operate. Society is composed of groups bound together, and separated from one another, by interests more or less divergent. The disruptive power of these divergent interests depends on the extent to which privileges have been established. Privileges are the bulwarks of classes and castes, the outward signs of class consciousness, and the objects round which class conflict centers. Class consciousness is more than the recognition of common ends in an exclusive group. It is a disposition to allow this correlation of mutual interests and group sympathy to dominate political, economic and industrial activity. If it were only what the former definition implies, it would have great value, sociologically considered. It would be a mode of internal discipline, whereby each group would be made to play its due part in the social process. The influence of an aristocracy in England, no less than that of the workers upon Australian social development, is due to the binding force of this sentiment of solidarity. But when a group of men feel that they are being discriminated against, and deprived of privileges which others enjoy, they tend to co-operate for the purpose of securing their share of those privileges. This co-operation dominates their social, political and economic outlook, creates class consciousness, and leads to social conflict. The free operation of social forces is checked by the barriers which are raised by stratification along the lines of class. Social prejudice and class bias stultify the operation and restrict the influence of all that would tend to bind society together and lead to its advance. Consequently, in the conflict which arises, social control is weakened, and either progress is realized, or a drift towards disorder and anarchy sets in.

Class conflict arises, therefore, as a result in part of the struggle against privilege. While privilege exists, and while educational advancement makes men more sensitive to its presence, class conflict will tend to perpetuate itself. On its worst side, this conflict will be aimed, as in the Marxian propaganda, at the destruction of privileges and their appropriation, without plan or purpose, by the unprivileged. On its better side, the conflict is over the assertion of what is deemed to be a right. It is actuated by a desire for a better adjustment of conflicting interests, a desire that, in its turn, is born of a higher ideal of social order, esteemed as juster or nobler in some sense. It is an attempt to bring about a readjustment which will establish this new relationship.

Understood in this sense, social conflict is recognized as a normal element in the process of social development, while class conflict and the class consciousness on which it depends lose their alleged necessity in the social order. Unless society is static, there is but slight ground for fixed opposition between groups. Such an attitude tends to increase hostility and widen the gap between classes rather than hasten social readjustment. The way out is not to be found through the overthrow and destruction of any one class, with all its influence and possessions, for that is the negation of social order and a challenge to social progress. Nor is the mere abandonment of special privileges all that is required to subdue social conflict. If its aim were the destruction or expropriation of privileges, this method would suffice. But with the insistence on a readjustment of social relationship as the aim of the social struggle, class above described will turn distrust into a discriminating recognition of the qualities which are the best equipment for leadership. The creation of a social as well as a political democracy will do much towards strengthening the dynamic power of the sentiment of democracy, and give democratic leadership a basis in feeling and group sympathy rather than in the vestiges of autocratic power that still remain. Thus will there tend to be created an organization in which a democratically-inspired minority guides, and an educated democracy ultimately determines, social action.

On the administrative side, social efficiency requires that organization shall be adequate to stimulate the energies, abilities and interests of the individual to the realization of the public good, and that there shall be a mechanism able to meet the changing purposes of government. To realize the first requirement, interest in the national welfare should be linked up with interest in local centers. The citizen of the democratic state can learn to function efficiently in a vital community group. There he will learn those habits of toleration and co-ordination that make social harmony possible and give social organization its meaning and purpose. The well-organized local community is the basis of the well-organized state. Political, social and industrial activity organized in the social cell will manifest itself in the social body. Hence the need of a strong local patriotism in the state, and of such a territorial division as will give scope to this sentiment.

Finally, there is needed a mechanism through which organization can be affected. All the institutions of social control, religion, education, morality, and laws are available. All have their part to play. For the purpose, however, of meeting the changing purposes of government, the supreme challenge to social organization, the most adequate one is that of legislation. To effect that end, however, the concept of its scope and of its relation to public opinion must be extended. It has long been held to be the expression of the public will and to lose its efficiency in proportion as it runs ahead of public opinion. But if it is to be an agent in the organization of a society that is consciously pursuing social values, it must become an instrument for the formulation of those values, a means of reconstructing intricate social and industrial conditions, a preparation for new economic and political developments, a consciously planned remedy for a well-analyzed situation. A society where civic efficiency is being promoted by education, where action is being both fostered in its inauguration and guided in its development by this concept of legislation, will have the insight to utilize the creative insight of the leader to secure social efficiency by organization on such lines.

CHAPTER XI

A Program of Social Efficiency

THROUGH discussion of the actual state of social organization in Australia and of the ideal content of social efficiency, we are now in a position to offer a program through which social efficiency may be advanced in that country. This program can be only a sketch without completeness or finality of form. Little argument will be advanced to demonstrate its urgency or practicability. If the foregoing analysis has been adequate, it should have made clear the urgency of such a program, and, by establishing its relation to the national temperament and to the line of the national development have furnished the surest proof of its practicability. For the secret of efficiency lies in the development of the national aptitudes in accordance with the stress and moment of the impinging forces of the social environment. The practicability of the program, however, is dependent upon the degree of organization and conscious collective effort manifest in society. For an unorganized society, much of the program would be a Utopian dream, or at best a series of valuable suggestions to be realized in the time-honored mode of reform, slowly and one by one. A country awake to its opportunities and to the demands made upon it by its admitted deficiencies can organize its citizens and its institutions so as to realize the program in a few years.

First must come a fuller use and development of the natural resources by scientific farming and dairying, conservation of water and forests, afforestation, and the development of the unsettled lands. Scientific agriculture must begin with a careful soil survey. By that means, scientists and settlers alike would know for what the land was suitable, what crops could be grown and in what rotation, and what social efforts would be necessary to encourage settlement. This would involve a great development in the attention given to agricultural chemistry, and a considerable use of expert scientists during a number of years. The work, however, would need to be done only once, but it is essential that it should be done thoroughly. Along with it should go an extension of the work done in breeding disease-resistant wheats which will ripen on dry or hot lands and possess high milling qualities. By this means it is possible that Australia might learn to grow wheat in her hotter areas which correspond to the wheat belt of India.

More pressing, however, is the problem of enabling the farmer to make the best use of the land already under cultivation. In wheat growing, he is faced with the uncertainty of the rainfall and with the need of replenishing the soil. The former compels him to resort to a form of dry-farming that differs greatly from that in vogue in the drier states of the mountain belt of the United States. It is practically a combination of fallowing with a rotation of crops that is effective in maintaining fertility, but not in securing the highest productivity. The oats and fodder crops that are inserted in the rotation cannot be grown as profitably as wheat. By a form of mixed farming, in which sheep are carried on the farm, the fodder crops can be utilized fairly effectively, but the market for oats is quickly supplied. The same problem arises in the matter of maize, the production of which in some of the subtropical areas has been discontinued. To market it "on the hoof," in the shape of cattle and pigs, would be a way conflict can be turned into social harmony, first, by transferring the emphasis from those factors that create class consciousness on to the rights which are at issue, and, secondly, by securing some general consensus of opinion as to those social ideals which are of the most value to society.

These two methods are related, in that they imply a fuller analysis and a far more widespread knowledge of the social process than is common. Without these, there can be no basis for the valuation of the right demanded nor for the readiness to shift the aim of the conflict from the preservation of vested rights to the establishment of a social ideal. These methods, therefore, because of what is required for their functioning, seem to have something ideal and fantastic about them. Yet they are logically necessary and far from impossible. They follow necessarily from the nature and aims of social conflict. For the conflict is not between fixed groups that differ widely in all, or most, interests, but between ideas that dominate men and women in various groups. When the emphasis is shifted to these dominant ideals, their acceptance by persons in different groups will become manifest. The worker will then find on his side many types of men whom class consciousness previously hindered from espousing his ideals. The wealthy and educated conservative will find among the workers some, at least, to whom his ideals appeal. Thus social harmony will be furthered so far as it can be by the resolution of a class consciousness based on feeling into a willingness to intellectually evaluate differences of standards and ideals.

Yet social harmony will not be assured till there is some relative agreement upon social ideals in the minds of those who compose the social group. Fundamentally, disagreement upon the ideals followed in the past is the real cause of social conflict. The more divergent are these ideals and the more fundamental the relations they involve, the more bitter will be the conflict. Of the truth of this statement the present European War is an illustration. A rapprochement between such conflicting ideals would ease some of the bitterness. But, in the last resort, the creation of social values, consciously recognized and pursued, into which divergent purposes are transmuted, alone can produce social harmony. The enunciation of these social values is the work of sociology. Through a clearer knowledge of the nature and purpose of society, of the conditioning environment in which it functions, and of the temperament and interactions of its component individuals, these ideals can be attained. The creation of a harmonious social order waits, then, their organization and realization in society.

Social efficiency includes, finally, the organization of society towards the realization of those social values on which progress towards industrial competency and group cohesion depends. Society is called upon to make a systematic effort to realize its own collective purposes. There is no reason to conceive of progress as either automatic, continuous or uninterrupted. An improved social state does not come about while nations slumber. Retrogression is as real a fact as progress. Societies have to effect some form of combination of the activities of all their members for the achievement of common ends. Efficiency depends, however, on the purpose for which this combined activity is created, and on the methods employed. The purpose has been described in terms of industrial competency and social cohesion. In organization the stress is laid on methods, since it is an organization of effort and activity. Social efficiency is therefore a matter of discovering and utilizing those factors in social control which will be effective in concentrating the energies, abilities and interests of each individual upon the public good, and those methods of administration which will make the public good realizable in concrete and detailed form.

The chief of the factors that have power to operate in forming efficient citizenship is education. Concerning its power to control and shape the fundamental impulses and instincts of the child the sociologist has no criticism. What he desires is that its promise and potency should be carried further afield into the socially significant years of adolescence and the more mature years of citizenship and industrial activity. He looks to it to further social efficiency by connecting the motor activities of youth with productive tasks, by creating interests that will save enhanced leisure from becoming a social menace and danger, and by definitely preparing men and women for the discussion and decision of the manifold problems in industrial, political and social life which citizenship covers. Industrial competency and social harmony will both be furthered by such an extension of education. Agricultural education that will be scientific and practical, that will show the dairyman and the farmer how, and how far, science may be brought to their aid, will tend to increase production and relieve some of the monotony of country life which, in Australia, as elsewhere, is responsible in part for the depletion of the countryside. The question of apprenticeship and of obtaining a supply of efficient artisans is to be solved by an education which links class-room and workshop. The health and welfare of the citizen in childhood, youth and maturity is to be secured by an education which links social hygiene with mental upbuilding. If effective citizenship be made its theme, it can not only stimulate and guide political activity, but can be made an instrument in the wise ordering of individual and social life. Standards of living, modes of the expenditure of wealth, and the supreme value of social obligations can thus be brought home to the community. In short, education can create those qualities of alertness, willingness to co-operate and sense of the value of social co-operation which are essential to group cohesion. It can give content and guidance to social activities, and furnish the situation in which leadership will be effective.

For leadership is the second factor in organization. Organization implies co-ordination, and leadership is its correlative. Real leadership wins recognition by a combination of insight and capacity. In organization generally the latter quality is sufficient, but both are needed in organization for social efficiency. Only thus can that distrust of leaders which is the bane of democracy be avoided. The natural leader of society is the man with insight sufficient to appreciate the changing social values and capacity enough to adapt the machinery of government to its changing purposes. Even the socialized education described above cannot guarantee any wide bestowal of insight into the meaning of the ever-present forces which are changing social values. Nor is democracy as a form of organization sufficient to dispense with the need of leaders. Membership of a democratic state does not guarantee the ability to decide wisely all questions concerning the whole, and certainly does not imply the probability that public opinion will organize itself spontaneously in the wisest direction. Even more than any form of political organization, democracy needs leaders to supply it with insight, if not with executive capacity.

The suspicion of leaders that democracy has, is not, however, without basis. The tendency on their part to obtain autocratic power is so natural and at the same time so contrary to democracy that suspicion awaits any attempt to strengthen their influence. There is a distrust born, too, of that wider experience and superior education or ability which fit for leadership. Nevertheless, both bases for mistrust can be removed. The wider diffusion of education and its extension along the line of civic efficiency out of this difficulty. This suggestion, however, does not do away with the necessity for a scientific survey of the relation of the whole of the agricultural, pastoral and dairying products to one another and to the effective use of the land. By scientific experiments in the feeding of stock on certain products, by other experiments on the value for food and manure of certain crops, and on the possible effective combinations of the above-named industries, the present areas and the present population can be made to yield and to obtain a greater quantity of production.

But two questions concerning the settlement and use of the land remain to be solved in Australia. One is to get more settlers upon the somewhat restricted amount of fertile land now occupied, the other is to use the unsettled lands. The former point has been given little consideration. Attention has been directed mainly to the question of what constitutes a living area. Especially is this so in those areas where wheat is the chief product, with sheep as a secondary product. Here, allowance has to be made for fallowing, and for a paddock for sheep. Hence, areas ranging from 500 to 2,000 acres comprise a one-man farm. Under the considerations of climate and the methods of operation this area may be necessary, but the system must be judged by its results. It is true that it has called for a great deal of courage and resourcefulness, and is made profitable only by a wide use of machinery in putting in and taking off the crop. But it is responsible for an average production of less than twelve bushels per acre. This is below that of Canada and the United States, where similar large-scale methods are adopted, and much below that of England, where intensive methods make the average yield per acre thirty-two bushels.[1] Apparently, there-

[1] *Cf. Commonwealth Year Book*, no. 9, pp. 314-17.

fore, this system can not be regarded as justified, while a higher productivity and more intensive settlement are both required. At least there is ground for an inquiry as to whether more science and more machinery will not make possible a more intensive system of production, increasing the yield per acre, decreasing the necessary size of the holding, and thereby making possible a larger population upon the soil. This inquiry should not be confined to the production of wheat, nor even to the agricultural industry. It can profitably be carried not only into agricultural production as a whole, but also into the pastoral and dairying industries.

The use of the unsettled lands is the most pressing problem facing the Australian people. At present, they are willing to let them remain unsettled. In view of the world situation, it is doubtful if they dare continue this policy. But no great influx of immigration can be received until a practical policy for the use of unsettled land is devised. Tropical Australia is the first problem. The Australian people are determined that it shall be settled by the white race. To effect that purpose, the question of tropical hygiene must be scientifically studied and the conclusions of the scientists made generally known, the occupation of the more temperate hinterland secured by the providing of railway communication and a wise allocation of the land, and attention given to the products and occupations possible in the coastal strip. After such preparation, a concerted plan of securing immigration from the agricultural classes of some one or other of the European countries could then be initiated. Without such preparation, nothing but disaster would follow the exposure of immigrant stock to the climatic terrors and economic hardship of such country. The use of the dry areas is a simpler problem. By following the results of experiments in dry farming as carried on in Arizona and Texas, it could be discovered how far the effective limit of settlement could be pushed. The rest is a matter of conservation of water supplies.

Conservation is one of the key words through which a program of social efficiency is to be interpreted. It is applicable to the storage of ensilage and fodder in dairying and in the pastoral industry for provision against the periods of drought. It is particularly applicable to the storing of water for the purpose of irrigation. In the case of artesian bores, it would seem as if their number will need to be regulated, as the steady diminution of flow therefrom indicates that the reserve underground supply is diminishing. This can be done by an extension of the system of artesian bore trusts.[1] Finally, the doctrine of conservation must be applied to the forests of the country. Possibly there has been greater waste of timber than of any other product of the country. The process of settlement was one in which forests were ruthlessly exterminated. Softwoods and hardwoods alike have been swept clear from large areas even where they would be valuable as shade trees. The consequence is that there is need for a jealous conservation of the forests that remain and a vigorous afforestation of the land so crudely and nakedly despoiled. Afforestation may even prove to be of some value in reclaiming the drier areas.

Next on the program must come an effort to overcome industrial strife. While much economic stupidity, much baseless class feeling and many false notions of the social purpose of industry obtain, there is present among employers and employed alike in Australia a sufficient basis of good sense and social idealism to make an effort towards industrial peace worth while. If our analysis in preceding

[1] *Cf. N. S. Wales Handbook,* "British Association for the Advancement of Science," 1914, pp. 546, 547.

chapters has been correct, industrial strife is to be overcome only by securing some measure of democratic control in industry. The first step in this process is to give employees, or, at least, their elected and delegated representatives, an opportunity for that training in responsibility, judgment and knowledge of the economic and technical side of business organization without which any participation on their part in industry would mean economic disaster. Industrial democracy can never be realized along the line of the Marxian dream, nor even as political democracy was achieved. In the stress of the international situation which will be dominant during the next quarter of a century, those nations will be powerful whose workers are entering into the processes of industry with knowledge, skill and judgment. To secure these qualities, countries like Australia, which have so many business enterprises and industrial undertakings, afford many opportunities to their workers. By " fathering " these undertakings, by making their success a collective aim, by seeking to understand their workings, their difficulties and their future development, there will be created that atmosphere and sentiment whereby much of the distrust of the present economic system will be destroyed and from which will arise the possibility of a reconstruction of the same. On this basis of development, the way would be prepared for something like a board of reference or a conciliation board, consisting of representatives from each side, to which subjects in dispute in factory and industry could be referred for adjudication. Such boards could be confined at first to State and municipal enterprises or to such an industry as coal-mining, where public utilities are concerned. A mere extension of the provisions of the Arbitration Acts in regard to such committees would bring them into existence, though the purpose and methods of the Federal Government in creating such boards recently in the ship-building industry affords a better illustration of what is suggested. To make clear to the workers the social value of industry, to secure their effective interest in the success of the specific trade or industry in which they are employed, is essential for the peaceful working of even a conciliation committee. This educational work, effected in the ship-building industry by the war and its lessons, may call in other industries for a vast extension of economic and sociological teaching, in class-room, study-circle, trade union and press. If such teaching is effective in revealing the inter-relatedness of industry and in making clear the elements, possible and ideal, of practical co-operation, it would be worth while. From it would spring the possibility of bringing all industry into a condition where democratic control through co-operation had stilled industrial strife.

A correlation between increased wages and increased production must be established if social efficiency is to be realized. At first sight, this appears to be a moral duty laid on the shoulders of the workers, implying that when they receive higher wages, they must work harder. It would also be possible to distort it into a statement that the worker must work harder before he should obtain higher wages. The trend of the argument of previous chapters would belie either interpretation. What is implied is the common and collective recognition of the fact that increased wages ultimately depend on the productivity of industry. Increased wages and increased profits are alike paid out of the proceeds of industry. Therefore, if, while wages are increasing, industry is becoming less productive, the very possibility of increased wages may ultimately be destroyed. It follows that increased production must go along with increased wages. The two must move in direct, not inverse relation. The practical task is to increase both production and wages. Three main factors are involved, labour, machinery and management. Labour may be awarded higher wages in an industry that increases its productivity without adding to the length or strenuousness of the day's toil. More and better machinery and better management are the necessary means for the increase. In fact, the social idealism which created the modern democratic movement in Australia looked to machinery to make possible the increased leisure held to be so desirable. Our analysis of recent developments shows that greater leisure has been attained, but that the workers are deliberately restricting their own toil and checking the employment of machinery, thereby making the problems of management greater and more irritating. None can deny the need of breaking up this vicious circle of inefficiency.

The first step must come through a more adequate economic analysis on the part of the trade unionists. Education has been the guide and safeguard of political democracy. Education in economics can be the only adequate guide and safeguard for industrial democracy. This education, however, must not be that which is issued to them, *ex cathedra*, like much of the teaching given to children. No university or teaching body can lay down a set of demonstrable truths in economics and require that they be accepted as the working principles of industry. On the contrary, the education referred to must be a fluid set of principles beaten out in study and debate in which practice and theory join. A trade unionism less obsessed with the problems of political manoeuvring, like that of England, has had time and opportunity within its own circle for such matters. But the economic views thus reached tend to become badly biassed by class considerations. What is needed is a combination of the theoretical precision and scientific accuracy of the trained student with the enthusiasm and practical knowledge of the worker. When the universities, from which the former come, link hands with the latter in the teaching to adult men and women of economics and the other social sciences, the first step will have been taken. A few years of such work would do much to efface the fallacy by which unionists justify increased wages and decreased production simultaneously, and would establish the value and place of machinery in socialized industry.

The second step must come from the *entrepreneurs*, and consists in the organization of industry so as to minimize waste and increase production. An increase in wages in an industry that can afford the increase is a challenge to the management to stimulate production, not so that interest, profits and wages of management should rise correspondingly, but so that society should be none the poorer. The obvious method for the *entrepreneur* is that of the application of science. Upon its liberal and increasing use the realization of industrial democracy depends. Machinery must be made to furnish the aid of natural forces, and, because it is unfeeling, non-human and capable of bringing much added power to man's aid, must be worked to its fullest capacity. A conscious realization of its place in the industrial order, of the human costs it saves, and of the conditions under which it works most efficiently would enable the worker to become its master, not, as he fears he is, its slave. Through the same mode of approach there could be worked out a system of scientific control of the conditions of labour, so that the economic and psychological objections to what is known as scientific management could be avoided, and a system evolved that would give a maximum production with a minimum of effort. Some form of scientific control is necessary for the realization of increased productivity. This waits mainly for the prior realization of social harmony through democratic control of industry.

A body of workers, educated in respect to the methods and costs of production, consulted through their representatives on the matters referred to above, and living in a society where industry is consciously directed to social ends, will find a means of putting the emphasis in scientific control upon self-conscious direction of their own toil. Finally, the *entrepreneur* will need to use the results of economic criticism so as to attain the best methods of accounting, finding costs, and checking the operation of each section of his plant, and to guide him in questions of location of plant, size and arrangement of building, transport of goods and materials, and size and organization of staff. Further, he will need the help of physical science in such matters as utilization of by-products. To this end, a scientific laboratory should be established in each large factory.

Next among the steps toward the realization of social efficiency stands the securing of skill in workmanship and its specific valuation. The first implies the training of skilled artisans. This, which was once the jealously guarded privilege and prerogative of the industry itself, has now become a matter for collective organization. The individual who may be desirous of making himself skilled and efficient may even yet forge his way against the indifference of employers and the veiled hostility of the workers on this matter. As stated in the discussion of the apprenticeship question, the form and direction of economic development and the strength and nature of the conflicting interests have produced an *impasse*. Industrial organizations have now no effective machinery for developing that skill which they so badly need. Trade unionists, in their better moments, recognize the need, in the interests of their own class, of adequate and careful training, but their own present interests predominate, and the situation remains one of drift and chaos. Society, as a whole, compelled to deal with it, must bring the situation within the scope of the education process.

A commencement must be made in the closing years of the primary school by vocational guidance. Talks to boys on the nature of modern industry, on its technical and mechanical achievements, and on the part which skilled intellects play in invention, control and direction of the vast machinery of production, will shift the emphasis from the well-paid "blind alley" job which lies outside the school doors waiting for the boy to seize it. If the school period were extended to the age of sixteen, it would give an opportunity for the effective use of two years that are most significant in the development of manual skill. A process of vocational selection, based on psychological grounds of interest and fitness, without being rigidly determinative, would enable the pupil during those two years to adjust himself to some type of occupation. With tools at his disposal, and definite tasks springing out of his own needs and desires or out of the collective needs of the school, such constructive tendencies as he manifested would be cultivated, while hand and eye were being trained. By coupling this more technical work with cultural training, corporate activity, some practical acquaintance with organized industry, and teaching concerning its needs, scope and social utility, there would be prepared a basis for the years of apprenticeship that ensue at the close of this period. The average boy, to whom work is drudgery, whose only end and measure of value are the wages earned, would come out of this preparation with a conscious recognition of the need and value of skilled work.

In the period of apprenticeship, the same inclusion of the apprentice in the educational process should be carried on. Society should, and society alone can, furnish those opportunities for education in the theoretical and scientific aspects of trade and industry without which the technical proficiency of the workshop is deficient. The practical problem is that of linking the class room and the workshop. Because of the almost equal value of the theoretical and the practical, an equal allocation of time is desirable. Apprenticeship should involve a contract between the individual, the employer and the State, making attendance at technical classes during either mornings or afternoons compulsory and essential to the fulfilment of the apprenticeship. Much, however, depends on the content of the instruction afforded in the technical classes. It can be made too intensive to awaken and stimulate powers of organization, or too broad to be of direct value in the technique of the workshop. The way out of this difficulty can be found by giving a broader training in the first two years of apprenticeship, when the youth is between sixteen and eighteen years of age, and a more specialized training in the three later years.

It is not sufficient that technical education should at this stage cease its efforts to produce skilled artisans. In fact, it is just at this point that the ordinarily excellent technical instruction that has been fostered in Australia will begin to operate. The courses provided have been carefully and definitely correlated with the various trades, and offer opportunities for the fullest acquaintance with the technique and organization of the most important of them.

When skilled men have been produced, they will demand a definite evaluation of their skill. As our analysis will have shown, this calls for an alteration in the methods of remuneration prevalent in Australia. Skill is a special and peculiar attribute of each distinct individual. It is not like his needs, common and general, and therefore a basis for a standard rate of remuneration. If it is to be rewarded proportionately, it must be measured by a method that takes account of its special and peculiar nature. This condition is met by the use of piece-work as a basis for remuneration. Piece-work, where practicable, is the appropriate stimulus and the logical form of remuneration for skill. In trades where piece-work is impracticable, the wages for skill can safely be left to competition. Skill is its own economic justification. In certain trades where piece-work has not been attempted, rates will have to be worked out. These should be the joint product of a board of reference, composed of equal numbers of representatives of employers and employees. Thus, two conditions essential to justice in the arrangement can be established. Piece-work rates must not be less than the minimum standard wage. In fact, as a recognition and encouragement of superior skill, the minimum piece-work rate should be above the minimum standard wage. Secondly, there must be sufficient stability about the rate to encourage skill. Unless the skilled man has some guarantee that the rewards of his increased efforts will come continuously to him, he will be thrown back on that distrust of the present economic system previously mentioned. The wages earned by piece-work may be far larger than those ordinarily paid on time rates, but that fact is no economic justification for regarding them as too high. If the economic position is sound that wages are ultimately conditioned by productivity, granting the variable factor of price, then employers must be prepared to elicit skill by guaranteeing that piece-work rates, possibly varying only in accordance with the price of the product, will be maintained for some reasonable period. The foregoing conditions of training and of remuneration being met, a country where class strife has been alleviated can be expected to develop a vigorous skilled artisan class.

A further suggestion towards the realization of social efficiency arises from the necessity in democratic countries of a strong local patriotism. The situation in Australia, as analyzed, furnishes a basis for the suggestion that the larger States be divided into smaller areas to secure their fuller and speedier development, and to give differences of climatic environment and of local interests, aptitudes and abilities their fullest sway. Australia is a land where cities occupy a dominating position in population, commerce and administration. The following table [1] shows clearly this phenomenal concentration of the population in the various metropolitan areas.

DISTRIBUTION OF POPULATION OF STATES OF AUSTRALIA IN THEIR CAPITAL CITIES, DECEMBER 31, 1914

States	Metropolis	Population of State	Population of Metropolis	Percentage of metropolitan population to total population
New South Wales	Sydney	1,861,522	752,500	40.38
Victoria	Melbourne	1,430,667	674,000	47.11
Queensland	Brisbane	676,707	154,011	22.76
South Australia	Adelaide	441,690	205,443	46.10
Western Australia	Perth	323,018	122,400	37.89
Tasmania	Hobart	201,416	40,000	19.86
Total for Commonwealth		[2] 4,940,952	1,948,354	39.43

This table shows how the capital cities have attained an abnormal size relatively to the unpeopled interior. Their growth, too, has been at a rate much greater than that of the population generally. The proportion of population in each capital compared with that of the whole State is shown below for the various census periods 1871-1911.

[1] *Commonwealth Year Book*, no. 9, pp. 91, 114.
[2] Two territories, Northern and Federal, are included in this total.

POPULATION OF THE CAPITAL CITY OF EACH STATE EXPRESSED AS A PERCENTAGE OF THE TOTAL POPULATION OF THE STATE FOR THE CENSUS PERIODS, 1871-1911 [1]

City	1871 %	1881 %	1891 %	1901 %	1911 %
Sydney	27.34	29.93	33.86	35.90	38.19
Melbourne	28.27	32.81	43.05	41.13	44.77
Brisbane	12.51	14.57	23.79	23.73	23.02
Adelaide	23.03	37.11	41.59	44.75	46.04
Perth	20.68	19.60	16.97	19.70	37.85
Hobart	18.76	18.25	22.81	20.08	20.88

Along with this aggregation goes dominant political power and the concentration of most of the manufactures and commerce of each State.

Our earlier analysis, together with these figures, suggest the need of developing the country areas. Decentralization of administration, of manufacturing and of commerce are requisite to that end. A preponderant city life, even though not built up at the expense of the country, but through immigration, nevertheless does rob the country-side. It makes rural centers unattractive to the man who has made his wealth in them, and upon whom they have a claim for civic service. Its needs and problems crowd out the claims of the country, and subtly affect such matters, vital to settlement, as the form and direction of railway communication, and the opportunities and costs of transportation. It makes the problems of local government secondary to those of the metropolis, and causes the commercial and industrial needs of the latter to absorb a large amount of the public funds. But, sociologically, its chief disadvantage is that under the conditions of Australian life it denies the opportunity to communities, far from devoid of social

[1] Coghlan, *Seven Colonies of Australia*, 1901-1902, p. 543, and *Commonwealth Census*, 1911, vol. ii, pp. 14, 41-43.

leadership, to develop along their own lines. States where the political capital is the commercial capital, where the only port developed is the commercial port, where the wealth of leadership, initiative and prestige are at the service of the capital, often without understanding of the problems of the country, cannot and do not adequately and efficiently develop. Differences of climate and environment, differences in occupation and employment, except so far as the latter refer to manufacturing, do not obtain their full scope. Local patriotism springs from the opportunity to react upon the stimulus of local needs, to organize for their satisfaction, and to work in face-to-face co-operation.

To furnish this opportunity, under the conditions of Australian life, there is needed some division of the larger States into smaller areas. Queensland, New South Wales and Western Australia could all be subjected, now, or in the future, to this process. The diversity of climate and products in the former state, the presence of several ports along the coast-line, the diverse problems which beset the tropical section, theoretically justify the consideration of the matter. New South Wales, is, administratively, a semi-circle, whose centre, roughly speaking, is the political capital. The areas lying on its farthest circumference are those which suffer most from this administrative concentration. At least one of these areas, that of the North Coast, with the adjacent tableland and wheat district behind it, has most of the essentials and all the above-named sociological differentia for a distinct State. The same is probably true of the Riverina district. In the case of Western Australia, there is not sufficient settlement to bring the matter even within the bounds of speculation, but it is certain that the tropical North-West of that State will differ fundamentally from the South-West section in its problems and needs.

Social efficiency requires also that education shall be extended, given a social content, made a training in citizenship, and a means of vocational guidance. In the school period it must create habits and interests that will enable the developing youth wisely to use the large amount of time and money which the industrial life of to-day places at his disposal. Industrial efficiency will depend as much on the rightful use of such leisure as on the technical training of the work-shop. It must awaken the imagination with subjects of wide range, it must stimulate interest in all that is noble in literature or beautiful in art. Until education has made the leisure hours of adolescence and early manhood interesting, they will remain a moral danger and a social menace. Education must awaken also the sense of social responsibility. To do that, it must train the youth, in the later stages of its school career, at least, in civic duty. It must itself become a factor in social betterment by means of its organic relatedness to the whole of life's experiences.[1]

Such a concept of education will involve re-organization of schools and re-adjustment of curricula. It may require such an effective combination of work, play, and social activity as the Gary schools afford. It will suggest a revaluation of the subject matter of instruction so as to secure at least an altered emphasis. It certainly does involve the furnishing of educational opportunities to those who have left formal instruction behind. What it means in regard to industrial competency has been stated before. Let it suffice to add that civic efficiency requires that the opportunity for instruction in the social sciences should be widely extended. The tutorial class movement, in conjunction with the Workers' Educational Association, supplies the method for this extension.

[1] This paragraph is adapted from a paper read by the author, before the 1911 meeting of the Australian Society for the Advancement of Science, entitled "The Sociological Concept of Education."

From this extension of education may be expected that development and recognition of democratically inspired leadership which was held to be essential to efficiency in a democracy. A leader is a gifted person whose personality has been developed by responsibility and by service towards the group of which he forms a part. The concrete factors in Australian social development have afforded abundant opportunities for the courage, the initiative, the executive power in which leadership partly consists. But they have given less scope to knowledge and social vision which are essential not only to the realization but to the social recognition of leadership. Herein comes the need and the opportunity of education as above defined. A socialized educational system that aims at civic efficiency will supply the guiding minority that has learned to use power in the interests of democracy and the higher-educated majority that can ultimately control, justly and wisely, the line of social action.

Finally, social efficiency requires some mechanism for this just and wise decision concerning the line of social action. Representative democracy is not sufficient. It is but a means to an end, namely, legislation. As suggested in the discussion of social efficiency, legislation can be made a means of preparing for new social growths and of making provision for them. To be effective it must be entered upon in a more scientific spirit than is much of the legislation of to-day. A bill presented to a legislative chamber should be a scientific hypothesis based on full survey of all the facts of the case and adequate to meet them. It is an attempt to meet a definite situation. If that situation is to be met efficiently, it must be studied in all its aspects. All similar situations and the resulting legislation in other countries should be brought under review. The views of experts in the fields on which legislation is being enacted should be consulted and considered. A society that is consciously seeking an efficient working of its legislative system will find some means consonant with its constitution for obtaining this scientific regulation of the national policy. In Australia, the establishment in each State of a legislative reference commission, composed equally of members of parliament and of men of expert knowledge in the social sciences, would meet this need. With a reference bureau for the collection, tabulation and study of the results of the experiments of Australia and other countries, and with sessions open on specified occasions to the public, this commission could put before responsible ministers, bills that would have some prospect of being adequate to meet a given situation.

Our discussion of a program must be left in this indefinite form. It is intended merely to suggest how the sociological point of view enables social action to be seen in the light of the past and the prospect of the future. It is the result of an endeavor to consider the problems of Australia in regard to the conditioning circumstances that thrust them, in their present form, intensity and purpose, into the arena of collective action. Sociology, as the science of society, is concerned with the stimuli that prompt to collective action, with the reaction that results, the measure of solidarity achieved, the nature of the organization set up and the value, potency and end of the forces of coercion and control that are an essential part of a collective organization. So little has been done in Australia towards study and research along these lines by the use of the psychological and statistical method, that this study lacks that basis of fact which is essential to broad generalizations. Its point of view may not therefore always be impartial. It is not a complete study of Australian life. It is a broad rather than a detailed study. It puts aside generally those differences in State organization that, because of their direct connection with special conditioning circumstances, are often of great sociological interest, with the proviso always that they are not of such great importance as to vitiate the general conclusions drawn. The homogeneity of the population of Australia precludes the possibility of such differences assuming predominant importance. The study has endeavored to see how the circumstances of the early settlement, the nature of the population and its psychic diversity, its relation to the land, and the opportunities of settlement, and the resulting diversity and conflict of interests have influenced the development of the country. The conclusion is reached that, through the diverse nature of the free settlers and of the nominated immigrants and through the influence of an early and persistent land-monopoly, there has been created in Australia a contrast between the practical and independent spirit of the pioneer and the radical socialized consciousness of the city dweller. This has manifested itself in the course of a struggle that has covered the years since 1890. In this struggle, which arose out of the opposition between the individualism typified by the pioneer and the socialism characteristic of the working masses of relatively large cities, there has arisen through reaction and counter-stimulation between these forces, a social idealism which is marked by intolerance of special privileges. This in its turn became the motive of an economic, political and social struggle that did much to establish social justice, that gave Australia a vast body of legislation marking a great advance towards social democracy. But in the struggle over methods, conflicting economic and political interests have set up a large measure of social disorganization. The struggle has proceeded so far as to challenge the enunciation of a program of social organization to further the attainment of the social values for which the Australian people are contending. Through the realization of industrial competency, social harmony, an effective citizenship and the conscious direction of social organization, advance toward that goal will be achieved.

BIBLIOGRAPHY
Books

Atkinson, M. (ed.), *Trade Unionism in Australia*, Sydney, 1915.
Barton, G. B., *History of New South Wales from the Records*, Sydney, 1889.
Buley, E. C., *Australian Life in Town and Country*, New York, 1905.
Coghlan, T. A., *Seven Colonies of Australasia*, Sydney, 1902.
Cramp, K. R., *State and Federal Constitutions of Australia*, Sydney, 1913.
Dewey, J., *Democracy and Education*, New York, 1916.
Epps, W., *The Land Systems of Australia*, London, 1894.
Fox, Frank, *Letters from an Old Dog*.
Giddings, F. H., *Principles of Sociology*, New York, 1916.
Hobhouse, L. T., *Liberalism*, London, 1911.
Hobson, J. A., *Work and Wealth*, London, 1914.
Hughes, W. M., *The Case for Labour*, Sydney, 1910.
Jose, A. W., *History of Australasia*, Sydney, 1913.
Knibbs, G. H. (ed.), *Federal Handbook of Australia*, Melbourne, 1914.
Mansbridge, A., *University Tutorial Classes*, London, 1913.
Marshall, A., *Economics of Industry*, London, 1905.
Mills, R. C., *The Colonisation of Australia*, London, 1915.
Money, Chiozza, *Riches and Poverty*, London, 1911.
Newsholme, A., *The Declining Birthrate*, New York, 1914.
New South Wales Handbook to the B. A. A. S. Meeting, Sydney, 1914.
Phillips, M., *A Colonial Autocracy*, London, 1909.
Reeves, W. P., *State Experiments in Australasia*, London, 1902.
Rusden, G. W., *History of Australia*, Melbourne, 1897.
Spence, W. G., *Australia's Awakening*, Sydney, 1909.
St. Ledger, A., *Australian Socialism*, London, 1909.
Taylor, G., *Australia in its Physiographic and Economic Aspects*, Oxford, 1911.
Wentworth, W. C., *Statistical Account of the British Settlements in Australia*, London, 1824.
Wise, B. R., *The Commonwealth of Australia*, London, 1909.

Public Documents, Journals and Pamphlets

American Journal of Sociology, Chicago, vol. xxiii.
Annals of the American Academy of Political and Social Science, Philadelphia, 1913.
Commonwealth Arbitration Reports, Melbourne, 1905-date.

Commonwealth Bureau of Census and Statistics, Labour Bulletins, Nos. 1-15, *Labour Reports,* Nos. 1-7, *The Private Wealth of Australia and its Growth,* Melbourne, 1918.
Fraser's Magazine, London, 1858, 1868.
Harvard Law Review, Cambridge, 1911.
Journal of the Statistical Society of London, London, vol. xi.
New South Wales Industrial Gazette, Sydney, 1912-date.
Nineteenth Century and After, London, 1904.
Notes on Australia for the Information of Intending Emigrants, Edinburgh, 1837.
Parliamentary Debates, Sydney, Melbourne.
Quarterly Journal of Economics, Boston, 1914.
Quarterly Review, London, 1911.
Report of the Chief Inspector of Factories, Sydney, 1901—date.
             Melbourne, 1896—date.
             Adelaide, 1900—date.
             Brisbane, 1901—date.
             Hobart, 1912—date.
Report of the Commissioner of Income Tax, Brisbane.
Report of the Department of Education, Sydney.
             Melbourne.
             Brisbane.
             Adelaide.
             Perth.
             Hobart.
Report of the Director of Public Health, Sydney.
Report of the Federal Land Tax Commissioner, Melbourne, 1910—date.
Report of the Royal Commission of Inquiry into the Alleged Shortage of Labour, Sydney, 1911-12.
Report of the Royal Commission of Inquiry into Apprenticeship, Sydney, 1912.
Report of the Royal Commission of Inquiry into the Hours and General Conditions of Female and Juvenile Labour, Sydney, 1912.
Report of the Royal Commission of Inquiry into Food Supply and Prices, Sydney, 1912.
Report of the State Children's Council, South Australia, Adelaide, 1914.
Report of the State Children's Relief Board, New South Wales, Sydney, 1916.
Rules of the Australian Labour Federation, Brisbane, 1890.
Sydney Morning Herald, Sydney, 1916.
The Argus, Melbourne, 1891.
The Bulletin, Sydney, 1901.
The Daily Telegraph, Sydney, 1915.
The Economic Journal, London, 1915.

Tariff Investigation—Report of the Inter-State Commission of Australia, Melbourne, 1914-5.
The Industrial Arbitration Reports, New South Wales, Sydney, 1901—date.
The Official Year Book of the Commonwealth of Australia, Melbourne, 1908—date.
The Official Year Book of New South Wales, Sydney, 1904—date.
The Sun, Sydney, 1916.
The Times, London, 1908.
The Worker, Sydney.
Victorian Year Book, Melbourne, 1902—date.
Westminster Review, London, 1910.

BIBLIOGRAPHICAL NOTE

Though no reference is made in the text to any American study of Australian labour conditions other than that of Professor Matthew B. Hammond, two such works deserve acknowledgment. In *The Labour Movement in Australasia* (New York, 1906), Dr. Victor S. Clark gives what was, and still remains, the best interpretation of the rise and policy of the Australian Labour party. Though unexpressed by references, the author of the present work owes much to his reading of Dr. Clark's monograph. His own differs from it in the stress laid on the sociological and economic foundations of Australian development as a whole, in its wider survey of social activity, and in its criticism of later tendencies.

Another admirable American study, which, though entirely from second-hand sources, conveys a correct interpretation, is Mr. Paul Collier, *Minimum Wage Legislation in Australasia* (Albany, N. Y., 1915). Mr. Collier attempts an intensive study of the history of the minimum wage laws in the several states of Australia and in New Zealand, together with their administrative working and the economic and social conditions forming the background of each system. It differs from the present work in its more specialised scope, in its emphasis on administration, and in the differentiated study of each state. It remains to be said that the several magazine articles of Professor M. B. Hammond, of the Ohio State University, remain the most recent first-hand American study of the arbitration laws and labour conditions of Australia.

The present work is the complement of all three. It sets the labour movement, conceived broadly, in its social perspective. It brings a first-hand knowledge of the trend and spirit of Australian social development. Finally, it not merely interprets the democratic tendencies of Australia, it subjects them to analysis, criticism and evaluation, concluding with a program of social efficiency.

INDEX

Added value, 224-5, 235, 236
Agriculture, 60, 212
Apprenticeship, 190, 218-20, 286-8
Arbitration, 81, 83-84, 97, 129, 207
Aristocratic trend in early settlement, 51, 64
Artesian Areas, 58, 210, 214
Assisted Immigrants, 37, 45, 48, 50, 52-54
Australia, physiography, 56-59
Australian Labour Federation, 80

Birth-Rate, 171, 251-4
Baby Clinics, 173

Caucus System, 149-50
Childrens' Courts, 197-8
Child Life, care for, 170, 172-4, 194
City Congestion, 53, 248, 290-2
Class Consciousness, 244, 269-72
Closer Settlement, 71-72, 214
Collective Bargaining, 79, 97
Coloured Labour, 156, 158-60
Commonwealth Conciliation and Arbitration Act, 97-98
Competition, limits on, in Arbitration, 102
Compulsory Voting, 153
Conservation, 278, 281
Continuation Schools, 189, 191
Convicts, 37-42

Democratic control in industry, 264-7, 282
Dependents and delinquents, 194, 196, 198-200
Division of States, 292

Education, 183-194, 246, 273, 287-8, 293-4
Efficiency, 256
English Officials, 51
Environment and social development, 31-2

Factory Legislation, 181

Female Labour, 138-9, 204-5, 249-51
Food, Pure, 172, 177-8
Franchise, 28, 152-4
Freedom of contract, 95-96, 103
Free Settlers, 37, 39, 42-5, 47, 49-50, 52-4

Girls in Factories, 181

Harvester Case, 107-8, 130
Health, 111, 170, 175, 179, 180-181, 249
Hours of Employment, 136, 180-1, 206-7, 249
Housing, 182-3

Immigration, 39, 45-9, 53, 136, 157, 160-2
Industrial competency, 260-8
 disputes, 118-128
 peace, 116, 128, 281-3
 undertakings, 165-6
Inefficiency, 229-230, 244
Infantile Mortality, 173
Irrigation, 214
Isolation, effects of, 55

Labour Bureau, 142-3
Labour Party, 23-27, 80-81, 85, 147, 148-50, 151-2, 254
Labour, restriction of, 136-41
Land monopoly, 68, 73-74, 154-6
 policy, 59-72
 tax, 154-5
Leadership, political, 147, 242, 274
Legislative Assemblies, 27-9
Legislative Reference Commission, 295
Leisure, 112, 207, 247
Liberal Party, 22-23, 25-26, 147, 150

Machinery, use of, 225-6
Maternity, care for, 171-2
Medical Inspection, 174-5

New South Wales, 37, 46, 48, 50-69, 70-71, 73, 76, 80, 120-121, 129, 137, 139, 142, 152, 153, 165, 166, 183, 187, 188, 191, 195, 205, 213, 214, 238, 292
New Zealand, 31, 83, 87, 200, 227, 251
Northern Territory, 58, 170, 212, 280

Occupations, 137-8
Old Age Pensions, 200-2

Pensions, Old Age, 200-2; Invalid, 202
Piece Work, 114, 220, 221, 229, 289
Playgrounds for Children, 248-9
Preference to Unionists, 98-100
Primary Industries, 210, 217
Prison Reform, 198-9
Production, Restriction of, 135, 231, 234-42
Profits and wages, 104-6
Psychological Characteristics, 18-20, 36
Public Debt, 164-5

Queensland, 57, 58, 68, 73, 128, 152, 153, 154, 156, 174, 186, 187, 189, 210, 292

Racial Assimilation, 31, 34-6
Religious instruction in schools, 187
Rest periods in industry, 250
Restriction of output, 232, 234, 236-40

Savings Banks, 133-4
School Attendance, 186
Scientific Management, 263
Skill, 218, 288-9
Social Considerations, 106, 110-16, 206-8
Social Efficiency, 255-295; ideals, 87-91, 169-170, 208

Sociological Problems, 29-33, 59, 257-60
Soil Survey, 278
South Australia, 28, 47, 56, 57, 64, 68, 70, 152, 153, 174, 186, 187, 190, 210, 212, 215
Standard of Living, 176-7
Standard Wage, 79, 81, 84, 102
State Interference, 100, 162-6
Strikes, 78, 117-28, 240
Supply of Labour, 136-41
Syphilis, 175-6

Tasmania, 28, 38, 56, 129, 186, 187, 190
Technical Colleges, 193
Trade Unions, 22n., 77-80, 87

Unemployment, 141-4
Unions, industrial, 217
Unskilled Labour, 109, 216

Value of Production, 72n., 235
Victoria, 28, 29, 47-49, 57, 58, 68, 70, 81, 120, 121, 128, 131, 137, 142, 152, 165, 166, 186, 187, 189, 212-214
Vocational Training, 191-4, 287-8

Wage Groups, 221-4
Wages, 108, 123, 128, 130-132, 135, 221, 226, 235
Wages Boards, 82, 129
Wages and Prices, 226-9
Wakefield, E. G., 64
Wealth, estimated, 233
Wentworth, W. C., 41, 43, 45
Western Australia, 28, 38, 47, 57, 58, 63, 64, 68, 78, 128, 129, 166, 186, 187, 190, 292
White Australia policy, 156-60
Women in Industry, 138-9, 204-205, 249-51
Women's Rights, 202-4
Workers' Educational Association, 244, 293
Workmen's Compensation Acts, 180